SCHOOL COUNSELING
RENEWAL

Strategies for the
Twenty-first Century

Rosemary Thompson, Ed.D., NCC, LPC

ACCELERATED DEVELOPMENT INC.
PUBLISHERS
3400 KILGORE AVENUE
MUNCIE, INDIANA 47304

SCHOOL COUNSELING RENEWAL:
Strategies for the Twenty-first Century

Copyright 1992 by Accelerated Development Inc.

10 9 8 7 6 5 4 3 2 1

Printed in the United States of America

Technical Development: Tanya Benn
                       Marguerite Mader
                       Sheila Sheward

Library of Congress Cataloging-in-Publication Data

Thompson, Rosemary, 1950-
    School counseling renewal : strategies for the twenty-first
century / Rosemary Thompson
    Includes bibliographical references and index.
    ISBN 1-55959-026-2
    1. Personnel service in education--United States. I. Title
LB1027.5.T46   1991
371.4'0973--dc 20   91-70333
                                           CIP

LCN: 91-70333

ISBN: 1-55959-026-2

Order additional copies from:

ACCELERATED DEVELOPMENT INC., PUBLISHERS
3400 Kilgore Avenue, Muncie, IN 47304-4896
Toll Free Order Number 1-800-222-1166

DEDICATION

In loving memory of my mother, Marie Teresa Ayres (1920-1986), who instilled in me early in life to "never start a job you cannot finish."

ACKNOWLEGEMENTS

Many counselors, directly or indirectly have contributed or influenced the development of this book. I offer special thanks for their ideas, encouragement, and support. An appreciation for the instructive feedback provided by the students and practitioners who participated in the field-testing of this book also is extended.

I also wish to thank Nina Brown, Old Dominion University, Norfolk, Virginia; Fred Adair; Kevin Geoffroy, The College of William & Mary, Williamsburg, Virginia; and Pamela Kloeppel, Norfolk Public Schools, Norfolk, Virginia. All are esteemed colleagues who through the years have shared their resourceful ideas and valued perspectives on the dynamic influence of school counseling.

Another significant influence for the development of this book has been C. Fred Bateman, Superintendent, Chesapeake Public Schools, Chesapeake, Virginia. As a fellow writer, his own contributions to the field of education inspires all those who benefit from his dedication and his leadership. A special acknowledgement also is extended to Joseph Hollis. His initial vision for the potential of this publication was patiently nurtured with timely suggestions, encouragement, and support.

Finally, I am most indebted to my family, Charles, Ryan, and Jessica. They unconditionally gave their love, patience, and support to make this book a reality.

TABLE OF CONTENTS

DEDICATION .... **iii**

ACKNOWLEDGEMENTS .... **v**

LIST OF FIGURES .... **xiii**

LIST OF TABLES .... **xv**

1 INTRODUCTION **1**

Changing Role of Guidance and Counseling *1*
Demand Exceeds Availability *2*
Role Expectations *3*
    Two Major Roles *4*
Influence of Changes in School Curricula *6*
Influence of Social Change *7*
Consumer/Community Focused Programs and Services *9*
Operationalizing Counselor Efforts *10*

**2 A PROFILE OF ADOLESCENT HEALTH AND
WELL BEING: IMPLICATIONS FOR
PRIMARY PREVENTION AND INTERVENTION** **13**

Overview *15*
Substance Abuse *15*
    Implications for Intervention of Substance Abuse *16*
Adolescent Pregnancy and Sexual Behavior *19*
    Implications for Intervention of Adolescent Pregnancy
    and Sexual Behavior *21*
Emotional Disorders and Adolescent Depression *22*
    Implications for Intervention of Emotional Disorders
    and Adolescent Depression *24*
Delinquency *29*
    Implications for Intervention of Delinquency *30*
Dropouts *30*
    Implications for Intervention of Dropouts *32*
Victimization *32*
    Acts of Commission *33*

Acts of Omission 33
Implications for Intervention of Victimization 33
Seven Explicit Dimensions to Assist At-Risk Students 34
Early Identification and Coordinated Program Delivery 35
Public/Private Collaboration 35
Parents as Significant Partners 36
Creating a Postive School Climate 36
Staff Development 37
Counseling 37
Assertive, Systematic, Attendance Program 38
Conclusion 38

3 SCHOOL COUNSELING
Definition and Benefits **41**
Toward a Definition of Counseling 42
Inherent Benefits of Counseling 44
In the Interpersonal Domain 45
In the Educational Domain 47
In the Vocational Domain 48
Summary 49

4 DEVELOPMENTAL GUIDANCE AND COUNSELING **51**
Characteristics of Children and Youth 51
Counseling Intentions and Interventions 53
Other Important Intentions of Counselors 55
Life Skills as Developmental Counseling 56
Life Skills Training Model 57
Life Skills Descriptors 61
Keenan Project 62
Efficacy of Small Group Counseling 63
Curative Factors in the Group Process 67
Empowering Youth as Peer Helpers 70
Functions of the Peer Helper 71
Training 72
Scope of Peer Helper Programs 75
Peer Helper Log 76
Conclusion 76

5 HELPING PEOPLE IN CRISIS:
THE SCHOOL COUNSELOR'S ROLE **79**
Crisis Intervention 80
School-as-Community 81
Behavior Manifestations of Loss 83
Common Vision of Shared Responsibility 86
Student Assistance Advisory Board 87
Early Intervention Procedures for Student Assistance Teams 88
Interviewing a Student in Crisis 89
Care for Suicidal Students 92
Empowering Families: The Family Safety Watch
An Intervention Strategy for Self-destructive Behavior 92

Contingency Plan in Case of a Student Suicide or Sudden Loss 98
    Identification of Key Helping Professionals and Staff 98
Guidelines for Deciding Whether to Counsel or Refer to Family Therapy 97
    Identification of Physical Resources 99
    Preparation of Teachers and Staff 99
    Mobilization of the Crisis Intervention Team 100
    Duties of the Case Manager/Team Leader 102
    Short-term Arrangements 102
    Role and Responsibilities of the Principal 104
The Crisis Communication Contingency Plan 105
    Clarification of Issues to the Media 106
Essential Components 109
Tasks of Mourning and Grief Counseling 110
    Special Treatment Issues with Adolescents 111
Post Traumatic Loss Debriefing Strategies 112
    Introductory Stage 113
    Fact Stage 114
    Feeling Stage 115
    Reactions Stage 116
    Learning Stage 117
    Closure Stage 117
Process Evaluation 120
Summary 121

6 SCHOOL COUNSELORS AS CONSULTANTS:
   A BRIEF INTRODUCTION 123
Consultation Models and Helping Orientations 126
    Adlerian-based Consultation 126
    Mental Health Consultation 128
    Behavior Consultation 128
    Organization Development Model 129
    DIRECT-Technique 129
Benefits of Consultation 131

7 CONSULTING WITH TEACHERS AND
   OTHER SUPPORT PERSONNEL 133
Consultation as Problem Solving 133
Counselors and Teachers as Partners
    Implementing a Teacher Advisor (T.A.) System 136
    Selection of Advisors 136
    Teacher Advisor's Role 137
    Student Advisor: An Advocate for the Student 137
    Benefits of a Teacher-Advisor 138
Motivation and Encouragement 140
    Skills to Foster Affective Growth 142
    Six Essential Concepts 143
    Fourteen Attitudes 144

8 CONSULTING WITH FAMILIES 145

Home School Partnerships 146
Value of Parent Conferences 148
  Student Led Conferences 153
Involving Parents in Their Child's Academic Performance
  and Career Development 156
Strategies to Improve Academic Performance 157
Involving Parents as Career Counselors 158
Primary Prevention and Early Intervention for Families 159

9 SCHOOL COUNSELORS AS PROMOTERS OF A MORE POSITIVE SCHOOL CLIMATE 163

Organizations and Change 163
Roles of Change Agent 164
Power or Influence: How to Influence Change 171
School Counselor as Facilitator of Organizational Health 172
Improving School Climate and Student Morale 176
School Climate Baseline Data 189
Productive Meetings Promote a Shared Commitment 191
Types of Meetings 194
Emotional Behavior in Groups 197
  Scoring the Inventory (Figure 9.9) 204
  Interpreting Your Score 204

10 EDUCATIONAL AND OCCUPATIONAL GUIDANCE 207

Future Forecasts 208
  Skills 208
  Computer Literacy 209
  Women and Minorities 209
  Information 209
  Services 210
  Technical Skills 210
  Sunbelt 212
  Flexibility 212
  Self-Reliance 212
  Choices and Decision Making 212
  Employers 212
  Change 213
  Flextime 213
  Marketing 213
  Work Style/Life-style 213
  Self-Employed 214
  Aging Workforce 214
  Diversity in Living 215
  Careers 215
  Old-fashioned Values 216
A Comprehensive System 216

Career Education Versus Career Development Education 218
Educational and Occupational Assessment 219
    Combined Instruments 222
Interpreting Test Data 223

11 COUNSELOR AS CATALYST FOR COLLEGE DECISION MAKING **231**

College and University Expectations 233
A College Education in the Workplace 236
Keeping Options Open 237
Bold Intervention Programs 244
    Upward Bound 244
    Options for Excellence 245
    Talent Search Programs 245
    Project Stay 245
    Business Communications Resources Utilized 245
    Cooperating Hampton Roads Organizations for
        Minorities in Engineering (Crome) 246
    P-ACT+ 246
School Based Programs 247
The Growing Complexity of Financing a College Education 249
    Nearly Half of All Post-Secondary Students Receive Financial Aid 249
Financial Aid Sources and Misconceptions 251

12 COUNSELOR AS OCCUPATIONAL CONDUIT FOR THE NONCOLLEGE BOUND **255**

Shifting Vocational Plans 256
Economic Barriers 257
Marginal Students 263

13 PROGRAM DEVELOPMENT **269**

Role Conflict and Role Ambiguity 271
Predictors of Quality Services 274
    A Comprehensive Consumer/Community Centered Model 275
Counselor Objectives Versus Program Objectives 276
Summary 280

14 PROGRAM EVALUATION **287**

Research Support 288
Program Evaluation 290
Evaluation of Programs 294
Program Audit 296
Evaluation of Services 297
Evaluation Design 307
    Experimental Research Approach 307
    Quasi-experimental Approach 309
    Tabulation Approach 309

Follow-up Approach 309
Case Study Approach 310
Expert Opinion Approach 310
Time/Cost Approach 311
Discrepancy Evaluation Approach 311
Summary for Evaluation Design 312
Evaluation of Professionals 312
Procedure 312

15 DEVELOPING EFFECTIVE PUBLIC RELATIONS 321

Marketing 322
Know Your Audience 326
Internal Marketing Strategies 326
External Marketing Strategies 331
Parent/Teacher Organizations: Alien or Ally 338
Parent Volunteers: Parents Actively Serving School (PASS) 340
Multimedia Approaches 343
Checklist of Vital Components of a
Public Service Announcement 343
Procedures for Photos and Captions 344
Newspaper or Organizational Bulletin Proposal Outline 345
A Systematic Approach for Organizing a Feature Column 347
Public Speaking 349
Enhancing Your Delivery 352
How to Get on Talk Shows 353
Developing a School Counseling Brochure 354
Evaluating Your Public Relations Strategies in Your School 355
Summary 357

16 ASSIMILATING THE PRINCIPLES OF
TIME MANAGEMENT 359

Analyzing Time Consumers 361
Time Management Exercise 363
Managing Your Paper Chase 363
Stress Management 365
Strategies for Leaving Stress at the Office 372
Is There a Neon "Do-Drop-In" Sign above Your Door? 373
Use Secretarial Assistance Efficiently 374
How to Say "No" and Help Others Assume Responsibility 374

REFERENCES 381

AUTHOR PROFILE 401

LIST OF FIGURES

4.1   Major developmental tasks of adolescence as identified by theorists 52
4.2   A developmental guidance model focusing on outcomes 58
4.3   Counselor interventions: Weekly scheduling plan 59
4.4   Group counseling skill classification systems 64
4.5   Classification system for group-focused counseling skills 68
5.1   Life events stressors in childhood and adolescence 82
5.2   Some significant indicators of crisis in students 91
5.3   An example of school counselor action plan 93
5.4   Administrative memo 94
5.5   Post traumatic stress reactions 118
5.6   Post traumatic stress disorder 119
6.1   School counselor as consultant—an adjective checklist 124
6.2   Consultation activities 127
7.1   Consultation model that follows a problem-solving approach 135
7.2   Student Assistance Program Behavior Report 139
8.1   The home-school partnership: A model for counselors 147
8.2   How welcome are parents in your school 149
8.3   Conference planning sheet 151
8.4   Elements of effective parent-teacher conferences 154
8.5   Effective Conference Continuum 155
9.1   Five roles of change agents 165
9.2   The organizational universe model 168
9.3   The diffusion process: The flow of information
      and influence toward decision making 170
9.4   Characteristics of a healthy organization 174
9.5   Organizational climate questionnaire 175
9.6   School climate profile baseline data 190
9.7   Evaluation of meeting 195
9.8   Emotional behavior in groups 199
9.9   Inventory of counselor potential for facilitating staff morale 200
10.1 Program of studies: Academic and career planning guide 220
10.2 Checklist on the organization and administration
      of the testing program (1986) 226
11.1 Financial aid misconceptions 253
13.1 Counselor objectives versus program development 277
13.2 A student-focused model for development of counseling services 279
13.3 Student Outcome Program Development Model 281
14.1 The Counselor's Time Study Analysis 291
14.2 Suggested code numbering for different counselor activities 292

14.3   Postcard follow-up 295
14.4   Teacher and administration evaluation of
        guidance program and counseling services 300
14.5   Student questionnaire of guidance and counseling services 300
14.6   Parent evaluation of guidance and counseling services 301
14.7   Critical steps in need analysis 303
14.8   Six-step checklist to evaluating your program 304
14.9   Relationship of effort, effectiveness, and
        efficiency to a program model 306
14.10   An exercise in identifying effort, effectiveness, and efficiency 308
14.11   Performance evaluation criteria: Administrator perspective 313
14.12   School counselor performance evaluation 315
15.1   Worksheet for implementing strategies 325
15.2   Internal and external advertising practices 327
15.3   Counselor's Kaleidoscope 334
15.4   Sample contact letter 335
15.5   Counselor's report card 336
15.6   When parents are partners 339
15.7   Partnership activities 341
15.8   Parent information night: A series of workshops 342
16.1   Irrational beliefs 367
16.2   Stress awareness exercise 368
16.3   Checklist of secretary's responsibilities 375

LIST OF TABLES

2.1 Indicators of Growing Youth Problems 14
2.2 Youth Suicides Nationwide 24
10.1 Some Traditionally Male Dominated Fields in Which
      Women Are Expected to Make Some Progress 210
10.2 Best Jobs for the Future Fact Sheet 211
10.3 How Do You Want Your Life to Be Different
      From Your Parents' Life 214
10.4 Life Values Seniors Consider Important 217
11.1 Applicant Credentials Considered Most Important or
      Very Important by Four Year Institutions
      in Making Admissions Decisions 235
11.2 Perceived Helpfulness of Resources
      for All Types of Colleges Combined 240

CHAPTER **1**

INTRODUCTION

Tighter than a string has
been our development.
Lurching on the edge of education
we have been fit in Procrustean
fashion into the forms of schedule
changers, information givers,
quasi-therapists, but always with
outsiders; strangely active with
unleavened affections and unlooked
for logic.
Groping through a wilderness of
role definition and an unresting
resentment we have asked in
Beckett's Godot, "What are we doing here?"

(Carroll, 1973, p. 326)

CHANGING ROLE OF
GUIDANCE AND COUNSELING

The early emphasis of guidance and counseling in school centered on a narrow concept of selected services rendered by a few specialists for a small population of students. During the twentieth century, school guidance has had three major emphases: occupational selection and placement (1900-1920), followed by school adjustment (1930-1960), and then personal development, psychodynamic methodologies, and interpersonal life-skills development (1960 to the present). The major focus today is on the acquisition and incorporation into one's self-

Ch 1 Introduction   1

system, life adjustment strategies that foster productive rather than self-defeating behaviors.

DEMAND EXCEEDS AVAILABILITY

In the later part of the twentieth century, approximately 80,000 to 90,000 guidance counselors in the nation work full or part-time in elementary and secondary schools. Idealistically, such figures perhaps look impressive, yet, in reality, a discrepancy exists between role and function, and programs and services. In terms of services rendered to student populations, counselors are assisting approximately 15,110,000 secondary students 21,875 school buildings and 31,819,000 elementary school students in 72,475 buildings (Pinson, Gysbers, & Drier, 1981). The counselor-to-student ratio at the secondary level across the nation is approximately 1 to 425 and as high as 1 to 1,000 in some urban areas. At the elementary school level, the ratio is one counselor for every six elementary schools.

By putting numbers into perspective, what becomes apparent is that many students and their families across the nation have no access to guidance and counseling services at either the elementary or secondary school level. Demands by students and their families for guidance services far exceed the availability. These disparities add to the relentless criticism that many school counselors are merely office clerks managing academic transcripts, schedule changes, scholarships, special program applications, discipline, attendance, or other routine administrative duties, precariously assigned by well meaning administrators.

In addition, while many school counselors define themselves on the basis that preparing students for college takes much of their time, a national study of 1,100 high schools found that college counseling was inadequate. The study found that a typical high school junior or senior received only 20 minutes of a counselor's time to plan the arduous chore of education and career (Tugend, 1984). The College Board further suggested in a recent report that improved guidance and counseling in our schools can contribute significantly to reducing the considerable waste of human talent that now exists. Disadvantaged children and a growing population of at-risk students also are in greatest need of the supportive environment counseling can promote.

ROLE EXPECTATIONS

More often than not, school counseling programs and corresponding counseling roles are instituted without a clear definition of mission, purpose, or goal. Within this context, the building principal often perceives an opportunity to assign other residual projects or mundane duties to the guidance and counseling program under the pretext that "you know all the children," or "you have all the files." Simultaneously, many counselors have been ill-prepared, rarely receiving any graduate training in program development and organization management, and thus, tend to deal with major issues in a case-by-case, crisis management manner. Others have sought the role of counselor as an exodus from the classroom and become quite comfortable with administrative tasks, with its institutional amenities of private office and private telephone.

Fundamentally, disparity with regard to role expectations adversely influences the perceived effectiveness of the school counselor, the value of the school district program, and ultimately the school counseling as a profession. This disparity perhaps is best illustrated by some of the competing philosophies of many proponents in the field. For example, Boyer (1983), in *High School: A Report on Secondary Education in America,* recommended that counselors be involved in short- and long-term educational and occupational decision making with caseloads that do not exceed 100 students. Counselors would assume the classic role of educational advisor rather than a therapeutic or crisis intervention role. Dagley and Gazda (1984) suggested that school counselors should strive to improve school climate and make it more conducive to learning. Pine (1976) recommended that counselors function more like consultants in the schools and work more collaboratively with teachers, administrators, students, and their families. Hays (1980) maintained that counselors should become human development specialists who would promote the worth and dignity of individuals within the context of the school-as-community. Herr and Pinson (1982) suggested that counselors become more articulate about counseling interventions that can empirically demonstrate improvement in student performance which in turn would demonstrate greater accountability. Peer (1985) maintained that counselors need to develop written goals and plans, in addition to clarifying their program responsibilities and outcomes. Ibrahim, Helms, Wilson, and Thompson (1984) reinforced this perspective and recommended that counselors embrace a consumer/community centered program model of counseling services. So many divergent perspectives create role conflict and role ambiguity which become debilitating individual and organizational stressors. The load, functions, and responsibilities of counselors must be more clearly delineated and collectively focused.

Role conflict is the simultaneous occurrence of two or more sets of inconsistent, expected role behaviors for an individual's task for function. Role ambiguity is the lack of clear, consistent information regarding the duties and responsibilities of a role and how it can best be performed. Chronic role conflict and ambiguity often result in a rather marked sense of futility. Role conflict also results when incompatible demands are placed on the counselor influenced by vague assumptions and differing expectations within the constraints of the school-as-institution.

Concurrently, school counselors are expected to be involved in a greater variety of unprecedented guidance and counseling activities. Role and function include work in the curriculum, conducting placement, and follow-up activities, intervention, remediation, identification of students with special needs, consultation, specialized testing, group work, and a growing interface with business and industry. In addition, they are expected to continue routine activities such as crisis counseling, teacher and parent consultation, assessment, scheduling, follow-up, and referrals.

Two Major Roles Evolved

Fundamentally, however, within the context of the school two different counselor's role orientations have evolved: the

administrator role and the ***therapeutic role.*** School counselors who devote a larger percentage of their time to planning programs, grouping, making schedule changes, helping in college selection, and job placement are performing the sorting, allocating, and selecting function of the counselor as ***guidance administrator.*** This orientation embraces the *National Defense Education Act of 1958* model for guidance and counseling in the schools. The therapeutic role, however, is more concerned with facilitating a relationship with a counselee to enhance his/her personal development and psychological competencies. The administrator role and the therapist role represent two major historical dichotomies that have influenced the present status of guidance and counseling in the schools. To focus solely on either may distort the perceived effectiveness of school counselors.

This distinct dichotomy is illustrated by Powell, Farrar, and Cohen (1985). Based on extensive interview and classroom observations, authors of *The Shopping Mall High School* found a typical day for the school guidance counselor to look as follows:

> A typical day included meeting with a learning disabled student who wanted to talk about the inherited disease that had already killed his sister; with a senior about college admissions; with a student leader who was attempting to explain the vandalism caused by other student leaders while on a school trip; with a therapist of a student suffering from anorexia nervosa; and with a student accused of cheating. (Powell et al., 1985)

Planning programs, grouping students by ability for instruction, making schedule changes, assisting students with college selection, course advising, and performing job placement services reflect the function of the administrator role. In the therapeutic role, counselors develop a trusting relationship with student(s) to enhance the student's personal development and strengthen psychological competencies. Inherently, the lack of clarity in a role and function persists because school counselors have attempted to embrace two different masters: education and psychotherapy.

A recent study by Brown, Thompson, Geoffroy, and Adair (1987) found additional discrepancies among the perceptions of counselors, teachers, and principals in secondary schools on ratings of **attainment, importance,** and **effectiveness** on such constructs as educational occupational guidance, counseling consultation, and program development. Disagreement about the priority of the tasks and the tasks themselves makes effective functioning very difficult. Indeed, considerable dissonance is created when counselors attempt to fulfill their role according to the standards that the profession dictates— a role that their co-workers perceive differently.

Brown et al. found that counselors are expected to have one set of tasks as a top priority by the state and profession, another set of tasks as a top priority by principals and teachers, and yet another set of tasks as a top priority by students and their families. The most important issues to emerge from their study were the need for (1) a formal endorsed model of guidance and counseling in the secondary schools, (2) a consensus definition of the role of the counselor in the schools, and (3) studies of the perceptions and needs of students in determining the role of counselor.

INFLUENCE OF CHANGES IN SCHOOL CURRICULA

This is further complicated with a close review of the changing school curricula. For example, as secondary school programs became more complex, and student populations became more heterogeneous, schools have implemented a variety of programs and services to maximize holding power, graduation percentages, and consumer satisfaction. With the thrust toward the more comprehensive high school, several curricula have emerged simultaneously: (1) **the horizontal curriculum** with differences in actual subjects, (2) **the vertical curriculum** with subjects of the same title offered at different levels of difficulty, (3) **the extracurricular curriculum** of sports and other nonacademic or vocational activities developed to attract students to an activity which makes them feel competent or successful, and (4) *the services curriculum* where the school addresses emotional and social problems deemed educationally valid (Powell et al., 1985).

Many school counselors have assumed increasing responsibility in all curricula with a growing tendency to become more involved in the services curriculum. The services curriculum is the fastest-growing component within the school curricula.

> Some services directly address social or psychological problems—grief, sudden loss, child abuse, depression, and alienation. Some schools also provide special programs depending on their populations such as daycare for children of students, health clinics, rehabilitation for teenagers in trouble with the law, support groups for unmarried teenage fathers and mothers; services for special needs of handicapped students; and remedial services such as tutorials, laboratories, and resource rooms for students in academic trouble. (Powell et al., 1985, p. 33)

Currently, across the nation a critical need exists to provide both early intervention and services which reflect the changing need of students and their families. From a primary prevention perspective, the role of the school counselor should assist individuals to gain insight about their personal characteristics, to understand their potentials, and to become educated to choose and plan constructive action for personal growth.

INFLUENCE OF SOCIAL CHANGE

In a period of rapid social change, single-parent families, dual-career households, chemical dependency, international unrest, shifting achievement profiles, greater occupational diversity, and changing population demographics, school counselors have come to represent a reservoir of stability and congruency of information. The school, which once was to educate, now must accommodate and facilitate psychological growth of both students and their families. This is not a new concept since:

> Schools have become the vanguard. They have always been expected to cope; to fuel the various social and economic revolutions, to assimilate the waves of immigrants, to integrate the races, to uplift the handicapped, to substitute for the family—all the while instilling the common culture. As the stabilizing and socializing influence of home and church has waned our reliance on the school has grown. (*Education Week*, 1986, June 4, p. 15)

Further, growing concern over the teenage suicide rate, adolescent depression, unemployment, alienation, dropout rates, and teenage pregnancy demonstrate the critical need for responsible adults to establish close, helping relationships with young people. Current data reveal some disturbing trends that seem to be alienating youth from participation in greater society. As a group, teenagers have an unemployment rate three times the adult rate. More than three million 16 to 24 year olds are looking for work and another 391,000 are classified as discouraged. Arrests of young people under 18 for drug abuse increased sixty-fold between 1960 and 1980. Arrests for drunkenness among high school seniors rose by 300% between 1960 and 1980. In addition, young people under 21 account for more than one-half of all arrests for serious crimes. Death by suicide among teenagers increased for all groups. Further, recent trends in adolescent pregnancy and parenthood are another concern with more than one million teens becoming pregnant each year and an increasing number of single teenage parents not returning to school, choosing to place their own children at risk.

This bleak profile is compounded by the changing demographics of future school populations. For example, in the fall of 1986, 3.6 million children began their formal schooling in the United States. The estimate was that one out of four of them were from families who lived in poverty; 14% were children of unmarried parents; 40% were or will be living in a broken home before they reach age 18; 10% have poorly educated parents, many of whom are illiterate; and nearly one-third were "latch key" children (*Education Week*, 1986, May 14).

CONSUMER/COMMUNITY FOCUSED PROGRAMS AND SERVICES

The school environment is perhaps viewed as the most structured and influential public integrative system to foster the transition to productive adult life. From an intervention perspective, the role of the school counselor can serve to assist individuals or groups to gain insight about their unique personal characteristics, and to choose appropriate life plans. This involves providing both a therapeutic process and program development which follows a systematic delivery component. The constant goal of counseling to achieve a sense of independence, integration, growth, competence, and responsibility can best be realized vis-á-vis the therapeutic relationship. The constant goal of accountability can only be realized if programs and services are consumer/community specific which will differ from a rural to urban population.

School counselors need to be encouraged to become involved in school and community programs and to systematically define their role and function within and outside the educational community. Also the need exists to break down the rigidity of the school-as-institution. This can be accomplished by more actively involving teachers, administrators, and parents. For example, teachers are a wealth and virtually untapped resource in the guidance and counseling process. Counselors also should enhance their role as human development facilitators. Teachers and counselors could both become committed to effective counseling programs with a shared philosophy. This involves providing therapeutic services which focus on life-skills within a program development model which reflects consumer/community need.

Moreover, teachers, administrators, and parents must become more involved in the guidance program. Educational and occupational planning, placement, and referral are three related areas that can become a shared responsibility of all members of the school staff. Counselors need to acquire more skills in consulting to provide essential staff development experiences and to learn how to use talents and resources of their colleagues. Inherently, school counselors, teachers, and administrators need to recognize they are members of the same team.

Further, the development and implementation of a comprehensive curriculum could be designed for the master of life-skills development such as self-competency, interpersonal development, communication, critical thinking, and personal mastery to assist a growing population of at-risk youth. Personal growth and development of students must be a curriculum objective. A curriculum that is experiential where students can share concerns in a secure and caring environment would be a more proactive intervention for preventing teenage suicide, substance abuse, and other impersonal adjustment maladies. This also would be an investment in the psychological well being of society's future. Perhaps the time has come to create a new model of accountability for school guidance and counseling. As recent reports have recommended, counselors might productively serve as coordinators of student's learning opportunities by working to improve the academic program and the climate of the school while also accessing school/community support services to assist all students.

OPERATIONALIZING COUNSELOR EFFORTS

Finally, counselors need to translate a counseling philosophy into concrete, observable program goals and communicate them to teachers, administrators, and families. Effective counseling programs measure the results of their counseling efforts and offer relevant data to the school and special interest groups. The survival alternative is what Jenkins (1986) termed the **Renaissance Counselor.** The Renaissance Counselor is a professional who demonstrates an intellectual comprehension of the guidance and counseling mission and charts a course that incorporates personal and professional development, inspires direction, accountability, and responsiveness to students, parents, and community.

The Renaissance Counselor is dedicated, innovative, and resourceful, possesses a high level of cognition and affective skills, manages and organizes, sets priorities, is a supportive team player, acts as a consultant and coordinator, demonstrates skill in interpersonal relationships, is a role model, is flexible, has integrity and maintains trust, is visionary, is protective and assertive, and has a global perspective. (Jenkins, 1986, p. 6)

This book nurtures the perspective of the Renaissance Counselor with comprehensive and proactive strategies for program accountability and program delivery. The present challenge of school counseling programs is how to broaden traditional areas of service. The need is to operationalize counselor efforts in a more consumer/community centered program model. As a catalyst to human growth and self-understanding, the school counselor who facilitates proactive strategies within a need-based context can anticipate potential problems and provide recipients with skills to promote social, emotional, and interpersonal well-being.

The growing importance and continued acceptance of guidance and counseling in the schools has evolved in sharp contrast to their initial intentions. Because of changing needs, expectations, and demands for accountability within the rapidly growing services curriculum, counselors are increasingly being called on to provide organizational stability and congruency of information. Within this context, an ever increasing need is to continue to refine and to develop an effective school model to assure that delivery systems promote both quality and equity in educational, occupational, and interpersonal domains.

Strategies, activities, and techniques which capitalize on the dynamic influence of the school counselor are provided in such areas as public relations, time management, program development, staff consultation, and school climate. All information is offered as pragmatic resources for the counselor-practitioner, the beginning counselor, and all who continue eagerly to embrace the possibilities and potentialities of a dynamic school counseling program.

CHAPTER 2

A PROFILE OF ADOLESCENT HEALTH AND WELL BEING: IMPLICATIONS FOR PRIMARY PREVENTION AND INTERVENTION

Today, within the context of school-as-community, the self-destructive potential of young people is a travesty of ambiguous proportion. The growing concern over adolescent suicide, substance abuse, alienation, teen stress, family dysfunction, and dropout rates demonstrate the critical need for responsible adults to establish close helping relationships with young people. All too many young people do not receive consistent, positive, and realistic validation of themselves from the adults on whom they depend.

The following statistical and demographic data provided in Table 2.1 have been gleaned from a variety of nationwide studies. Most of the information, however, can be found in the following reports: American Medical Association's White Paper on Adolescent Health (1987), U.S. General Accounting Office (1986), U.S. Department of Education (1987), U.S. Department of Commerce (1984), and National Educational Association (1985).

Table 2.1
Indicators of Growing Youth Problems

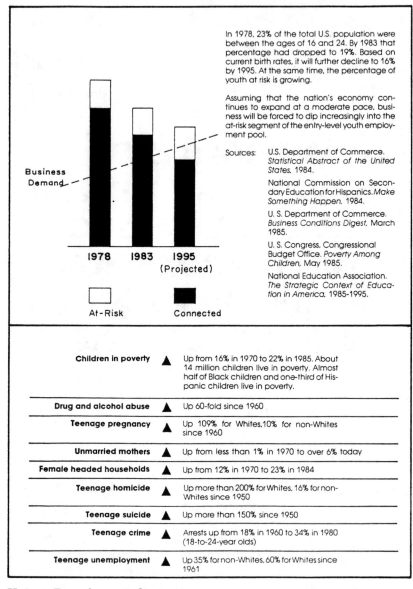

In 1978, 23% of the total U.S. population were between the ages of 16 and 24. By 1983 that percentage had dropped to 19%. Based on current birth rates, it will further decline to 16% by 1995. At the same time, the percentage of youth at risk is growing.

Assuming that the nation's economy continues to expand at a moderate pace, business will be forced to dip increasingly into the at-risk segment of the entry-level youth employment pool.

Sources: U.S. Department of Commerce. *Statistical Abstract of the United States.* 1984.

National Commission on Secondary Education for Hispanics. *Make Something Happen.* 1984.

U. S. Department of Commerce. *Business Conditions Digest,* March 1985.

U. S. Congress, Congressional Budget Office. *Poverty Among Children,* May 1985.

National Education Association. *The Strategic Context of Education in America,* 1985-1995.

Business Demand

1978 1983 1995 (Projected)

☐ At-Risk   ■ Connected

Children in poverty	▲	Up from 16% in 1970 to 22% in 1985. About 14 million children live in poverty. Almost half of Black children and one-third of Hispanic children live in poverty.
Drug and alcohol abuse	▲	Up 60-fold since 1960
Teenage pregnancy	▲	Up 109% for Whites,10% for non-Whites since 1960
Unmarried mothers	▲	Up from less than 1% in 1970 to over 6% today
Female headed households	▲	Up from 12% in 1970 to 23% in 1984
Teenage homicide	▲	Up more than 200% for Whites, 16% for non-Whites since 1950
Teenage suicide	▲	Up more than 150% since 1950
Teenage crime	▲	Arrests up from 18% in 1960 to 34% in 1980 (18-to-24-year olds)
Teenage unemployment	▲	Up 35% for non-Whites, 60% for Whites since 1961

Note: Based on information appearing in *AMA Whitepaper on Adolescent Health.* American Medical Association. (1987). Reproduced with permission.

OVERVIEW

A recent report by the National Drug Policy Board, an arm of the U.S. Department of Justice, also reflects the magnitude of the problems facing high-risk children.

> Federal crime statistics for 1986 revealed that 250,000 juveniles were arrested for drug-related offenses.

> According to the National Institute on Drug Abuse, About 3 million 17 to 20-year olds use marijuana or cocaine.

> Nearly 12 million children were reported to be victims of neglect or of physical or sexual abuse in 1985, according to the American Human Association.

> More than 1 million teenage girls become pregnant each year, and only one-half of them complete high school, according to the Center for the Study of Social Policy.

> According to the National Governors' Association, the national dropout rate ranges from 14% to 25%. And, the U.S. Department of Education estimates that as many as 80% of school dropouts may use illegal drugs on a regular basis.

Inherently, we must proceed beyond pontificating about the maladies of at-risk youth and begin implementing strategies that provide viable outcomes which can be evaluated.

SUBSTANCE ABUSE

The truth about the use of drugs by students is elusive. Self-reported data are sometimes of dubious validity, but they do represent an important source of information on substance use and abuse. Substance abuse among adolescents increased explosively in the 1960s and 1970s. Alcohol and drug use also remain prevalent in this population group.

Two-thirds of American youth (64%) try an illicit drug before they finish high school.

Over one-third of adolescents, by 12th grade, have illicitly used a drug other than marijuana.

Approximately 1 in 16 high school seniors drink alcoholic beverages daily and, when surveyed, 41% had consumed five or more drinks on a single occasion in the preceding two weeks.

Heavy drinking older adolescents report they first drank at age 12.

Teenage drinkers account for nearly 50% of all fatal automobile accidents (Sherouse, 1985).

Children are beginning alcohol use at an earlier age— the average beginning age is 12.5 years, and children as young as 9 years old are being treated for alcoholism (Horton, 1985).

Alcohol and substance abuse have correlated significantly to school vandalism, absenteeism, tardiness, truancy, discipline, classroom disruption, violence, declining academic achievement, dropout rates, and automobile related deaths. In addition, the site for virtually all primary prevention or early interventions activities is in the schools. The schools are perceived by both those who sell drugs and those who would prevent their sale as the single most important point of access to young people. The activities of both groups intrude on the time available for teaching and learning.

**Implications for Intervention
of Substance Abuse**

The National Drug Policy Board and other researchers have suggested that local and national strategies should coordinate existing youth programs and expand them with a shared responsibility to improve family and peer relationships.

The board identified 10 factors that increase a child's vulnerability to the lure of drugs:

> having parents who use drugs,
>
> being the victim of physical, sexual, or psychological abuse,
>
> dropping out of school,
>
> becoming pregnant,
>
> being economically disadvantaged,
>
> committing a violent or delinquent act,
>
> experiencing mental health problems,
>
> attempting suicide,
>
> running away from home, and
>
> being homeless.

These same factors place the child at high risk for dysfunctional or self-defeating behaviors.

Furthermore, our efforts at drug prevention must concentrate on the "gateway" drugs, particularly alcohol. Programs to prevent alcohol and drug abuse must be comprehensive and all inclusive. Schools and communities must identify ways to integrate the prevention message into multiple services areas. Inherently, we must find more innovative ways to include community agencies, medical personnel, the clergy, businesses, and educators in providing the leadership and collective commitment for primary prevention and early intervention programs. Until the alcohol and drug problem is controlled, we cannot expect other adolescent problems— pregnancy, suicide, violence, poor academic performance, and juvenile crime—all of which are often rooted in drug use, to significantly diminish.

Providing awareness, information, and motivation to "just say no" is not enough. Programs that emphasize assertive approaches that build resistance skills should have a longer developmental effect (Hansen, 1988). Such approaches include the following:

Peer pressure resistance training which explains the nature of peer pressure and teaches youth (through role playing) skills to cope with pressure to try drugs. Training includes didactic descriptions and demonstrations of resistance techniques accompanied by methods of practicing them. The emphasis is on developing personal coping skills that will be effective in real situations.

Normative education which counters the false perceptions of drug use by giving youth accurate information about true rates among peers.

Inoculation against mass media messages in which youth are taught critical analysis skills to counter the influence of such messages.

Training dealing with parental influences in which youth learn a simple message that they need not use substances even though their parents choose to do so.

Peer leadership training uses peer opinion leaders to reach more rebellious youth who are more likely to pay attention to the message if respected peers advocate its goals. Research data continue to support the efficacy of using youth to deliver all or some of such messages (Votdin & McAlister, 1982). More specific interventions are provided by Capuzzi and Lecoq (1983).

Because of parental drinking patterns, communication of caring and interest, and use of social control seem to be linked with adolescent substance abuse, educators and counselors should give some thought to designing programs around family counseling or parent education models.

Peer group support is very influential in the process of using and abusing drugs, hence, group counseling with adolescents may be a viable intervention strategy. Structured opportunities to practice peer resistance skills also can be effective.

The perception of experiencing increased pleasure or decreased internal psychic pain may reinforce use and abuse of substances. Intervention strategies must facilitate examination of such perceptions and foster awareness of other options for producing such outcomes.

Low self-esteem seems to be one predictor of substance use and abuse. Educators and counselors should design treatment modalities to restore or develop a sense of self-worth. Policies that are punitive or disenfranchise youth from meaningful participation should be re-examined.

Low impulse control and lack of ability to delay gratification are correlates with chemical use and abuse. Assisting young people to exert control and postpone satisfaction may provide them with the help they need to overcome drug and alcohol related difficulties.

Intervention strategies with young people should explore whether the feeling of independence from parents or other adults can be achieved through options other than the use and abuse of drugs and alcohol.

Adolescents who are insecure or ambivalent about peer and parental relationships may need help in developing interpersonal trust, and socialization skills to initiate and maintain relationships.

Once a model for intervention is designed, based on reported research, an evaluation component to assess its effectiveness also should be implemented so the model can be refined and improved.

ADOLESCENT PREGNANCY AND SEXUAL BEHAVIOR

While statistics on sexual behavior do not summarize adolescent sexuality, they do confirm that many adolescents initiate sexual activity during a developmental stage characterized by risk-taking behavior and a propensity to act without a full sense of the potential consequence of their actions.

Of the 29 million adolescents over age 12, about 12 million are sexually active.

Mean age at first intercourse is less than 15 years.

Yearly, 30,000 girls younger than 15 become pregnant. Girls under 15 make up the only group of women in the country for whom the birth rate is not declining.

The younger a female is at her first pregnancy, the more children she will have, and the closer spaced they will be.

In 1985, an estimated 1 million teenagers became pregnant in this country. Of these pregnancies, less than one-half (477,705) resulted in births, an estimated 40% ended in abortion, and an estimated 13% ended in miscarriage.

Teens with poor basic skills are five times as likely to become mothers before age 16 as those with average basic skills. Adolescent males with poor basic skills are three times as likely to be fathers as those with average basic skills.

Almost all racial differences in the incidence of teen parenthood disappear when poverty and basic skills are taken into account.

One of five poor teens with lower than average basic skills is a mother, regardless of race.

Poor white teens with lower than average basic skills are 6.5 times as likely to be teen mothers as white teens above poverty with higher basic skills. (Children's Defense Fund, 1988)

According to the Alan Guttmacher Institute (1984), an independent research corporation based in New York, the

United States now has higher teenage pregnancy, birth, and abortion rates than most developed countries in the world. The teenage pregnancy rate has been 9.8% in the United States, while most European countries have shown an average of approximately 3.5% (Olson, 1989). Caught between peer values, parent values, and the image of sex portrayed in the media, adolescents frequently act impulsively without thought to the consequences of their actions.

**Implications for Intervention
of Adolescent Pregnancy and Sexual Behavior**

> Make maternity programs more accessible by simplifying the eligibility process and bureaucratic red-tape.

> Develop a system to track high-risk infants from birth, so that case managers can effectively guide them into appropriate services.

> Create half-day preschool programs and coordinated child care programs for "at-risk" 4-year olds.

> Create health clinics for youth that are school-based or located near schools.

> Provide critical services for adolescent mothers such as (1) personal counseling, (2) basic education, (3) assistance in obtaining social services, (4) pregnancy/ parental counseling, and (5) early childhood enrichment programs for their offspring.

High quality sex education programs are now offered to a small minority of adolescents through the schools. Yet, fewer than 10% of all U.S. teenagers have an opportunity to participate in such program. The literature does support, however, that successful programs focus on teaching the skills necessary for responsible and informed decision making.

> Students are exposed to good decision-making models and are given opportunities to make decisions in real or simulated situations.

Students are encouraged to explore their values and behavior and to confront discrepancies between the two.

Students are given accurate information about acquiring and using contraceptives.

Students take part in classroom discussions that explore alternatives to sexual activity.

Students are exposed to the realities of such situations as teenage marriage and parenting, about which they may have idealistic concepts.

Students are taught that sexual thoughts, feelings, and emotions are normal, but behavior must be monitored for its appropriateness.

Students are taught, and practice, effective communication skills.

EMOTIONAL DISORDERS AND ADOLESCENT DEPRESSION

The escalating rate of emotional disorders can be attributed to several precipitating variables. For example, many teenagers from dysfunctional families are often products of alcoholism, violence, and incest. Add to these risk variables, rapid social change, cultural pluralism, occupational diversity, and international discord, then a teenager's hopelessness and disillusionment with planning for the future are understandable.

The number of teenage suicides has tripled in the last 30 years (Pfeffer, 1986; Strother & Jacobs, 1986).

Suicide is the second leading cause of death among teenagers, after automobile accidents (Strother & Jacobs, 1986).

Each year, 500,000 teenagers attempt suicide (Cohen-Sandler, Berman, & King, 1982); attempts outnumber actual completed suicides 50 to 1.

Seventy-eight percent of teenage suicide victims actually gave some type of warning within three months prior to the act (Shafii, Carringan, Whittinghill, & Derrick, 1985).

Each year, 5,000 teenage suicides are reported (Strother, 1986).

Females attempt suicide three times as often as males; however, males are two to three times more likely to "succeed" in their attempt (Cohen-Sandler, Berman, & King, 1982).

Depression is becoming increasingly acknowledged as a serious disorder of childhood and adolescence and perhaps the most common impetus to suicide. The pattern of a teenager's life, and how he/she ultimately feels about it, continues to punctuate their attitudes and actions.

As applied to adolescents, the term depression describes behavior ranging from common mood swings or short-lived situational episodes to chronic recurring feelings of worthlessness, helplessness, and hopelessness. Depression is often characterized by withdrawal from normal social interactions, sleep disturbances, poor concentration, feelings of inferiority, and self-blame. The severity of the depression often profiles the equation—Severity equals Distress times Uncontrollability times Frequency ($S = D \times U \times F$). The variables of depression and hopelessness appear to be the important factors that are associated with both suicidal ideation and suicidal behavior in adolescents (Kazdin, French, Unis, Esveldt-Dawson, & Sherick, 1983).

Most recently Cohen-Sandler et al. (1982), Gispert, Wheeler, Marsh, and Davis (1985), and Pfeffer (1981) suggested that suicidal children and adolescents have experienced higher levels of stress than "normal" adolescents. Generally, they have experienced more dysfunctional families and losses of significant others, witness repeated trauma (e.g., family violence, and/or chemical abuse), and were themselves subject to more abuse and neglect.

Hawton (1986) found that predominant problems immediately preceding adolescent suicide include school failure, a loss of status among family and/or friends, a feeling that one has let others down, being publicly reprimanded or humiliated and/or a significant love loss. Escalating problems lead to an increasing sense of helplessness and impotence about effecting solutions eventually ending in a suicidal mental set. (See Table 2.2).

Table 2.2
Youth Suicides Nationwide

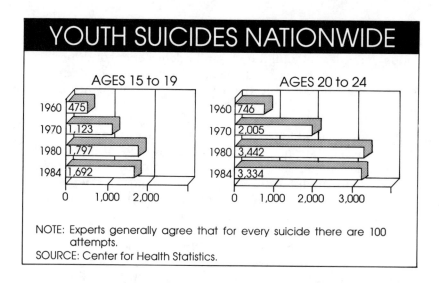

Note: Based on information appearing in *AMA Whitepaper on Adolescent Health.* (1987). American Medical Association. Reproduced by permission.

Implicaitons for Intervention
of Emotional Disorders and Adolescent Depression

A critical need exists for school personal to identify and implement primary prevention programs and activities within the school-as-community that foster a positive school climate and enhance school morale. Promoting and validating the self-worth for such a program is emphasized by such proponents as Sprinthall (1984), and Dinkmeyer (1971) who stated, "The lack of a required sequentially developmental program in self-understanding and human behavior testifies to an educational paradox: We have taught children almost everything in school except to understand and accept themselves and to function more effectively in human relationships."

In addition, a majority of adolescent suicide attempts appear to be related to "adjustment reactions" or "adolescent crises." Hawton, O'Grady, Osborn, and Cole (1982) also maintained that suicide attempters had experienced twice as much stress (measured on a scale of social readjustment or adaptation) as had other young people. Earlier in their lives, the suicide attempters had experienced increasing and significantly greater amounts of stress as they had matured through various developmental stages. Especially common stressors were chaotic and disruptive family events that resulted in losses and separations from important people, particularly parents and other relatives (Hawton, 1986). Concurrently, studies have found live stressors of children and adolescents to be significantly related to measures of anxiety and depression and to be correlated with decreased levels of self-esteem, external locus of control orientation, delinquent behavior, poorer school performance, and an increase in behavioral dysfunctions.

The following activities (not all-inclusive) are offered with the understanding that variations will be needed to (1) meet the various maturity and developmental needs of student populations, and (2) meet the various responsive communities.

Use more adults in the classroom as volunteers, aides, paraprofessionals, or parents.

Involve students in all major aspects of school operations. Expand students' lines of communication to faculty and administration; allow for student input and influence on decisions and regulations that affect them.

Provide more effective counseling programs, including specialized student assistance counselors who work exclusively with targeted at-risk student populations such as potential dropouts, etc.

Offer appropriate parent education courses in such areas as preventing drug and alcohol abuse, setting achievement goals, and improving school work habits.

Develop a "student adoption program" where each member of the instructional staff adopts an at-risk student (with behavioral adjustment problems, attendance problems, family problems, etc.) to meet with on a daily basis to discuss problems, progress or barriers to success, to develop short-term strategies to enhance success rather than failure, and to provide unconditional support.

Promote clubs and service organizations that are altruistic and other-centered with community service contributions. Students often rediscover their self-importance by learning their value to others. To do so gives a student an opportunity to feel they have worth and can affect change, as well as enhance the quality of life. The tendency exists to become "other-centered" rather than "me-centered." To invest energy in another person or cause provides a purpose and a reliable goal for the adolescent. Organizations or participation in such activities as Students Against Drunk Driving (SADD), "Just Say No" clubs, Operation Prom/Graduation (OPG), Rock Against Drugs (RAD), The Special Olympics, Sub Teens Recreational Activities to Educate (STATE), and Responsible Educated Adolescents Can Help America (REACH America) are selected examples.

Implement an ongoing student support group as part of the student services of the school counseling program. Provide students with the opportunity to share anxieties in a secure environment. To achieve validation, from a caring adult in a helping capacity, provides needed support for adolescents. Topics could include:

dealing with life-transitions and change;

academic pressure;

parental separation and divorce;

competition and achievement;

death, loss, or separation: necessary losses to personal growth;

aptitude, interest, and achievement: finding your career niche; and

maintaining interpersonal relationships.

In addition, school after care groups following intervention for drug, alcohol, or other self-destructive behaviors can help the adolescent make the fragile transition to a more productive life, as well as reduce recidivism. Other support groups serve to address multiple needs in the school and the community. Selected examples of some community support groups include descriptors such as the following: Adolescent female/male support group for ages 15 to 18 "who want to enhance their self-esteem, and who need support in coping with the stress of adolescent years"; Adolescent survival skills for school; Boys' therapy—"group for boys 8 to 12 who are experiencing stress in their families and face adjustment problems"; Children of alcoholics—"group for children from ages 5 to 12"; Children's sexual abuse—"for children ages 8 to 12 who have been sexually abused"; Our children's hope—"group therapy for young cancer patients, their parents, and siblings"; Teen music therapy— "group focusing on peer relationships and common adolescent problems"; and Young adolescents—"group for ages 11 to 15 to explore identity issues, peer relationships, emotional awareness and to learn ways to deal with anger, sadness, and rejection."

Develop a student stress reduction program which can be preventive, and serve to circumvent the direct discussion of suicide with students focusing on many of the factors found to precipitate self-destructive behaviors. Classes on suicide are often not as successful as student classes and programs about stress, followed by small group discussion and other group activities. Emphasis should be placed on the social, emotional, and curative factors that adolescents possess as a group to manage personal, social, or academic disappointments or frustrations. Through the mutual sharing of problems in a secure environment, the adolescent discovers a commonality of fears, fantasies, hopes, and needs. Similar problems are no longer unique; they are universal.

Train volunteer teachers to serve as positive role models, and to lead group discussions on subjects of time-management, stress, and academic problem-solving strategies. Many caring educators welcome an opportunity to interact with students on a more affective domain.

Mental health professionals can serve as resource people to the school to present 4 to 6 week group counseling units in targeted classes on identified needs.

Institute a peer counseling program. The range of peer helper programs available today includes cross-age tutoring, peer counseling, educational advisement, and special interest self-help groups. Development of a peer counseling problem is based on the premise that adolescents invariably turn to their peers for needed support and understanding, as well as a validation of their perceptions and feelings.

Integrate a comprehensive "services curriculum." Ideally, the development and implementation of a comprehensive "services curriculum" could be designed for the "mastery of daily problem-solving skills such as self-competency, enhancement of interpersonal relationships, commun-ications, values, and the awareness of roles, attitudes, and motivation" (Worrell & Stilwell, 1981). Personal development could become an integral part of the school curriculum and evolve as a required course which is integrated into the student's program of studies much like computer literacy, driver education, or fine arts. Powell et al. (1985) lend credence to this potential maintaining that along with the horizontal, vertical, and extracurricular, the "service curriculum" directly address social or psychological problems such as grief, child abuse, depression, and alienation or emotional and social problems deemed educationally valid.

DELINQUENCY

Research thus far has shown a correlation between delinquent behaviors and certain situations and/or experiences of the adolescent in his/her development. These include poor performance in school, negative labeling, poor peer relations, multiple health problems (speech, vision, motor impairment, hearing, or neurological), drug and alcohol use, and involvement with the police.

Adolescents are responsible for 35.9% of all reported arrests for major crimes (U.S. Department of Justice, 1981);

Thirty-six percent of all reported arrests for major crimes in 1981 were youth under the age of 18; 57.9% were under the age of 21.

Almost 13% of all arrests for major crimes are of individuals under the age of 15. For youth under 18, these percentages translate into

1,742 homicides,

4,346 forcible rapes,

41,997 robberies,

38,135 aggravated assaults,

215,387 burglaries,

58,798 motor vehicle thefts,

421,082 other thefts, and

8,161 cases of arson.

The leading crimes committed by adolescents include vandalism, motor vehicle theft, burglary, larceny, robbery, and other stolen property. Vandalism and theft often correlate highly with drug and alcohol use in order to pay for a drug habit.

Implications for Intervention
of Delinquency

The following rehabilitative programs and appropriate treatment plans for troubled youth were outlines from a judge's perspective:

Individual/Family Counseling;

Substance Abuse Evaluation and Treatment;

Referral to a Child Development Center for Multidisciplinary Evaluation;

Parenting Skills Classes for Dysfunctional Families;

Law-related Education or "Street Law" Program;

A Quarterly Probation Care Review;

Youth Assigned to Non-profit Community Service Programs;

Jail Tour as a Diversion Program;

Residential Placements and Community-based Services;

Volunteer Emergency Foster Care;

Prescriptive Teams which include representatives from education, corrections, mental health, and social services, agencies to integrate treatment efforts and to coordinate resources;

Big Brothers/Big Sisters Program for Troubled Youth; and

Public/Private Coordination for School/Community Programs and Services.

DROPOUTS

Statistical manipulations have the effect of trivializing a significant social and educational program. For example, the underestimation of dropout rates on the local level raises serious issues of public accountability. In addition, dropout rates in nearly all large U.S. cities are tabulated annually, rather than according to how many starting freshmen actually received diplomas four years later.

One reliable estimation is provided by the U.S. General Accounting Office (GAO). The GAO reported that in 1985 4.3 million young people between the ages of 16 and 24 dropped out of school, 13% of the age group. The most common reason for leaving school was poor academic performance.

A variety of studies have identified a number of conditions as major risk variables for a potential dropout:

> behind in grade level and older than classmates; (by grade 4, one year behind in reading and mathematics and by grade 7, two years behind in reading and mathematics);

> poor academic performance, i.e., reading poorly;

> dislike of school, often precipitated by fear of attending school;

> frequent detention and/or suspension;

> pregnancy;

> welfare recipient and/or member of single-parent household;

> the attractiveness of work;

> undiagnosed learning disability;

> views school as irrelevant and unchallenging;

> poor teacher-student relationships;

> little involvement in extracurricular activities;

> low self-esteem;

hostility;

resentment of authority; and/or

punitive/abusive families.

Implications for Intervention of Dropouts

Influential factors, objectives, and services needed for successful dropout program from an instructional perspective include

a caring and committed instructional staff,

a non-threatening environment for learning,

low student-teacher ratio, and

basic education.

Critical services include

personal counseling,

job search assistance,

job skills training, and/or

GED preparation.

VICTIMIZATION

Child maltreatment is one of the most critical problems that exist in the United States today. Each year tens of thousands of children are maltreated in ways that lead to serious developmental, psychological, or medical problems that sometimes culminate in death.

Because of the vast range of maltreatment acts, this phenomenon is more readily understood if classified into categories representing both acts of commission (i.e., physical abuse) and/or acts of omission (i.e., emotional neglect) (Halperin, 1979). These categories plus multiple maltreatment and physical and behavioral signs are listed in the following subtopics.

Acts of Commission

Physical Abuse: Infliction of physical injury (e.g., burns, bites) to the child.

Sexual Abuse: Subjection of a child to sexually stimulating acts by the adult.

Physical Neglect: Failure to provide a child with a nurturing home environment that supplies the basic necessities of life (i.e., food, clothing, shelter, supervision, and protection from harm).

Medical Neglect: Failure of a caretaker to provide medical treatment in cases of suspected or diagnosed physical ailments (except for religious reasons).

Acts of Omission

Emotional Abuse: Speech and actions by a caretaker that inhibit the healthy personal and social development of the child.

Emotional Neglect: Failure of a caretaker to show concern for a child or his/her activities.

Educational Neglect: Failure of a caretaker to ensure that a child is provided with the opportunity to learn.

Abandonment: Failure of a caretaker to make provisions for the continued sustenance of the child.

Multiple Maltreatment: A severe and complex combination of several types of abuse and/or neglect.

Implications for Intervention of Victimization

The following collective and collaborative efforts also are necessary to demonstrate a commitment for change.

Institutionalize primary prevention in a broad-based national family policy statement.

Modify current programs to earmark more funds for primary prevention and establish the importance of the family in legislation.

Coordinate preventive efforts across human services programs. Coordinate federal, state, and local programs in education, health, mental health, juvenile justice and social services. Education in particular offers the ideal nonproblem-oriented setting for primary prevention.

Establish community networks and resource centers. Self-help resource centers have grown out of the desire of citizens to be involved in local planning, decision making, and problem solving. Networks and resource centers can operate in a wide variety of local settings; hospital, schools, community mental health centers, recreation centers, libraries, community colleges, civic center, day-care centers, social service agencies, and churches.

Draw network members from the medical, educational, law enforcement, and social work disciplines including key leaders from business, political, and volunteer segments of the community. Committees of network members should concentrate on such as a speaker bureau; media liaison and publicity; parenting and mental health education programs; legislative and family advocacy; staff for hot lines, crisis nurseries, shelters for victims of family violence; and the development of self-help groups through churches and community centers.

SEVEN EXPLICIT DIMENSIONS TO ASSIST AT-RISK STUDENTS

Furthermore, seven explicit dimensions can be targeted to assist the growing population of at-risk students. These explicit dimensions are (1) early identification and coordinated program delivery; (2) public/private collaboration; (3) parents as significant partners; (4) creating a positive school climate; (5) staff development; (6) counseling; and (7) assertive, systematic attendance program.

Early Identification and Coordinated Program Delivery

The onus of responsibility for at-risk youth rests with the school division, the school board, the superintendent, district administrators, principals, teachers, students, parents, and the business community. The need for coordinated program planning in the following areas include

early identification of at-risk youth;

a district-level plan that assesses need, identifies school/community resources, and suggests intervention strategies;

a local school-based plan for early intervention and primary prevention strategies; and

a vigorous united front to promote private/public collaboration with community agencies, businesses, and schools.

Public/Private Collaboration

A new mentality of collaboration must be developed to reach contemporary youth. Emphasis must be placed on creating linkages between schools, families, community agencies, businesses, and institutions of higher learning. A coalition of services as well as linkages with resources outside of the school could include the following:

establishing an adopt-a-school program to involve the business community in school activities with youth;

creating a "cities-in-schools" program to integrate community resources in the schools;

identifying community volunteers to provide nurturing to at-risk youth; and

developing a "student assistance advisory board" to review programs, services, and policies.

Parents as Significant Partners

Parental involvement strategies should create opportunities to bring teachers, parents, and administrators together to better understand and serve the developmental needs of youth. Selected activities include

planning and conducting parent education seminars addressing such concerns as stress, peer pressure, chemical dependency, etc.;

scheduling home visits with parents of students who have a high absentee rate with the belief that parents might be more willing to work with the school if they feel the school was genuinely concerned; and

distributing school news and information to community agencies and churches to provide continuity in the notion of shared responsibility for youth.

Creating a Positive School Climate

The school-as-institution (i.e., the assembly line-cell-and-bell school) clearly alienates youth from active participation. Some strategic efforts to create a more caring, nurturing school include

evaluating suspension, attendance, and eligibility policies that exclude students from participation;

enlisting mentors from the business and community to provide more one-on-one contact with students who have a high risk profile;

encouraging and motivating youth to participate in cocurricular and extracurricular activities and eliminating some simple barriers such as lack of school transportation after participating in these activities;

working closely with community services and agencies to coordinate service delivery; and

revitalizing parent/teacher outreach efforts that focus on positive feedback regarding student effort or performance. (See Chapter 9 for more school climate ideas.)

Staff Development

Intervention with at-risk youth demands a staff commitment to a student-centered approach that actively involves students in the learning process both academically and interpersonally. Suggested means to do so are to

facilitate staff development opportunities for all instructional and support staff (include cafeteria workers and bus drivers) to create strategies to raise student expectations for success;

provide ongoing staff development in responsible discipline, facilitative communication, crisis counseling, and behavior improvement strategies; and

collaborate with teacher education centers and local higher education institutions to include preservice training components for reaching at-risk youth.

Counseling

The school counselor's role in early intervention strategies is central to the success of all school/community efforts. Counselors have an important role in all seven dimensions targeted to assist at-risk youth by providing short-term counseling and intervention. They also can refer students to critical support services and referral sources in and out of school serving as the pivotal link between the school and the community.

Assertive, Systematic Attendance Program

The perceived relevance of school can be improved with an assertive, systematic attendance program. Suggested activities include the following:

> before school opens in the fall, send a postcard with a brief note to students who had elevated absentee rates the previous year and by means of the card invite them to come to school to review their plans for the coming year, and to discuss any problems they may be anticipating (e.g., delinquent fees, transportation, part-time work schedule, childcare needs, etc.);

> initiate a "peer" calling network in which upper level students "who made it" call their younger counterparts to encourage a quick return to school . . . "no hassle man, honest"; and

> delegate someone to review attendance records weekly to alert the counseling department of emerging patterns.

CONCLUSION

To be successful in reducing the debilitating attitudes and destructive behavior manifestations of today's youth, a school-as-community approach could have long-range implications. According to Joyce, Hersh, and McKibben (1983) the school/community develops distinctive normative patterns that draw students toward or away from particular activities and domains of development (social, academic, physical, emotional, and interpersonal). These normative patterns will have a profound long-term effect on the self-concepts, values, and skills that will ultimately be developed. Personalities will interact within the social system productively or unproductively with long-term effects on motivation and learning style (p. 114).

Collective efforts invested around structured activities to discuss adjustment anxieties in a secure environment could enhance the self-worth of the struggling at-risk youth. Providing ongoing programs in the schools are crucial for all so they may be given an opportunity to express feelings and to know that significant adults care about their well-being, emotionally as well as intellectually.

CHAPTER 3

SCHOOL COUNSELING
DEFINITION AND BENEFITS

If For Counselors

If you can sit and give your full attention
To each new student whom you meet and greet,
Without neglect of files and information
And keep in mind the student data sheet;

If you can sense his feelings, oft unspoken,
And let him know how deeply you do care,
That you can keep his confidence unbroken
Despite responsibilities you share;

If you can keep in place your own temptation
To give advice you think he wants to hear,
And stimulate instead his own creation
Of new ideas and goals toward which to steer;

If you can help each one gain understanding
Of self, of world, of plans and future hope,
And yet maintain a goal of still expanding
Concepts of self with the social scope;

If you can help to build a strong profession
In spite of all your critics have to say,
In belief and pride support your own confession
That your feet, too, are only made of clay;

If you achieve such heights of aspiration
With half of those who knock upon your door.
Then you can say, regardless of your station,
I'm surely proud to be a counselor.

Author Anonymous

The early emphasis of guidance and counseling in secondary schools centered on a narrow concept and selected services rendered by a few specialists for a small population of problem students. The results were measured by the number and frequency of tests administered, the use of occupational and educational information, and the emphasis of cumulative record data. The primary function of the counselor was to sort, select, and allocate students within the educational system.

In the early years, counseling per se was not a major emphases in many programs. No mention of counseling was made in the professional literature until 1931 (Proctor, Benefield, & Wrenn, 1931). The post World War II years dramatically affected guidance and counseling in schools. New psychological theories and techniques evolved with the predominant advancement of psychodynamic methodologies of therapy (Aubrey, 1983). The influence of Carl Rogers and counseling orientation of person-centered therapy (Rogers, 1942) led counselors to consider counseling as their primary function.

TOWARD A DEFINITION
OF COUNSELING

From the client-centered perspective, Rogers (1951) defined counseling as the process by which the basic nature of the self is relaxed in the safety of the relationship with the counselor and where previously denied experiences are perceived, accepted, and integrated into an altered self. Shertzer and Stone (1974) combined self-concept and behavioral orientations in their definition: "counseling is an interaction process which facilitates meaningful understanding of the self and environment and/ or clarification of goals and values for future behavior" (p. 20). From a psychodynamic perspective, King and Bennington (1972) described an essential goal of counseling as one "to reduce the anxiety of the client to manageable limits in order for the ego to function in a more discriminating and effective manner" (p. 187). Adlerian psychology maintains that the primary goal of professional counseling is "behavior change within the existing life style and differentiates it from the goal of psychotherapy for which a change in life style is the desired outcome" (Sweeney, 1989, pp. 239-40).

Counseling also, is viewed as a goal-setting and planning process. Smith (1982) described counseling as a "process in which the counselor assists the counselee to make interpretations of facts related to choice, plans, or adjustments which he needs to make" (Smith, 1982, p. 802). Similarly, Smaby and Tamminen (1978) stated that "counseling is a process in which counselees learn how to make decisions and formulate new ways of behaving, feeling, and thinking. Egan (1986) maintained that counseling involves both choice and change evolving through such distinct stages as exploration, goal setting, and action planning.

More recent definitions have reflected a movement toward a balance between remediation and personal development. Pietrofesa, Hoffman, and Splete (1984) defined counseling "as a relationship between a professionally trained, competent counselor and an individual seeking help in gaining greater self-understanding and improved decision-making and behavior-change skills for problem resolution and/or development growth" (p. 6).

Furthermore, contemporary practitioners such as Dyer and Vriend (1977) provided pragmatic components of effective counseling. Dyer and Vriend (p. 17) maintained that

> Counseling is an interpersonal helping procedure which begins with counselee exploration for the purpose of identifying thinking, feeling, and doing processes which are in any way self-defeating or which require upgrading.
>
> The counselee determines and declares to the counselor what the counter-productive behaviors are and makes decisions about which one can be worked on.
>
> The counselor helps the counselee to set goals in which more positive thinking and feeling will lead to the acquisition of self-enhancing behaviors which had not previously been a part of the counselee's repertoire.
>
> The counselor helps the individual to identify significant behaviors which are self-defeating; helps to move the counselee toward self-understanding by examining with the counselee why such self-crippling behavior persists,

as well as the psychological maintenance system for such behavior.

The counselor then moves the counselee to explore possible alternatives to self-defeating thinking, feeling, and doing.

Setting goals which are specific and realistically attainable are introduced.

The counselee tests proposed alternate behaviors in the counseling session where helping intervention, structures, activities, or simulations are provided by the counselor; psychological homework assignments are mutually initiated and agreed upon, and the client tries the new behavior in his/her personal world, outside the counseling session. Selected counseling strategies include consultation, modeling role reversal, journals/logs, assertiveness training, stress management, relaxation training, imagery, contracts, positive self-talk, role playing, goal setting, testing and assessment, bibliotherapy, homework, thought shopping, and acquisition of new coping skills.

In subsequent sessions the counselee reports on the new thinking, new feelings engendered by the new thinking and new behaviors. This is followed by revised behavioral goals which are established as a result of analysis and evaluation in the counseling. The individual either incorporates the new thinking and behavior or rejects it or get recycled for additional exploration, self-understanding, and goal setting. The total emphasis is on the acquisition and incorporation into the self-system productive new behavior. Virtually every significant theory of counseling states that creating some kind of change toward growth in the counselee is the ultimate intended outcome of the counseling experience.

INHERENT BENEFITS OF COUNSELING

Fundamentally, counseling is not a singular process. The term counseling outlines a group of processes based upon a variety of philosophical orientations that occur in many different settings intending to serve persons composed of a wide range of individual differences. The importance of the counselor-counselee relationship and interactions also is supported.

A review of what has been empirically revealed about the counseling process and potential benefits also is important for the practicing school counselor. Although not all inclusive, a compendium of empirical studies over the last two decades reveals information in three domains.

In the Interpersonal Domain

Longitudinal follow-ups of persons exposed to counseling and related guidance processes in high school can be distinguished from their peers who did not participate in guidance and counseling on such criteria as higher income and contributions to society (Campbell, 1965).

In follow-up studies of high school students at 2, 5, and 10 year intervals, differences were found between those who received extensive counseling and guidance services from those who received no special counseling efforts. The experimental students had better academic records after high school; made more realistic and more consistent vocational choices; made more progress in their employment; and were more satisfied with their lives (Prediger, Roth, & Noeth, 1973).

During periods of sociocultural transition, counselors who are specially trained to provide personal counseling resolve interpersonal conflicts, and coordinate classes designed to improve students' human relations skills and their understanding of different racial/ethnic groups can assist in reducing prejudice and conflict (Gordon, Brownell, & Brittell, 1972; Higgins, 1976; Katz & Zalk, 1978; Lewis & Lewis, 1970).

The higher the degree of therapeutic conditions provided by the counselor, the more likely it is that the counselee will achieve constructive change (Carkhuff & Berenson, 1976; Egan, 1980; Egan & Cowan, 1979; Herr, 1976; Lewis & Schaffner, 1970).

Students who have been helped by counselors to evaluate, break into components, and master their problems gain self-confidence (Bennett, 1975; Herr, 1976).

Guidance and counseling activities can help children with self-concept development, peer relationships, improved adult/youth relationships, academic achievement, and career development (Thompson & Poppen, 1979).

As a function of behavioral modification techniques, delinquent boys in a community based home tend to improve dramatically in self-esteem, and to move from external to internal locus of control as compared with a control group (Bryan & Pearl, 1981; Higgins, 1976; Tesiny, 1980).

Affective education designed to improve racial understanding provided by trained school counselors does achieve such a goal (Sue, 1978; Sue & Sue, 1977).

A rise in the self-esteem of students exposed to guidance and other counseling process is related to reduction in dropout rates, absences, and improvement in conduct and social adjustment (Bennett, 1975; Wiggins, 1977).

Students exposed to the guidance process tend to organize their concepts about themselves in a more coherent way and reconcile their differences between ideal and real self-concepts more effectively than persons without such experiences (Schunk, 1981; Washington, 1977).

Middle school students exposed to guidance processes designed to improve their interpersonal skills experience improved general behavior and interpersonal relationships (Hutchins & Cole, 1986).

Minority students who are assisted in deciding upon vocational objectives are typically found to have more positive self-concepts and higher ideal selves than those who do not have such objectives (Bennett, 1975).

Individual counseling in combination with counselor connected training programs designed to develop interpersonal, physical, emotional, and intellectual skills which are transferable to home, school, and community can reduce the recidivism rate of youthful offenders (Lewis & Boyle, 1976).

Secondary students have been assisted through counseling to overcome debilitating behaviors such as anorexia, depressions, and substance abuse (Beck, Rush, Shaw, & Emery, 1979; Burns, 1981; Halmi, 1983; Johnston, Bachman, & O'Malley, 1982; Jones, 1980; Lazarus, 1981).

In the Educational Domain

Either group or individual counseling extended for a reasonable amount of time helps students whose ability is adequate or better to improve their scholastic performance. Greater results are likely if intervention focuses on the variables that predict underachievement rather than relying on more general approaches (Laport & Noth, 1976; Schmidt, 1976)

Counselor teams that work closely with teachers, principals, and parents in dealing with emotional or social problems interfering with the use of their intellectual potential by children are helpful in increasing general levels of student academic achievement (Bertoldi, 1975; Thompson, 1987).

Guidance and counseling processes integrated with remedial instuction in mathematics and reading have been found to increase academic achievement significantly (Bertoldi, 1975; Thompson, 1987).

Through group problem-solving methods, students can be helped to understand the relationship between educational and vocational development, to clarify goals, to acquire skills in identifying and using relevant information for their decision making (Babcock & Kauffman, 1976; Martin & Stone, 1977; Steward & Thorenson, 1968).

In the Vocational Domain

Students utilizing computer based career guidance systems make larger gains than non-users in such characteristics as degree of preparedness, knowledge, and use of resources for career exploration, awareness of career options available to them, and cost benefit risks associated with these options (Meyer, Strowig, & Hosford, 1970).

Short-term counseling (three sessions) with high school students has been found to facilitate the career maturity of these students with regard to such emphasis as orientation to decision making, preparedness, and independence of choice (Flake, Roach, & Stenning, 1975).

Comprehensive programs involving self-awareness activities, job-seeking skills, peer interaction through group sessions, counseling, career materials displays, and testing information meetings cause observable, positive change among rural youth (Herr, 1976; Meyer, Strowig, & Hosford, 1970; Wiggins, 1977).

Students exposed to systematically planned career/ guidance classes dealing with topics such as values clarification, decision making, job satisfaction, sources of occupational information, work-power projections, and career planning make greater gains on self-knowledge and the relations of self-knowledge to occupations and engage in a greater number of career-planning activities than students who have not participated in such classes (Griggs, 1983; Krumboltz & Thoresen, 1964).

SUMMARY

From this perspective, programs and amenities proliferated from the counseling process have been diverse and numerous. They demonstrate that support for and the availability of guidance and counseling programs, services, and processes do make a significant difference in the lives of children, youth, and adult populations. Fundamental techniques and processes have demonstrated universal utility in a wide arena of human problems and can be applied and modified to respond to changing populations and social conditions. These significant differences are particularly critical in view of the growing concern over at-risk adolescents.

CHAPTER 4

DEVELOPMENTAL GUIDANCE AND COUNSELING

Developmental guidance and counseling assumes that human nature moves individuals sequentially and positively toward self-enhancement (Myrick, 1987, p. 31). The developmental approach considers the nature of human development, including the general states and tasks that most individuals experience as they mature from childhood to adulthood. It centers on positive self-concepts and acknowledges that one's self-concept is formed and reformed through experience and education. It further recognizes that feelings, ideas, and behaviors are closely linked together and that they are learned. The ultimate objective is to help students learn more effectively and efficiently from a developmental perspective.

CHARACTERISTICS OF CHILDREN AND YOUTH

Many theorists of human development exists, each of which contributes to the understanding of student behavior at various age levels. In Figure 4.1 is a list of major theorists and respective development tasks for adolescents. Fundamentally, theories of human development focus our attention on the sequence of patterns that occur such as biological, social, cognitive,

(Continued on page 53)

Theorist	Developmental Domain	Developmental Task
Freud	Psychosexual	Sexual energy is invested in socially accepted activities
Erikson	Psychosocial	Self identity; image of self as a unique individual
Piaget	Cognitive	Formal operations; engaging in abstract thought; consider hypothetical situations
Maslow	Human Needs	Ego, esteem needs; confidence sense of mastery; positive self-regard; self-respect, self-extension
Super	Vocational	Crystallizing a vocational preference; tentative choices are made; appropriate career fields are identified; generalized choice is converted to specific choice
Sullivan	Interpersonal	Personal security with freedom from anxiety; collaboration with others; increased sensitivity to needs of others; establishment of a repertoire of interpersonal relatioships
Kohlberg	Moral	Defines moral values and principles; decisions of conscience are congruent with self-held ethical principles
Egan & Cowan	Life-style Systems	Family, peer group, school and community are key systems life-style management; gain emotional independence from nuclear family
Havighurst	Stages of Childhood Development	Gaining emotional independence from nuclear family; assimilate appropriate sexual identity; finding an educational/vocational direction; setting goals; acquiring a set of values and ethical system to guide behavior

Figure 4.1. Major developmental tasks of adolescence as identified by theorists.

moral, affective, interpersonal, and vocational. From this perspective, they reflect the unfolding of individual development within the life cycle.

The major developmental tasks of adolescents is to achieve a sense of identity and self-esteem (Havighurst, 1973). For youth to accomplish this life transition, they need to acquire skills, knowledge, and attitudes which may be classified into two broad categories—those involving self-development and those involving other people.

COUNSELING INTENTIONS
AND INTERVENTIONS

Unless group counseling is an integral component of the school counseling program, most school counselors may not see a counselee more than three times during the calendar year. Assistance is usually provided in a short amount of time with the presenting problem remediated contingent upon the degree of counselor expertise. Critical problems in a school setting predominately focus upon academic or interpersonal concerns.

For the most part, however, most counselors find themselves gathering information, providing support, exploring feelings, generating alternatives, or merely providing a secure environment to share developmental anxieties. One means school counselors might utilize to clarify their intended purpose and to provide a focus for their intervention could revolve around Hill's List of Therapeutic Intentions (Hill & O'Grady, 1985). The 18 intentions along with statements written as objectives are presented in the paragraphs that follow:

> **Set Limits.** To structure, make arrangements, establish goals and objectives of treatment, outline methods.

> **Get Information.** To find out specific facts about history, counselee functioning, future plans, and present issues.

> **Give Information.** To educate, give facts, correct misperceptions or misinformation, and give reasons for procedures.

Support. To provide a warm, supportive, empathic environment; increase trust and rapport and build a relationship; help counselee feel accepted and understood.

Focus. To help counselee get back on track, change subject, channel or structure the discussion if he/she is unable to begin or has been confused.

Clarify. To provide or solicit more elaboration; emphasize or specify when counselee or counselor has been vague, incomplete, confusing, contradictory, or inaudible.

Hope. To convey the expectations that change is possible and likely to occur; convey that the counselor will be able to help the counselee; restore morale, build the counselee's confidence to make changes.

Cathart (achieve catharsis). To promote a relief from tension or unhappy feelings; allow the counselee a chance to talk through feelings and problems.

Cognitions. To identify maladaptive, illogical, or irrational thoughts or attitudes (e.g., "I must perform perfectly").

Behaviors. To identify and give feedback about the counselee's inappropriate or maladaptive behaviors, and/or their consequences; to do a behavioral analysis, point out discrepancies.

Self-control. To encourage the counselee to own or gain a sense of mastery or control over his/her own thoughts, feelings, behaviors, or actions; help the counselee become more appropriately internal in taking responsibility.

Feelings. To identify, intensify, and/or enable acceptance of feelings; encourage or provoke the counselee to become aware of deeper underlying feelings.

Insight. To encourage understanding of the underlying reasons, dynamics, assumptions, or unconscious motivations for cognitions, behaviors, attitudes, or feelings.

Change. To build and develop new and more adaptive skills, behaviors, or cognitions in dealing with self and others.

Reinforce Change. To give positive reinforcement about behavior, cognitive, or affective attempts to enhance the probability of change.

Resistance. To overcome obstacles to change or progress.

Challenge. To jolt the counselee out of a present state; shake up current beliefs, patterns, or feelings; test validity, adequacy, reality, or appropriateness.

Relationship. To resolve problems; to build or maintain a smooth working alliance; to heal ruptures; to deal with dependency issues; to uncover and resolve distortions.

Other Important Intentions of Counselors

Objectivity. To have sufficient control over feelings and values so as not to impose them on the counselee.

Implementation. To help the counselee put insight into action.

Insight. To help the counselee become more aware of his/her cognitive, behavioral, affective, and spiritual domains.

Structure. To structure the on-going counseling sessions so there is continuity from session to session.

Inconsistencies. To identify and explore with the counselee contradiction within and/or between counselee behaviors, cognitions, and/or affect.

Goals. To establish short and long range goals which are congruent with the counselee's potential.

Reinforcement. To identify and use reinforcers that facilitate the identified counselee goals.

Flexibility. To change long and short term goals within a specific session or during the overall counseling process as additional information becomes available.

Behavioral Change. To develop specific plans, that can be observed, for changing the counselee's behavior(s).

Homework. To assign work to the counselee to reinforce change.

Problem Solving. To teach the counselee a method for problem solving.

LIFE SKILLS AS
DEVELOPMENTAL COUNSELING

As educators, we often feel compelled to create a comprehensive initiative to remediate the broad spectrum of threats to the physical, intellectual, emotional, and social well-being of contemporary youth. The growing concern over adolescent subpopulations who are at-risk demonstrates the critical need for responsible adults to establish close helping relationships with young people.

Ideally, the development and implementation of a comprehensive "services curriculum" could be designed for the mastery of daily problem-solving skills such as self-competency, enhancement of interpersonal relationships, communications, values, and the awareness of rules, attitudes, and motivation (Worrell & Stilwell, 1981).

Personal development could become an integral part of the secondary school curriculum and evolve as a required course which is integrated into the young person's program of studies much like computer literacy, driver education, or fine arts. Powell et al. (1985) lend credence to this potential maintaining that along with the horizontal, vertical, and extracurricular, the "service curriculum" is the fastest-growing component within the comprehensive high school.

Targeted programs within the "services curriculum" directly address social, psychological, or interpersonal problems such as grief and mourning, child abuse, depression, dysfunction, COA's (Children of Alcoholics), bulimia, anorexia, underachievement, loss of significant others, or emotional and social problems deemed educationally valid. Some schools provide special services depending on their particular needs such as day care for children of students; rehabilitation for delinquent teens; services for special needs students such as the handicapped; and remedial services such as tutorials, laboratories, and resource rooms for students in academic trouble.

A developmental guidance model which focuses on outcomes is listed in Figure 4.2 by competencies: personal effectiveness, lifelong learning, and life roles. In addition, in Figure 4.3 are listed counselor interventions and means by which changes can be achieved.

Life Skills Training Model

Essentially, life skills training is a strategy for sharing psychological knowledge and expertise. It is considered "the most recent and most robust of the approaches to the remediation of human problems, the enhancement of interpersonal effectiveness, and the general improvement of the quality of life" (L'Abate & Milan, 1985, p. 11). Influenced by society's growing interest in and concern with psychological principles and knowledge life skills are being converted into teachable skills and disseminated by means of systematic methods and programs" (Larson, 1984, p. 5). The effect of the program is to make counseling/learning available on a larger scale to the many groups that need help but are not currently receiving it.

(Continued on Page 60)

Personal Effectiveness Competencies

Self-
  understanding
Identity
Autonomy
Acceptance and
  validation

Human
  relationships
Respect and
  empathy
Social interest
Conflict
  resolution

Health
  development
Intimacy
Leisure
Growth stages

Lifelong Learning Competencies

Communication
Reading and
  Writing
Listening
Expressiveness
  and
  assertiveness

Information
  processing
Study and
  analysis
Evaluation
Problem solving

Personal
  enrichment
Time
  management
Renewal
Change

Life Roles Competencies

Daily living
Child rearing
Consumer
Community
  involvement

Career planning
Values
  clarification
Decision making
Planfulness and
  goal setting

Employability
Self-assessment
Work habits
Educational and
  occupational
  preparation

Source: Dagley, J.C. (1987). A new look at developmental guidance: The hearthstone of school counseling. *The School Counselor, 63,* p. 124. Reprinted by permission.

Figure 4.2. A developmental guidance model focusing on outcomes.

Counselor Intervention	General Caseload	Weekly Time Commitment (Hours)
Direct Service		
Individual Counseling	4-6 cases, including high priority or targeted students meeting no less than twice a week during one grading period.	2-6
Small Group Counseling	4-5 groups, preferably meeting twice a week for 6-12 structured learning sessions in 3-6 weeks.	4-10
Large Group Classroom Guidance	2-3 large groups, usually meeting once but sometimes twice a week.	2-3
Indirect Services		
Peer Helper Programs and Projects	Trainer/Coordinator of PH program and/or service projects such as SADD.	1-5
Consultation	(Group)—Teacher or parent group meetings (30 minute seminars or conferences)	Variable
	(Individual)—Teachers or parents (about 30 minutes or less)	1-2
Coordination of Guidance Services	Other guidance related duties (e.g., orientation, testing, career information, educational placement)	Variable
	Total	10-26 Hours

Source: Myrick, R.D. (1987). *Developmental guidance: A practical approach.* Educational Media Corporation, PO Box 21311, Minneapolis, MN 55421. Reprinted by permission.

Figure 4.3. Counselor interventions: Weekly scheduling plan.

Life skills training could provide adolescents with supportive services in an attempt to intervene in academic, behavior, emotional, or interpersonal problems. Students who could benefit from this systematic delivery of skills include those who have the following:

School-behavior Difficulties

- recent behaviors unlike the student's typical behavior;

- disruptive behavior in the class or in building;

- fear of attending school; unusual phobic or anxiety reaction;

- beginning truancy, tardiness, cutting classes;

- unusual negative attitude toward school;

- resistance to school rules; and

- frequent suspensions.

Personality Difficulties

- recent depression,

- age-inappropriate behavior,

- recent isolation and withdrawal,

- negative change in self-perception or self-esteem, and

- psychosomatic complaints.

Social Difficulties

- increase in peer conflict or poor peer relations,

- conflicts with authority,

- increase in physical aggression, and

- increase in verbal aggression.

Educational Difficulties

- evidence of knowledge gaps,

- lack of interest in work,

- inconsistent and erratic performance,

- drop in grades,

- inability to concentrate,

- unwillingness to finish work, and

- alienation from the classroom.

The Life Skills Training (LST) model (Gazda, Childers, & Brooks, 1989) is a comprehensive delivery system designed to facilitate effective functioning throughout the life span (hence, a developmental model of helping). The model, according to Gazda can be implemented by all practitioners, regardless of their disciplinary focus.

Life Skills Descriptors

Interpersonal communication/human relations: skills necessary for effective verbal and nonverbal communication, e.g., attitudes of empathy, genuineness, clearly expressing ideas and opinions, and giving and receiving feedback.

Problem solving/decision making: skills of seeking, assessing, and analyzing information, problem solving, and implementation.

Identity development/purpose in life: life skills that contribute to the on-going development of personal identity, enhancing self-esteem, and life transitions.

Physical fitness/health maintenance: skill necessary for nutrition, sexuality, stress management, and wellness.

Keenan Project

The Keenan Project (Cooper-Haber & Bowman, 1985) further differentiates the life skills model with their exemplary high school program:

Decision Making (8 sessions). The goals are to provide students with information on dating relationships, including sexuality, and to help students acquire skills in making responsible decisions.

Communication Skills (8 sessions). The goals are to help students develop more effective interpersonal skills and to expand guidance services by training potential peer facilitators as natural helpers.

Career Awareness (6 sessions). The goals are to introduce students to skills for obtaining and maintaining desired jobs and to give students opportunities to practice these skills.

Conflict Resolution (7 sessions). The goals of this group are to present effective problem-solving techniques and to build more effective interpersonal skills.

Study Skills (6 sessions). The goals are to improve students' academic work by developing greater academic mastery and enhance study skills.

Family Concerns (8 sessions). The goals are to provide opportunities for students to share concerns they have in relating to family members and to improve students' abilities in communicating with parents, stepparents, and siblings to bring about a more harmonious family life (p. 53).

EFFICACY OF
SMALL GROUP COUNSELING

The efficacy of small group counseling for helping people change attitudes, perspectives, values, and behavior is well documented (Dyer & Vriend, 1977; Egan, 1982; Ohlsen, 1977; Yalom,1975). Yet many helping professionals especially those who work in the school setting want to be able to identify group helping behaviors to provide structure for service delivery. Gill and Barry (1982) provided a more comprehensive classification of counseling skills for the group process. Such a classification system can assist the school counselor by delineating an organized, operational definition of group-focused facilitation skills. A classification of specific group-focused facilitation skills has a number of significant benefits such as clear objectives, visible procedures, competency based accountability, and measurable outcomes.

In Figure 4.4. is provided the evolution of researchers' attempts to classify group counseling skills from their own group counseling experiences. Ivey (1973) proposed a taxonomy of group skills consisting of 10 skills which are appropriate to both individual and group counseling. He added four "phases" of skill focus: group, individual, self, and topic.

Lieberman, Yalom, and Miles (1973) generated a list of what they considered to be critical group facilitation skills under the auspices of four basic leadership functions—emotional stimulation, caring, meaning attribution, and executive function.

Dyer and Vriend (1977) identified 20 behaviors for group leaders that could be viewed as important competencies for counselors in both one-to-one interactions and in group settings. Ohlsen (1977) outlined a classification system of ten facilitative behaviors for group leaders. Many of these earlier classification systems evolved from experiential rather than empirical data, with group leaders using individual counseling techniques to help one person at a time within a group setting.

Gill and Barry (1982) recommended a more group-focused classification system which provides a more practical and

(Continued on Page 66)

Ivey (1973)	Lieberman, Yalom, and Miles (1973)

1. minimal encouragers
2. open questions
3. closed questions
4. paraphrase
5. reflection of feeling
6. summary
7. directions
8. expression of content
9. expression of feelings
10. cognitive restructure
 	
1. group focus
2. individual focus
3. self focus
4. topic focus
	1. emotional stimulation
	  a. revealing feelings, beliefs
	  b. confrontation
	  c. stylistically emoting
	  d. risk taking
	2. caring
	  a. friendship
	  b. love, affection
	  c. acceptance, support, praise
	  d. invitation to seek feedback
	3. meaning attribution
	  a. explaining
	  b. cognitizing behavior
	  c. interpreting of reality
	  d. labeling behaviors
	4. executive function
	  a. limit setting
	  b. rules, norms setting
	  c. goal setting
	  d. group management

Source: Gill, S.J., & Barry, R.A. (1982). Group-focused counseling: Classifying the essential skills. *The Personnel and Guidance Journal, 60,* 5, p. 303. Reprinted by permission.

Figure 4.4. Group counseling skill classification systems.

Figure 4.4. Continued.

Dyer and Vriend (1977)	Ohlsen (1977)
1. identifying, labeling, clarifying, and reflecting feeling	1. developing readiness
2. identifying, labeling, clarifying, and reflecting behavioral data	2. relationship building
3. identifying, labeling, clarifying and reflecting cognitive data	3. relationship maintaining
4. questioning, drawing out and evoking material appropriate for counseling focus	4. problem identification
5. confronting	5. definition of counseling
6. summarizing and reviewing important material	6. definition of criteria to appraise client's growth
7. interpreting	7. resistance
8. restating	8. countertransference
9. establishing connections	9. feedback
10. information giving	10. termination
11. initiating	
12. reassuring, encouraging, and supporting	
13. intervening	
14. dealing with silence	
15. recognizing and explaining nonverbal behavior	
16. using clear, concise, meaningful communications	
17. focusing	
18. restraining, subduing, and avoiding potentially explosive and divisive of group happenings	
19. goal setting	
20. facilitating closure	

integrative framework that outlines what should be done. They outline specific behaviors that are appropriate, operational, developmentally related, group-focused, and composed of progressive interdependent stages.

Gill and Barry (1982) proposed that if counselors wish to utilize the group as a medium for learning and change, dynamics such as group member interaction, group support, group decision making, and group problem solving should receive greater emphasis. The researchers suggest the following selection criteria for building a system of group-focused counseling skills. Group focused counseling skills should be as follows:

> ***Appropriate.*** The behavior can reasonably be attributed to the role and function of a group counselor.

> ***Definable.*** The behavior can be described in terms of human performances.

> ***Observable.*** Experienced as well as inexperienced observers can identify the behavior when it occurs. The behavior can be repeated by different people in different settings.

> ***Measurable.*** Objective recording of both the frequency and quality of the behavior can occur with a high degree of agreement among observers.

> ***Developmental.*** The behavior can be placed within the context of a progressive relationship with other skills, all contributing to movement of the group toward its goals. The effectiveness of the behaviors at one stage in the counseling process is dependent on the effectiveness of the skills used at earlier stages.

> ***Group Focused.*** The target of the behavior is the group, or more than one participant. The behavior is often related to an interaction between two or more participants. The purpose of the group is to facilitate multiple interactions among participants, to encourage shared responsibility for helping to promote participation,

or to invite cooperative problem solving and decision making (Gill & Barry, 1982, pp. 304, 305).

In Figure 4.5 is provided a more germane group-focused classification system of counseling skills. Gill and Barry differentiate three stages and 22 different group-focused behaviors. Such a system provides a practical reference for school counselors. A developmental and group-focused target of behaviors is a very pragmatic approach to use with adjustment concerns of adolescents allowing them to share anxieties in a secure environment and to enhance their self-sufficiency.

Curative Factors in the Group Process

Further, Yalom (1985), Hansen, Warner, and Smith (1980), as well as others, have stressed the "curative" and "therapeutic factors" which are responsible for producing change in productive groups. The eleven primary factors are as follows:

> ***Instillation of Hope.*** Group members develop the belief that their problems can be overcome or managed.

> ***Universality.*** Group members overcome the debilitating preconceived notion that their problem is unique only to them.

> ***Imparting Information.*** Group members learn new information, as well as advice, suggestion, or direct guidance about developmental concerns. Guidance, advice-giving and advice-seeking behavior is central to the school counselor's role.

> ***Altruism.*** Group members offer support, reassurance, and are helpful to one another.

> ***Corrective Recapitulation of the Primary Family Group.*** The group environment promotes a replay, both consciously and unconsciously of experience typical of one's primary family group.

(Continued on Page 69)

Stage I	Stage II	Stage III
Group Formation: Facilitating Cooperation Toward Common Goals Through Development of Group Identity	*Group Awareness:* Facilitating a Shared Understanding of the Group's Behavior	*Group Action:* Facilitating Cooperative Decision-Making and Problem-Solving
1 *Norming* stating explicitly the expected group behavior	1 *Labeling Group Behavior* identifying and describing group feelings and performance.	1 *Identifying Group Needs* asking questions and making statements which clarify the want and needs of the group.
2 *Eliciting Group Responses* inquiries or invitations to members which encourage comments, questions, or observations	2 *Implicit Norming* describing behavior which has become typical of the group through common practice	2 *Identifying Group Goals* asking questions and making statements which clarify group objectives
3 *Eliciting Sympathetic Reactions* inquiries or invitations to members which encourage disclosure of experiences or feelings similar to those being expressed	3 *Eliciting Group Observations* inquiries or invitation to members which encourage observations about group process	3 *Attributing Meaning* providing concepts for understanding group thoughts, feelings, and behavior
4 *Identifying Commalities and Differences* describing comparative characteristics of participants	4 *Eliciting Mutual Feedback* inquiries or invitations to members which encourage sharing of perceptions about each other's behavior	4 *Eliciting Alternatives* providing descriptions of possible courses of action and inviting members to contribute alternatives
5 *Eliciting Empathic Reactions* inquiries or invitations to members which encourage reflection of one member's expressed content or feeling	5 *Identifying Conflict* labeling discordant elements of communication between members	5 *Exploring Consequences* inquiries or invitations to the group which evaluate actions and potential outcomes
6 *Task Focusing* redirecting conversation to immediate objectives; restating themes being expressed by more than one member	6 *Identifying Non-Verbal Behavior* labeling unspoken communications between members (facial expression, posture, hand gestures, voice tone and intensity, etc.)	6 *Consensus Testing* requesting group agreement on a decision or course of action
	7 *Validating* requesting group confirmation of the accuracy of leader or members' perceptions	
	8 *Transitioning* changing the group's focus on content or feelings being expressed	
	9 *Connecting* relating material from group events at a particular time or session to what is happening currently	
	10 *Extinguishing* ignoring, cutting-off, or diverting inappropriate talk or actions of members	

Source: Gill, S.J., & Barry, R.A. (1982). Group-focused counseling: Classifying the essential skills. *The Personnel and Guidance Journal, 60,* 5, p. 304. Reprinted by permission.

Figure 4.5. Classification system for group-focused counseling skills.

Development of Socializing Skills. The development and rehearsal of basic social skills is a therapeutic factor that is universal to all counseling groups.

Imitative Behavior. Group members learn new behaviors by observing the behavior of the leader and other members.

Interpersonal Learning. Group members develop relationships typical of their life outside the group within the social microcosm of the group.

Group Cohesiveness. Group membership offers participants an arena to receive unconditional positive regard, acceptance, and belonging which enables members to fully accept themselves and be congruent in their relationships with others.

Catharsis. Learning how to express emotion reduces the use of debilitating defense mechanism.

Existential Factors. As group members face the fundamental issues of their life, they learn that they are ultimately responsible for the way they live no matter how much support they receive from others.

Waldo (1985) differentiated the curative factor framework when planning activities in structured groups. In a 6-session structured group, activities can be arranged in relation to the group's development so that group dynamics could foster curative factors. The group can be structured as follows:

Session I: Establishing goals and ground rules (installation of hope) and sharing perceptions about relationships (universality).

Session II: Identification of feelings about the past, present, and future relationships (catharsis, family reenactment).

Session III: Demonstrating understanding of other group members' feelings (cohesion).

Session IV: Feedback between group members (altruism).

Session V: Confrontation and conflict resolution between group members (interpersonal learning).

Session VI: Planning ways group members can continue to improve relations with others, and closure (existential factors).

Each session involves lectures and reading materials (imparting information), demonstrations by the leader (imitative behavior), and within and between meeting exercises (social skills and techniques) (Waldo, 1985, p. 56). This model provides a conceptual map that can be utilized in school counseling for structured groups on conflict resolution, decision making, interpersonal relations, or any intervention that needs to be structured in order to learn important life skills.

EMPOWERING YOUTH AS PEER HELPERS

Sprinthall and Ojemann (1978) aptly stated that our present adherence to curriculum negatively affects how students make decisions, how they feel about themselves, and how they learn. They conclude that a rigid school climate increases students' reliance on the peer group, external locus of control, and stereotypical thinking. Schools often maintain an environment that perpetuates the denial of feelings and thwarts personal growth; generating rejection, rebellion, and indifference among students. The learning environment in most classrooms are excessively content-oriented, frequently hindering both intellectual and psychological well-being.

The responsibility for promoting a student's psychological and personal well-being becomes the central function of the school guidance and counseling program. To increase the effectiveness and visibility of school counseling programs, it becomes more important to systematically utilize the natural sources of influence within the educational setting, such as the peer group. A peer group in which youth are trained as peer helpers meets both the concern of responsible school counseling programs and the needs of young people.

Functions of the Peer Helper

An effective peer helper program can serve as a bridge between feelings and intellectual behaviors—an important function, as feelings and emotions play a critical role in blocking or enhancing learning. The need for such a program was emphasized by Dinkmeyer as early as 1971:

> The lack of a required sequentially developmental program in self-understanding and human behavior testifies to an educational paradox; we have taught children almost everything in school except to understand and accept themselves and to function more effectively in human relations. (p. 62)

Alschuler and Ivey (1973) further noted that "a major problem in the guidance movement, and education in general, has been the separation of personal growth from academic learning." In this context, peer helper programs could be facilitative in providing a more comprehensive approach to meeting personal needs of individual students, in addition to clarifying the role of the school counseling program. One of the best vehicles to accomplish these goals is to harness the unlimited potential of the peer group.

> Adolescents respond better when there is support from their peers. The likelihood of a program's success is increased when the program comprises a peer approach.

> Adolescents typically respond well to informational programs, as long as their emotional needs have been taken into account. Developmentally, because the adolescent is capable of "formal operational thought," the provisions of information and the exchange of ideas can be conducted on a relative high level.

> The group is an effective arena for reaching adolescents. Positive changes occur in the group context because adolescents are given an opportunity to release their

tensions and to examine their behavior with the help of their peers. The peer group serves a number of useful functions such as

- replacement for family support,
- stabilizing influence,
- social status,
- source of self esteem,
- source of behavioral standards,
- source of security,
- opportunity for role taking and feedback, and
- opportunity for modeling.

Peer helper training facilitates self-awareness and self-sufficiency. Adolescents often come to a training program with distortions in their self perceptions. These distortions are what Kottler (1983) identified as self-defeating behaviors such as procrastination, unrealistic expectations, self-pity, anxiety, guilt, rigid thinking, ethnocentricity, psychological dependence, or an external locus of control orientation.

The nature and scope of the training process encourages self-assessment, risk-taking, confrontation, feedback, and goal setting. Interpersonal socialization techniques are a critical component. Peer helpers learn such skills as establishing a relationship, suspending critical judgment, listening attentively, communicating empathy, and expressing warmth and genuineness. Once systematically assimilated, these skills create the opportunity for personal growth and more rewarding interpersonal interactions. As peer helpers feel more self-sufficient they are often "first finders" for students in distress. Fundamentally, adolescents are trained to help others as effective leaders, group listeners, and positive role models. A peer helper program also extends the school counselors reach to the school population as skillful listeners and special friends.

Training

The training in a peer helper program may address the following issues:

- academic planning,

- decision making,
- career information,
- social and emotional concerns,
- community resources,
- information about referral sources,
- issues of codependency,
- assessing crisis situations,
- confidentiality,
- communication skills, and
- improving students' help-seeking behavior.

The ultimate goal for peer helper programs is to use a heterogeneous group of representatives of the student body as a resource for assistance to others, and as a role model of positive influence for younger youth. The training goals include the following:

- developing increased awareness of self and others,
- developing facilitative communication skills,
- developing problem-solving and decision-making skills,
- more clearly defining students' value systems,
- developing small group helping skills and techniques, and
- providing accurate information from the school counseling program.

Peer helper programs utilize the natural resources of influence that the peer network maintains to promote personal growth. Conceptualized as an extension of the school counseling program, it also serves to promote the therapeutic or curative needs of adolescents. The guided training experiences for peer helpers also embraces the curative factors of Yalom (1985). Specific applications are as follows:

> **Instillation of Home.** By learning new skills such as listening, paraphrasing, and expressing empathy, the peer helper develops a stronger sense of self, as well as, a belief in the efficacy of the process of helping i.e., that they have meaning and relatedness to their school community.

> **Universality.** Through the mutual sharing of problems

in a secure environment, the peer helper discovers a commonality of fears, fantasies, hopes, needs, and similar problems. Problems are no longer unique; they are universal and shared with others.

Disseminating Information. This category includes instruction and information. By providing specific information such as establishing a group community, developing communication skills, and sharing concrete information from the counseling office, peer helpers feel more self-sufficient. They also become articulation agents for the school counseling program, and they often are "first finders" for students in distress.

Altruistic and Other Centered. The peer helper becomes other-centered rather than "me-centers," often rediscovering their self-importance by learning that they are of value to others. They feel a sense of purpose and that others value their expertise.

Corrective Reassessment of the Primary Family Group. During the peer helper training experience, the focus is on the vitality of work in the "here-and-now." Outside of the group experience, the peer helper may internalize and shift their perspective to rectify their earlier experiences which may have created problems in their own family relationships.

Development of Interpersonal Socialization Skills. Peer helpers learn such skills as establishing a relationship, refraining from critical judgment, listening attentively, communicating empathy, and expressing warmth and genuineness. Once assimilated, these skills create an opportunity for personal growth, and more rewarding interpersonal interactions which are transferred to daily living.

Imitation. In training, the process of modeling serves to create behavior that the peer helper can assimilate, e.g., body language, tone of voice, eye contact, etc. The peer helper not only sees the behavior in action but also experiences the effects of it.

Interpersonal Adjustment. Peer helper group training facilitates self-awareness and interpersonal growth. Adolescents often come to a training program with distortions of their self-perceptions. The nature and scope of the training process encourages self-assessment, risk-taking, confrontation, feedback, and goal-setting.

Group Cohesiveness. The group community creates a cohesiveness, a "we-ness" or a common vision. Once a group attains cohesiveness with established norms, members are more receptive of feedback, self-disclosure, confrontation, and appreciation, making themselves more open to one another. An effective training process facilitates this component.

Humanistic/Existential Factors. Contributions of the peer helper are validated, stressing issues of personal responsibility and consequences of life, urging choice and the development of one's potential.

Scope of Peer Helper Programs

Fundamentally, the development of a peer helper program is based on the concept that young people invariably turn to their peers for needed support and understanding, as well as, validation of their perceptions and feelings. The range of peer helper programs available include cross-age tutoring, educational advisement, and support groups. Peer counseling programs extend the counselor's reach to the school population as skillful listeners and special friends. Across the literature, students have shown improvement in such areas as attitude, self-esteem, academic achievement, behavior and leadership ability.

Another way of looking at what is required of a peer helper is to consider the kinds of skills and methods a helper uses in contrast to some common misperceptions of the role of the peer helper. These are outlined in Figure 4.5. Although developed for peer helper programs sponsored by the Center of Human Development in Lafayette, California, these assumptions are shared by most peer counseling programs across the nation.

One of the successful peer helper programs for middle and high school was developed, starting in 1978, by Judy Tindall (1985, 1989a, 1989b). The program consists of a Leader Manual and two sequential books for participants. Eight peer helping skills are learned in Book 1 and application of those skills in ten areas plus ethical considerations is achieved in Book 2. A new peer helper program by Tindall and Salmon-White (1990a, 1990b) has just been released for preadolescents (grades 4 through 6).

Peer Helper Log

One means of assisting youth in recognizing the impact of their assistance is to have them keep a journal or log. Summarizing what has been done is often a very positive reinforcer. If shared in the peer helper group, the importance of what they are doing becomes even more apparent. some members may not be achieving their goals. Other members, however, can apply their skills to help one of their own members. This can be done under supervision and with the help of the group leader.

CONCLUSION

Developmental guidance and counseling is a more proactive approach to school counseling. By identifying specific tasks and age-appropriate life skills, students are systematically provided with opportunities to assimilate these skills for their transition into adulthood. The guidance and counseling curricula (e.g., the "services curriculum") evolves as an integral part of the academic curricula (e.g., both horizontal and vertical).

Ultimately, students are provided with an on-going, sequential opportunity to learn new interpersonal skills and try them out among their peers. Skill building in the developmental guidance and counseling approach is related directly to developmental tasks and learning conditions. Robert

D. Myrick, one of the nation's leading proponents of developmental guidance and counseling aptly stated:

> When the developmental approach to guidance and counseling is used, it incorporates preventive, remedial, and crisis approaches. The developmental approach looks at teaching, coaching, tutoring, instructing, informing, and counseling as part of the helping process. It is a flexible approach that draws upon whatever is appropriate to meet student needs. Interpersonal relationships are an essential part of the approach and everyone in the school is considered a facilitator of personal, social, and academic growth. (Myrick, 1987, p. 16)

CHAPTER 5

HELPING PEOPLE IN CRISIS: THE SCHOOL COUNSELOR'S ROLE

waking in the morning
he returns home
no longer confused
just battered
and
empty.

sent to school
and directed
to a room without windows
he waits.
the counselor
late in arriving
switches on a small lamp
and together
they begin
to take the light in slowly . . .

Nicholas Mazza
Florida State University

CRISIS INTERVENTION

Crisis is usually defined as a variant of stress that is so severe that the individual becomes disorganized and unable to function effectively (Janosik, 1983). According to Baldwin (1977), crisis intervention is a "sound body of principles that provides an effective framework for professional practice" (p. 659). Crisis intervention is not synonymous with emergency services. It differs from traditional counseling interventions in a number of ways. Slaikeu (1984) defined crisis intervention as a "helping process to assist an individual or group to survive an unsettling event so that the probability of debilitating effects (e.g., emotional trauma, post-traumatic loss reactions or physical harm) is minimized, and the probability of growth (e.g., new coping skills, new perspectives on life, or more options in living) is maximized" (p. 5).

Sandoval (1985) maintained that the goal of crisis counseling is "to restore the counselee to equilibrium," with the number of counseling sessions ranging from one to eight. A secondary therapeutic role involves "taking action rather than listening and allowing the client to take responsibility and control over his/her decision making and understanding" (p. 260). Crisis reactions often become cycles of mounting tension, anxiety, and ineffective coping. The ability to think clearly, to plan decisively, and to act responsibly becomes impaired.

Crisis intervention and counseling is considered much more directive, with the counselor taking an active role in giving information, educating about typical post-traumatic stress reactions, and offering strategies for coping with the crisis situation. A temporary dependency on the counselor (which is discouraged in traditional counseling) is often required to restore equilibrium. The therapeutic relationship has facilitative powers for most counselees, and in many cases, the therapeutic relationship itself is curative and permeates all current approaches to brief psychotherapy.

Crisis often fall into two major categories: (1) developmental crises, which are universal and are often experienced while negotiating developmental tasks (as presented in Chapter 4); and (2) situational crises such as injury, disaster, death, divorce, or illness. In an extensive study, Sandler and Ramsay (1980) found that loss events (e.g., death of a parent, sibling, or friend; divorce and separation) were the main precursors of crisis reactions in youth, followed by family troubles (e.g., abuse, neglect, parent loss of job). Lower on the scale were primary environmental changes (e.g., moving, attending a new school, or mother re-entering career), sibling difficulties, physical harm (e.g., illness, accidents, and violence), and disasters (e.g., fire, floods, hurricanes, and earthquakes).

As a primary prevention and early intervention effort, we need to provide youth with coping skills before a crisis occurs. Such skills might include (1) an understanding of what constitutes a crisis event; (2) an awareness of feelings, thoughts, or unfinished issues that can be reactivated by a crisis; (3) changes in feelings and thoughts that occur over time; and (4) coping strategies and behaviors useful in a time of crisis (Allen & Anderson, 1986, p. 145). In Figure 5.1 is a list of life events with related extent of stress produced when they occur in childhood and adolescence.

SCHOOL-AS-COMMUNITY

Fundamentally, within the context of the school-as-community, the self-destructive potential of young people is a travesty of ambiguous proportion. Classmates, parents, teachers, and relatives experience both the direct implications of a student's death and the residual long-term effects of a significant loss. The devastating feelings of loss at a young age can be a traumatic experience. Inherently, personal loss or threat of loss increases a person's suicide risk. This is a very significant indicator among at-risk adolescents. Hawton (1986) found that peers of adolescents who attempted suicide are vulnerable because suicide is higher:

- among persons with unstable social relationships,

(Continued on Page 83)

	Life Change Units			
Life Events	Pre-School	Elementary	Middle School	High School
Beginning school	42*	46	45	42
Change of school	33	46	52	56
Birth or adoption of sibling	50	50	50	50
Sibling leaving home	39	36	33	37
Hospitalization of sibling	37	41	44	41
Death of sibling	59	68	71	68
Change of father's occupation requiring increased absence	36	45	42	38
Loss of job by parent	23	38	48	46
Separation of parents	74	78	77	69
Divorce of parents	78	84	84	77
Serious illness of parent	51	55	54	55
Death of parent	89	91	94	87
Death of grandparent	30	38	35	36
Marriage of parent to step-parent	62	65	63	63
Jail sentence of parent 1 year	34	44	50	53
Inclusion of third adult in family	39	41	34	34
Change in family financial status	21	29	40	45
Mother beginning career	47	44	36	26
Decrease in parent arguing	21	25	29	27
Increase in parent arguing	44	51	48	46
Decrease in arguing with parents	22	27	29	26
Increase in arguing with parents	39	47	46	47
Discovery of being adopted	33	52	70	64
Acquiring a deformity	52	69	83	81
Having a visible deformity	39	60	70	62
Hospitalization	59	62	59	58
Change in acceptance by peers	38	51	68	67
Outstanding personal achievement	23	39	45	46
Death of close friend	38	53	65	63
Failure of a year in school		57	62	56
Suspension from school		46	54	50
Pregnancy on unwed teenage sibling		36	60	64
Becoming involved in drugs/alcohol		61	70	76
Becoming a member of church/ synagogue		25	28	31
Not making extracurricular activity/team			49	55
Breaking up with a boy/girlfriend			47	53
Beginning to date			55	51
Fathering an unwed pregnancy			76	77
Being an unwed adolescent mother			95	92
Being accepted by college of choice				43
Getting married				101

*The higher the number, the greater the stress.

Source: Johnson, J.H. (1986). *Life events as stressors in childhood and adolescence.* Beverly Hills, CA: Sage Publications. Reprinted by permission.

Figure 5.1. Life events stressors in childhood and adolescence.

- when a population is self-contained (as in school-as-community and school-as-institution),

- when imitative behavior is common,

- when the element of bravado exists, and

- when the act is sure to be noticed.

BEHAVIOR MANIFESTATIONS OF LOSS

What continues to be clear is that when one suicide death or sudden loss occurs within a school, other students are immediately put at high risk. For example, Balk (1983) identified acute emotional responses of students after the death of a peer. He revealed that while peer support and chances to talk with friends about the death at such a time of loss were important aids in coping with death, many peers feel uncomfortable talking about death. They frequently avoid the survivors to decrease their discomfort of not knowing what to say or how to say it. Balk maintained that young people sometimes hide their feelings of grief because such feelings often are not considered acceptable in public, and as a result, adolescents are often confused about the source of their reoccurring grief reactions.

The reactions of survivors who have experienced a suicide (deliberate death) or sudden loss (accidental loss) are likely to be complex, but typically include some or all of the following behavioral characteristics.

DENIAL, dominates during the first twenty-four hours and includes refusal to accept the fact of death or that it was due to suicide; preferring to consider it an accident; or selective denial of painful memories.

ANGER, which may be directed toward the deceased, as well as toward medical services, family, friends, teachers, administrators, and others in positions of authority.

BLAMING OTHERS / BLAMING SELF, with the presence of a "suicide note" for example, the family may blame teachers, counselors, administrators; or teachers and administrators may blame parents, stepparents, or estranged siblings, if the family has a history of dysfunction.

SHAME, because of the stigma associated with the death, if it was a suicide.

GUILT, about what the survivors might or should have done to prevent the suicide or sudden loss, as well as, about how he/she may have contributed to it; feeling responsible for the death; regretting other relationship issues or disappointments in the past such as not making the athletic or scholastic team, or a romantic breakup.

FEAR, about one's own self-destructive impulses; fear of being alone, fear of being found out, fear of loss of control.

INTELLECTUALIZATION (particularly among adults), to search to make sense of the suicide or sudden loss; to seek an explanation for the death; to seek justification and to go over the incident over and over in one's mind.

HOSTILITY, to the person who designated the cause of the individual's death as a suicide (medical examiner, police, or attending physician) and to groups or systems (such as the school, the family, the church, the juvenile justice system, the class, or the team).

UNFINISHED BUSINESS, a sudden death or tragic loss often creates the potential emergence of unresolved conflicts or abuses of the past (especially among at-risk youth).

A suicide note also eliminates the opportunity for the survivor(s) to say goodbye or communicate unresolved conflicts with the deceased.

A survey by Tishler, McKenry, and Morgan (1981) of 108 adolescents revealed that 20% had experienced a recent death of a friend or relative; and 22% were exposed to a recent suicidal episode of a family member. The young people surveyed stated that their inability to cope with the loss led them to begin having suicidal thoughts themselves. Rappeport (1978) maintained that counseling intervention with survivors needs to include structured opportunities to talk about the death as a means to test and retest reality. Validation of feelings as a perceptual check is particularly important to adolescents. Talking about the death and related anxieties in a secure environment provides a means to "work through" the experience. It also serves to prevent destructive fantasy building which often occurs when young people cannot test their perceptions and feelings in a secure environment against the real world.

Stanford (1978) further suggested the need for direct intervention in schools with survivors. Shneidman (1972) noted that "when a death occurs, particularly of an unexpected nature, there is no pattern of behavior to draw upon, and confusion results" (p. 105). Teachers need help in understanding and handling young people's normal, yet often inappropriate reactions to death. Glasser (1978) stated that young people often take cues as to how to react from the adults around them more than from the event itself. A paramount need is for counselors, educators, and other support personnel to process the emotional needs of survivors. Intervention to enhance coping skills could ultimately prevent future suicides, or related self-destructive behavior.

In addition, school personnel need to understand and respond to adolescent anxiety related to asking for help. Adolescents, like adults, often do not assimilate intervention efforts from helping professionals to alter their stress or pain. For example, Garfinkel, Frose, and Hood (1982) found that 63% of completed suicides had not made contact with a caregiver or helping professional. Powell et al. (1985) in the analysis of the high school environment found that "the risk a student must take to talk to a significant adult in the school is to be considered a problem case." Adolescents also manifest resistance to seeking help related to feelings of loss of control and fear of dependency, "being found out," having to "tell everything," or submission to a powerful authority such as a school principal or a quasi-administrator.

Students' concern for privacy and confidentiality is very genuine. They frequently fear that their personal problems might become a part of the school record, or worse, the "school grapevine." Often they don't seek adult help because they are apprehensive about the outcome. Will they be hospitalized? Will their parents be contacted? Consequently, it becomes critical to any intervention or prevention program that adolescents be provided with detailed descriptions of the school and community resources that are available to them as well as the services provided.

COMMON VISION OF
SHARED RESPONSIBILITY

Fundamentally, to be successful in reducing the debilitating attitudes and destructive behavioral manifestations of today's youth, a school-as-community approach could have long range implications. According to Joyce et al. (1983) the school community develops distinctive normative patterns that draw students toward or away from particular activities and domains of development (social, academic, physical, and interpersonal). These normative patterns will have a profound long-term effect on the self-concepts, values, and skills that will ultimately be developed. Personalities will interact with the social system productively or unproductively with long-term effects on motivation and learning style (p. 114).

Lightfoot (1983) further described the deterioration of a sense of community within the school-as-institution. Students in this type of environment tend to feel isolated and alone as they move through their day. The tone of the school is dominated by a superficial sophistication with the primary preoccupation in finding the right clothes, the right kind of car, and the right friends. Troubles inside the school reflect a "depressive core in the community" where hostility is directed inward and divisions intensify (e.g., cliques and gangs) (p. 137). Inherently, building a sense of community is the most fundamental step to arrest the self-destructive behaviors of today's adolescents. A sense of caring and commitment should permeate the school and extend to the parents and the community. One means of demonstrating caring and commitment is to implement a "Student Assistance Advisory Board."

Student Assistance Advisory Board

The general purpose of the Student Assistance Advisory Board is to provide educators and youth serving professionals in the community with information and innovative programs to facilitate comprehensive division-wide education and intervention services for youth. The goals are to (1) provide a collective perspective and school/community commitment to the needs of youth, especially those who are at-risk; (2) identify resources, educational programs, and services to assist students, parents, teachers, and administrators; and (3) develop strategies and community resources for primary prevention and intervention in areas of critical need such as drug education, suicide prevention, and crisis intervention.

Responsibilities include (1) identify specific needs of youth in the community; (2) review potential programs for intervention and prevention services; (3) articulate and disseminate information of programs and services to parents, teachers, students, and administrators; (4) periodically provide educational programs for parents, teachers, and councils such as the PTA/PTO; (4) plan future programming together to address student needs and to evaluate ongoing pilot programs; and (5) maintain a professional network to share knowledge, training opportunities, and local expertise.

Potential points of focus could include the following:

Establish community-based activities that concentrate on the developmental needs of youth and involve young people in the planning and implementation of programs that serve their needs such as field experiences or career shadowing opportunities.

Develop a city-wide education, primary prevention and early intervention program.

Target populations of students who need additional counseling services and develop intervention plans.

Develop an annual school plan for the delivery of programs and services based on consumer need, not educator preferences.

Provide more public service opportunities for young people. Today, more than 3,000 school-based service programs demonstrate a growing awareness of the value of service projects as a means to engage youth into meaningful participation in school and community.

Encourage public/private partnerships among business organizations, the chamber of commerce, and employers to expand apprenticeships and on-the-job training programs that have demonstrated their usefulness.

EARLY INTERVENTION PROCEDURES FOR STUDENT ASSISTANCE TEAMS

Each school in a district should organize it's own school crisis intervention team which could include members of the local administration, school counselors, identified teachers, and other significant adults based on local skills, resources, and limitations. All local teams should be collectively assembled routinely for training in suicide intervention and crisis management skills. The school crisis team's primary responsibility would be to mobilize local resources and to follow specific procedures in the event a student is identified to be suicidal. These procedures are often supported by administrative directives or school board policy. For example, when a student verbalizes suicide ideation, the following steps may be outlined by administrative policy:

The staff member or student immediately should refer the student to the appropriate counselor or administrator.

The counselor or administrator should interview the student to determine the accuracy of the suicide threat. If the threat is confirmed, the counselor or administrator should immediately involve the parent or guardian to discuss the situation and explain that intervention is an alternative.

Documentation of the suicide threat and intervention procedures should be maintained by the counselor or administrator in the student's confidential file.

The counselor or administrator should provide the names of professional resources and helping professionals to the parent or guardian. If parents fail to respond to the suicide potential of their child or fail to contact a professional resource for the student, the counselor or administrator should contact the coordinator of pupil personnel or psychological services of the school district. Psychological services in cooperation with the counselor or administrator should contact the coordinator of pupil personnel or psychological services of the school district. Psychological services in cooperation with the counselor or administrator of the school should evaluate the situation and determine whether child protective services should be contacted.

If during the interview the student, the counselor, or the principal determine that the student is not in imminent danger or at high risk for a potential suicide, appropriate monitoring, follow-up, and documentation should be provided.

Interviewing a Student in Crisis

Assisting, interviewing, and counseling a suicidal youth ultimately involves utilizing the principles of crisis intervention. Nondirective approaches to therapy or intervention should be avoided during the initial stages of intervention. Essentially, nondirective approaches lack the control that school personnel (counselors, school psychologist, etc.) will need to guide the young person through the crisis. A high degree of perceptiveness on the part of the interviewer is necessary to sense the state of the student's crisis and to intervene adequately. The interviewer's approach should focus on resolution of the immediate problem with the mobilization of personal, educational, social, and environmental resources. The primary outcome is to explore more concrete and positive alternatives to help the student re-establish a feeling of control over his/her life.

The positive resolution of a crises depends on crisis intervention, that aspect of crisis management carried out by resource people in or outside of school such as the school's crisis team leader, nurse, teacher, principal, counselor, minister, or mental health professional. Essentially, crisis intervention is a short-term helping process. It focuses on resolution of the immediate problem through the use of the student's personal, social, and environmental (school and home) resources. Unfortunately, many students choose suicide as a resolution of their own personal distress or as a means to gain control or to communicate to others.

When a student contacts an adult, the following six step procedure (Sue, Sue, & Sue, 1981) can be useful:

- maintain contact, rapport, and establish a therapeutic relationship with the student that is student centered;

- obtain necessary information and documentation;

- evaluate suicidal potential;

- clarify the nature of the stress and focal problem;

- assess the student's present strengths and resources;

- recommend and initiate an action plan; and

- notify the parent or guardian, as well as identify referral resources.

In Figure 5.2 are listed routinely significant indicators of crisis in students. These could be duplicated and distributed to students, teachers, and parents.

(Continued on Page 92)

SOME SIGNIFICANT INDICATORS OF CRISIS IN STUDENTS

Crisis can occur in all students regardless of age. Most frequently the student in crisis may attempt or commit suicide. Some significant indicators of a student in crisis may include one of the following.

Significant Indicators

Suicide threat

Verbal hints indicating self-destructive behavior or that life would be better if student did not exist.

Preoccupation with thoughts of suicide or death.

Previous suicide attempt.

Family member or close friend has attempted or completed suicide.

Making final arrangements, giving away possessions, unexplained cheerfulness after prolonged depression.

Keeping guns, knives, or lethal medicines in student's possession.

Breakup with boyfriend or girlfriend and withdrawal from other friendships.

School Indicators

Failing or drop in grades.

Difficulty concentrating on school work.

Loss of interest in extracurricular activities.

Social isolation.

New to school.

Frequent referrals to office because of behavior, tardiness, truancy.

Academic learning difficulties.

Significant Times of Danger

Changes in eating or sleeping patterns.

Weight gain or loss.

Neglect of personal appearance.

Lethargy, listlessness.

Frequent physical complaints.

Pregnancy.

Prolonged or terminal illness.

Drug or alcohol abuse.

Family Indicators

Loss of family member (or anniversary of loss) through death, separation, or divorce.

Rejection by family members.

Financial change, job loss.

Recent household move.

Family discord.

Change in immediate family or household membership.

Alcoholism or drug use in the family.

Student is a victim of sudden physical, sexual, and/or emotional abuse.

Running away from home.

Family history of emotional disturbance.

Social and Emotional Indicators

Noted personality change.

Depression, feelings of sadness.

Withdrawal, does not interact with others.

Agitation, aggression, rebellion.

Sexual problems (promiscuity, identity, pregnancy).

Feelings of despair, hopelessness, helplessness.

Feelings of being bad or the need to be punished.

Unexplained accidents, reckless behavior.

Recent legal involvement.

Physical Indicators
Rites of Passage

Graduation

Completion of parental divorce.

Anniversaries of unhappy events (parental deaths, severe losses).

Holidays, particularly family holidays.

Vacation times, especially if child is isolated.

Change of season.

Custody disagreements.

Note: Help cards or crisis cards are a highly visible information that serves to provide a measure of security for young people and adults. School divisions might consider investing inpriting and circulating help cards as a prevention alterative.

Adapted from D. Capuzzi and L. Golden (1988). *Preventing Adolesscent Suicide.* Muncie, IN: Accelerated Development Inc.

Figure 5.2. Some significant indicators of crisis in students.

CARE FOR SUICIDAL STUDENTS

To provide maximum care for suicidal students, a strong recommendation is that the counselor or helping professional (1) document the problem and intervention procedures; (2) share the information and the responsibility with the appropriate adults (parents, principals, support personnel); (3) recognize the importance of knowing how, when, and where to refer students appropriately whose concerns fall beyond the counselor's or helping professional's area of knowledge or intervention skills; (4) have a network of mental health professionals to confer or consult; (5) undergo training or re-education for crisis prevention and intervention skills; and (6) obtain adequate supervision, or develop a crisis team approach to facilitate intervention and prevention.

In Figure 5.3 is an example of a school counselor action plan. Completion of this material will provide the essential documentation that needs to be maintained.

In Figure 5.4 is an example of an administrative memo that spells out procedures to be followed.

EMPOWERING FAMILIES:
THE FAMILY SAFETY WATCH
An Intervention Strategy for
Self-destructive Behavior

The Family Safety Watch (Stanton, 1984), is an intensive intervention strategy to prevent self-destructive behavior. The safety watch can apply to such problems as child abuse, self-mutilation, eating disorders, and drug or alcohol abuse. The procedure is as follows:

> Family members conduct the watch. They select people to be involved in the watch from among their nuclear family, extended family, and network of family friends.

> An around-the-clock shift schedule is established to determine what the adolescent is to do with his/her

(Continued on Page 95)

SCHOOL COUNSELOR ACTION PLAN

Support Resources   Support Resources
   (identified by student)   (identified by counselor)

_____   _____

_____   _____

Lethality of Method	____ High	____ Medium	____ Low
Availabity of Means	____ High	____ Medium	____ Low
Specificity of Plan	____ High	____ Medium	____ Low
Suicidal Risk	____ High	____ Medium	____ Low

ACTION TO BE TAKEN

Date: _____   Time: _____

Crisis Team Member:

	YES	NO	N/A	PERSON RESPONSIBLE	DATE COMPLETED
Contact Parents	___	___	___	_____	_____
Notify Principal	___	___	___	_____	_____
Notify Community Mental Health	___	___	___	_____	_____
Consult with local school/ community mental health liaison	___	___	___	_____	_____
Notify Social Service	___	___	___	_____	_____
Notify police or youth service officer	___	___	___	_____	_____
Is it safe to let student go home?	___	___	___	_____	_____
Is the student in need of 24 hour supervision?	___	___	___	_____	_____
Is student provided with contact person and phone number?	___	___	___	_____	_____
Is student scheduled for contact with school counselor for the following day?	___	___	___	_____	_____
Other (specify)					
_____	___	___	___	_____	_____

Source: R. A. Thompson (1988). Crisis intervention. In D. Capuzzi & L. Golden, _Preventing adolescent suicide_, p. 399. Muncie, IN: Accelerated Development Inc.

Figure 5.3. An example of school counselor action plan.

To: All Principals and Support Personnel

Re: Suicide Referral Procedures

When a student threatens to commit suicide or a staff member believes a student plans to attempt suicide, the following steps are to be taken:

1) The staff member should immediately refer the student to the appropriate counselor or principal.

2) The counselor or principal should interview the student to determine the accuracy of the suicide threat. If the threat seems real, the counselor or principal should call the parent or guardian to discuss the situation and explain that intervention is necessary.

3) Documentation of the suicide threat and intervention procedures should be maintained by counselor or principal in the student's category II record.

4) The counselor or principal should provide the names of professional resources to the parent(s) or guardian. If the parent(s) or guardian fail(s) to respond to the suicide threat of their child or fails to contact professional resources for their child, the counselor or principal should contact the Coordinator of Psychological Services of the school division for professional support. Psychological Services, in conjunction with the counselor or principal of school, will review the current situation and determine whether court services and/or child protective services should be contacted.

Figure 5.4. Administrative memo.

time over a twenty-four hour period, i.e., when he/ she is to sleep, eat, attend class, do homework, play games, view a movie, etc., according to a structured planned agenda.

The intervention team leader (counselor, parent, teacher, or principal) consults with the family to

- determine what the family resources and support systems are;

- arrange ways for involving these support systems in the effort (e.g., "How much time do you think Uncle Harry can give to watching your son/ daughter?);

- design a detailed plan for the safety watch; and

- plan schedules and shifts so that someone is with the at-risk child 24 hours per day.

A back-up system also is established so that the person on the watch can obtain support from others if he/ she needs it. A cardinal rule is that the child be within view of someone at all times, even while in the bathroom or when sleeping.

The family is warned that the first week will be the hardest. They also should be warned that the youth may try to manipulate situations to be alone or pretend to be fine.

A contractual agreement is established that if the watch is inadvertently slackened or compromised, and the youth makes a suicide attempt or tries to challenge the program in some way, the regime will consequently be tightened. This is a therapeutic move that reduces the family's feeling of failure should a relapse occur during the week.

The primary goal of the watch is to mobilize the family to take care of their "own," and feel competent in doing so.

With tasks surrounding the watch, the family, the adolescent, and helping professionals (as a team) collaborate in determining what the adolescent must do in order to relax and ultimately terminate the watch. Task issues should focus around personal responsibility, age appropriate behavior, and handling of family and social relationships, such as to

- arise in the morning without prompting,

- completing chores on time,

- substitute courteous and friendly behavior for grumbling and sulking,

- talk to parents and siblings more openly, and

- watch less TV and spend more time with friends and significant others.

The decision to terminate the watch is made conjointly by the family and the therapeutic team. It is contingent upon the absence of self-destructive behavior, as well as the achievement of an acceptable level of improvement in the other behavioral tasks assigned to the adolescent. If any member of the therapeutic team feels a risk still exists, the full safety watch is continued.

This approach appeals to families because it makes them feel potent and useful, and reduces the expense of an extended hospital program. It also re-establishes the intergenerational boundary, opens up communication within the family, reconnects the nuclear and extended families, and makes the adolescent cared for and safe. In addition, it functions as a compression move which pushes the youth and family members closer together and holds them there awaiting the rebound or disengagement that almost inevitably follows. This opens the way for a more stable family structure—a structure that does not require a member to exhibit suicidal or self-destructive behavior as a means of communication.

GUIDELINES FOR DECIDING WHETHER TO COUNSEL OR REFER TO FAMILY THERAPY

To differentiate families experiencing reactions to recent stress from those with chronic, long-standing problems is important. The former is probably appropriate to counsel, the latter to refer to other helping professionals.

All families experience temporary stress associated with predictable life crises in the family cycle (e.g., birth, loss, separation). Healthy families may need only supportive counseling during these times, whereas unhealthy families probably need referral because they have fewer coping mechanisms.

In general, the following situations are appropriate for supportive counseling:

- families in transition (e.g., adjustment to a birth or remarriage) and

- behavior problems of recent origin (e.g., child who just begins to show behavior problems).

The following situations reflect families with more chronic problems and should be referred for more intensive help:

- chemical dependency or abuse (Therapy for this problem is highly specialized and the problem is often transgenerational.);

- longstanding family problems (e.g., chronic marital difficulties, a child with serious behavioral problems);

- history of psychiatric disturbance in family (e.g., debilitating depression, anxiety, psychosis, other conditions requiring medications and/or hospitalization); and

- serious, acute problems, particularly child abuse, spouse abuse, or incest. (These are life threatening situations which are more appropriately managed by professionals with special training.)

CONTINGENCY PLAN
IN CASE OF A
STUDENT SUICIDE OR SUDDEN LOSS

In order to prepare adequately for a crisis situation, the **School Crisis Intervention Team** should have made the necessary anticipated logistical arrangements before a crisis occurs. These arrangements include, but are not limited to, the subheadings that follow.

Identification of Key
Helping Professionals and Staff

Identify members of the faculty who are willing to talk to students in small groups. These groups are intended for students who are not experiencing intense problems, but who do need to obtain accurate information about the death of a classmate from a responsive and caring adult. Teachers should provide general information and answer questions and facilitate concerns. They also could assist in identifying students who are experiencing more intense adjustment problems or students who have fewer support resources. Other school personnel resources could include the administrative staff, school nurse, school psychologist, and school or community counseling personnel. The specific action is to

- identify personnel who can provide more in-depth one-to-one counseling,

- designate a contact person to facilitate communication with central office personnel,

- activate the **Crisis Communication Contingency Plan** and the contact person who is designated to work with the media,

- designate a person to serve as case manager or team leader (depending on professional orientation) of the School Crisis Intervention Team to schedule departmental meetings or individual and group sessions for students, and

- designate a person to work with and organize community resources.

Fundamentally, the number of persons needed to accomplish the first two items will depend on the size of the student population and the number of students in crisis. Facilitating the remaining roles do not necessarily have to be filled by different individuals.

Identification of Physical Resources

The specific resources within the school must be made available.

Designate specific rooms to hold small group sessions of consultation with staff, students, and parents;

designate specific rooms that can be available for community consultation and information;

free a telephone line in order to contact parents, central office personnel or community mental health resources;

identify appropriate literature, films, and other educational materials for students, parents, faculty, and community groups; and

provide guidelines, structure, and resources for teachers to use in small educational groups.

Preparation of Teachers and Staff

Teachers need to have preparation ahead of time as well as structured procedures to deal with students on the first day after a crisis. The procedures may be as follows:

Conduct a faculty meeting before school on the first day after a suicide or sudden death.

Discuss the situation and explain specific procedures for the day.

Introduce school counselor(s) from neighboring schools and other personnel who will be involved in counseling students.

Explain the role and function of the Student Crisis Intervention Team and provide teachers with a schedule of the counseling sessions which may occur.

Hand out written procedures to be discussed with students at the beginning of the school day. Thoroughly discuss procedures to be sure all teachers understand their roles in communicating and processing information for students. The first hour of the school day should be spent providing students with accurate information as well as processing the death in small groups.

Encourage teachers who may feel uncomfortable discussing the situation with students (e.g., if the teacher was particularly close to the child) that they have the option to request a member of the School Crisis Intervention Team to be present in their rooms to answer student questions.

Confirm that teachers and members of the School Crisis Intervention Team know whom to report to, and to who to refer students or families in crisis.

Establish support groups for the deceased's present and previous teachers who may need assistance in coping with their own feelings, and arrange for their classes to be covered while they are in the individual or group debriefing sessions. Confidentially inform teachers involved of the plans or provisions that have been made available for them.

**Mobilization of the
Crisis Intervention Team**

All members of the School Crisis Intervention Team should determine student needs and personnel needs. They should also outline procedures to follow. Suggested procedures on the first day of school after a suicide or sudden death is for teachers or School Crisis Intervention Team members to conduct the first hour session as follows:

announce the death of the student using accurate, objective facts;

let students know that they will be (1) informed of funeral arrangements, and (2) excused from classes to attend the funeral with written permission from parent or guardian;

maintain the traditional ethnic and cultural mores regarding procedures and protocol of students from different cultural or ethnic backgrounds regarding the deceased (The cultural diversity in many school settings cannot be ignored. Education and responsiveness to different roles and rituals will help diffuse rigidity and expectations of other ethnic groups for the deceased. Prepare participants when possible.);

announce that friends of the deceased will be allowed to meet in a group at _____ a.m. in room _____ (Excuse friends of the deceased to go to the meeting.);

open the discussion with any remaining students and let them know it is normal to be upset [Try to maintain a calm climate. Direct the discussion, if appropriate, toward identifying ways the class members might do something positive in remembrance of their peer. Caution must be taken to prevent any collective activities that would glamorize a suicidal act or make it appear as a heroic alternative on the part of the adolescent. Types of innocuous activities may include writing a poem to be read at the funeral of the deceased, or other choose-life or living alternative activities (Joan, 1986).];

announce that adults will be available to students for counseling, talking, and listening and record the names of students who express interest in counseling or further processing and submit them to the School Crisis Intervention Team Leader or case manager;

inform students that they will be called to the office and escorted to the appropriate counseling area throughout the course of the day; and

inform students that for the remainder of the day, they should follow their routine schedule of classes.

Duties of the
Case Manager/Team Leader

The case manager or team leader of the School Crisis Intervention Team should do the following things:

contact teachers and other staff members who volunteered and were trained to work as group facilitators before school begins so they can be prepared. (The focus should stress the communication of feelings, recognition that others have faced similar anguish and have survived, and normal reactions to loss and stress);

make arrangements to notify concerned community leaders, agencies, churches, and parents of the actions being taken by the school or the programs provided;

schedule, if necessary, meetings for parents and community resource people;

contact other members of the city-wide School Crisis Intervention Team if necessary to assist in debriefing activities; and

contact other resources within the district such as psychological services, and private counseling agencies with whom the school has already made arrangements for assistance.

Short-term Arrangements

Make short-term arrangements for the first day that include the following:

- allow students with questions to talk in small groups with selected teachers, members of the School Crisis Intervention Team, and mental health professionals in the community;

- provide for the most severely affected students to be seen individually by the school counseling staff, School Crisis Intervention Team, and/or mental health professionals; and

- identify students and/or adults who could be at-risk.

Research continues to support the notion that a number of children and adults may experience suicide ideation themselves. Students and/or adults who are potentially at-risk may be

- any student who was involved in any way with the youth who committed suicide, i.e., called the crisis center, called the police, helped write the suicide note, provided the lethal means, or were involved in a suicide pact;

- any student or adult who knew of the suicidal ideation and suicide intent, but chose to ignore or kept it a secret;

- survivors such as best friends and relatives;

- any peer or adult who assumed the role of rescuer for the student or assumed the responsibility to keep the student alive;

- any student or adult with a history of suicidal ideation, depression, or arrested attempts;

- any student or adult who appears to have identified with the student;

- any student or adult who demonstrates feelings of guilt about communication or interaction with the deceased prior to the death; and

- others who are distressed by the experience because of past events.

Divide student population into the following categories as soon as possible:

- those students who need to be seen by a counselor immediately;

- those students with less severe problems, but who need follow-up work such as a referral to community agencies or parental conferences (Very often, when a student commits suicide, many students become identified as high risk because of reoccurring suicide ideation or some other underlying personal dysfunction such as abusive relationships or other self-destructive behavior.);

- those students who are experiencing mild or moderate coping problems whose progress needs monitoring; and

- those students who are adjusting adequately and do not need further monitoring.

Meet daily for staffing meetings with the School Crisis Intervention Team to discuss student needs and to assign responsibilities for counseling, consulting, referral, or monitoring of students.

Role and Responsibilities of the Principal

At the time of an actual suicide crisis, the School Crisis Intervention Team should be assembled immediately, and the principal or principals should do the following:

- contact the central office liaison in order that they can adjust their schedules to meet at the local school if necessary;

- contact the individual designated to work with the media in order that statements can be prepared before being contacted by the media;

- meet with the family of the deceased to offer assistance and condolence;

- arrange for a morning faculty meeting for the first day of school after the suicide or sudden loss;

- finalize procedures for the first day of school after a crisis; and

- make arrangements for substitutes or parent volunteers who may be needed for teachers who are to facilitate discussions and to debrief for students.

THE CRISIS COMMUNICATION CONTINGENCY PLAN

Community awareness programs are the areas over which the school has the least control, especially at the secondary level where parents become less involved in their child's activities. School personnel, however, must try to communicate and educate their constituents about debilitating issues such as teen stress, suicide, chemical dependency, and other self-destructive or self-defeating behaviors. This approach is important for two fundamental reasons: (1) parents made aware of the problem in a non-threatening environment may be more responsive to school personnel should their child ever be involved in a suicidal crisis; and (2) community support may be more easily obtained in the event of a crisis, if the community perceives the school as a proactive institution which continually demonstrates competence in preventing a crisis situation.

When confronted with a crisis situation, one person, preferably the principal, must assume responsibility for implementing a Crisis Communication Contingency Plan. A Crisis Community Contingency Plan demonstrates responsibility and responsiveness. It also is a systematic procedure to disseminate information more efficiently, and to foster school/community stability. Proactively, a Crisis Communication Contingency Plan anticipates events that could occur with specific procedures to manage rumor and misinformation, as well as, foster congruency of accurate information. Fundamentally, effective public relations in the school should encompass much more than merely reacting to reporters and the media. The following investment procedures could be implemented annually and systematically to provide objective and timely information:

> write a comprehensive Crisis Communication Contingency Plan that details whom to contact, designates human resources, and utilizes a communication tree (who calls whom) to facilitate the flow of information;

> routinely distribute copies of the Crisis Communication Contingency Plan to all school personnel annually such as during back-to-school orientation activities for teachers and support personnel;

> develop a "fact sheet" about school programs, resources, and services for students and their families as a handout at regularly scheduled meetings for community groups and organizations that interface with the school (PTA/PTO boards, advisory committees, and feeder schools);

> designate a central office area (clinic, attendance office, etc.) to coordinate information gathering and dissemination in the event of an emergency; and

> be assertive and take initiative with the media.

Clarification of Issues to the Media

A statement should be made as soon as the crisis occurs to show that school officials are perceptive and responsive to community and school needs. Remind faculty and staff that only designated spokespeople are authorized to talk with news media. The *school should* (a) decide what to say, define the ground rules, issue a statement and answer questions within the limits of confidentiality; (b) advise students of the media policy of not having to talk to the media, therefore saying no is okay; (c) if the crisis is a death, consult with the deceased staff member's family before making any statement. Explain school system policy and assure them confidential information is being protected. Also, have the following public relations plan for your school:

get to know the reporter(s), who are likely to cover your school, early in the academic year;

respond to all medial inquiries or telephone calls promptly;

when asked to react to a statement or event ask if you can call right back; write down the reporter's question, make notes for your answers, and then return the call;

periodically provide the media with contact people, resources, and services that are both routine and unique to your school;

write appreciation letters to staff writers when they portray a difficult or sensitive assignment well and forward a copy of the letter to their editor; and

be aware of reporters' deadlines and assist them in their information gathering with any written information about a prevention or intervention program.

Perhaps one of the most subtle defenses against the occurrence of a future suicide is for a school official to be firm and assertive with information given to the media. News reporters can influence the public's perceptions about school, people, events, and decisions. The excitement, the lurid, and the romantic depiction of a student's suicide seems to attract troubled adolescents, and reinforce the act as a viable alternative. Displaying a student's death on the front page of the local newspaper (complete with picture and quotes from grieving family or classmates) gives the victim a "fame-in-death" that he/she may not have achieved in life. Perceived as a hero or martyr, many adolescents may personalize the act and see themselves in place of the victim. A number of precautions should be sensitively heeded:

don't put suicide stories on the front page of the newspaper; placing the story on the inside page, or near the bottom may reduce the "copycat" phenomena;

don't use the word suicide in the headline;

don't use photographs or intimate descriptions of the victim's life because this often promotes over identification with the victim; and

don't fail to mention alternatives to suicide. If suicide is the only alternative mentioned, it serves to exclusively advertise this self-destructive method.

Fundamentally, when communicating information to the media or the community, maintain a "unified position and a uniform message." Keep messages concise, clear, consistent, and tailored to each targeted group with accuracy and sensitivity. Hannaford (1987) maintained that an important procedure is to develop a **SOCO—single overriding communication objective** when dealing with the media. The role of the designated contact person and a SOCO is to focus upon a communication objective, bringing the topic back to the objective and reinforcing it with accurate information as much as possible. The more a topic is framed and the objective is discussed, the more it is likely to appear as part of a reporter's focus in the story, or community members' perception of the event.

In addition, the principal or designee may wish to appoint a community steering committee or task force composed of clergy, health professionals, community leaders, or PTA representatives. This group can assist in arranging programs on the subject of preventing self-destructive behaviors at churches, synagogue, clubs, and organizations. Community support systems also can assist in providing the same uniform message and reinforce information about programs and services the school can provide for families and their children.

To foster additional continuity, associations and groups that sponsor programs or adolescent stress, and related concerns could be encouraged to hold their program when in-school educational programs are scheduled so that families who wish to discuss the topic further would be equally informed. School personnel can be supportive and resourceful to groups organizing parent programs, especially in the selection of appropriate speakers.

Reciprocal attendance of teachers and school administrators at the programs sponsored by parents can help reinforce the importance of the subject and provide an opportunity for parents to ask questions about the in-school programs for teachers and students. In some instances, members of the Student Assistance Advisory Board could serve as speakers at community programs. This can serve as an evaluation of the effectiveness of a program. Other questions to consider for evaluation purposes are the following:

> How effective are educational and awareness programs giving information, raising consciousness or changing attitudes?

> Are the goals of the community education approaches realistic and related to consumer needs?

> Is the material up-to-date and related to specific populations?

> Are education and awareness programs developed to reach all of sub-populations?

> How effective is school policy working to identify, assess, and intervene with a student?

> Are education and training opportunities systematic and repetitive?

ESSENTIAL COMPONENTS

Finally, during the crisis period the following components must be systematically facilitated:

- a calm, organized atmosphere should be maintained;

- all involved be kept informed of the status of plans, events, actions, and schedules;

- daily crisis team debriefing meetings should be held to review and modify plans and communication to promote accountability;

- sufficient helping professionals be involved so that a few people are not overworked;

- staff members should routinely be reminded to take time for themselves and engage in stress reduction activities during the course of their day;

- counseling services should be made available for faculty and staff members who may need to share their anxieties and frustrations in an environment that is nonjudgmental and allows them to debrief the experience;

- all students and faculty members expressing difficulty in maintaining adequate coping skills during and after the suicide crisis should be taken seriously and appropriate assistance be made available; and

- a normal schedule of extracurricular and instructional periods be maintained for the majority of the student body to provide routine and structure, as well as promote institutional equilibrium and interpersonal stability.

TASKS OF MOURNING
AND GRIEF COUNSELING

A number of tasks of mourning and grief counseling need to be reviewed. These are summarized as follows:

To accept the reality of the loss and to confront the fact that the person is dead; initial denial and avoidance becomes replaced by the realization of the loss.

To experience the pain of grief. It is essential to acknowledge and work through this pain or it will manifest itself through self-defeating behavior.

To adjust to an environment in which the deceased is missing. The survivor(s) must face the loss of the many roles the deceased person filled in their life.

To withdraw emotional energy and reinvest it in another relationship. One must become open to new relationships and opportunities.

To accept the pain of loss when dealing with the memory of the deceased.

To overtly express sorrow, hostility, and guilt, and to be able to mourn openly.

To understand the intense grief reactions associated with the loss; for example, to recognize that such symptoms as startle reactions, including restlessness, agitation, and anxiety may temporarily interfere with one's ability to initiate and maintain normal patterns of activity.

To come to terms with anger which is often generated toward the one who has died, toward self, or toward others; to redirect the sense of responsibility that somehow one should have prevented the death.

Special Treatment Issues with Adolescents

Allow regression and dependency,

realize their lack of life experience in handling trauma,

allow expression of feelings,

encourage discussion,

allow fluctuations in maturity level,

watch for emergence of unfinished business or unresolved conflicts of the past,

answer questions and provide factual information,

correct distortions,

avoid power struggles with adolescents or own professional peers,

focus on strengths and constructive adaptive behaviors,

act as a mediator between adolescents and family and staff,

mobilize family members and peers for a supportive community,

address conscious and unclear guilt, and

identify and help resolve adolescent's sense of powerlessness.

POST TRAUMATIC LOSS
DEBRIEFING STRATEGIES

The sudden, unexpected death by suicide or the sudden loss from an accidental death often produces a characteristic set of psychological and physiological responses among survivors. Persons exposed to traumatic events such as suicide or sudden loss often manifest the following stress reactions: irritability, sleep disturbances, anxiety, startle reactions, nausea, headaches, difficulty concentrating, confusion, fear, guilt, withdrawal, anger, and depression.

Diminished responsiveness to one's immediate environment with "psychic numbing" or "emotional anesthesia" usually begins soon after the traumatic event. Sometimes the stress reactions appear immediately after the traumatic event or a delayed reaction may occur weeks or months later. The particular pattern of the emotional reaction and type of response will differ with each survivor depending on the relationship of the deceased, circumstances surrounding the death, and coping mechanisms of the survivors.

Post traumatic loss debriefing is a structured approach to understand and manage the physical and emotional responses of survivors and their loss experiences. It creates a supportive environment to process blocked communication which often interferes with the expression of grief or feelings of guilt, and to correct distorted attitudes toward the deceased, as well as discussing ways of coping with the loss. The purpose of the debriefing is to reduce the trauma associated with the sudden loss, initiate an adaptive grief process, and prevent further self-destructive or self-defeating behavior. The goals are accomplished by allowing for ventilation of feelings, exploration of symbols associated with the event, and enabling mutual support.

Post traumatic loss debriefing is composed of six stages: introductory stage, fact stage, feeling stage, reaction stage, learning stage, and closure. Post traumatic loss debriefing is a structured approach to the management of the acute emotional upset affecting one's ability to cope emotionally, cognitively, or behaviorally to the crisis situation. Successful resolution and psychological well-being is dependent upon interventions that prepare individuals for periods of stress and help survivors return to their precrisis equilibrium.

A debriefing should be organized 24 to 72 hours after the death. Natural feelings of denial and avoidance predominate during the first 24 hours. The debriefing can be offered to all persons affected by the loss. The tone must be positive, supportive, and understanding.

Introductory Stage

The introductory stage is where brief introductions are provided to the debriefing process and establishment of rules for the process. The school counselor is more directive as caregiver and as a group facilitator.

The caregiver-as-facilitator defines the nature, limits, roles, and goals within the debriefing process.

The caregiver clarifies time limits, number of sessions, confidentiality, possibilities, and expectations to reduce unknowns and anxiety for survivors.

Members are encouraged to remain silent regarding details of the debriefing, especially details which could be associated with a particular individual.

Participants in a debriefing need to be assured that the open discussion of the feelings will, in no way, be utilized against them under any circumstances.

Give reassurances that the caregiver-as-facilitator will continue to maintain an attitude of unconditional positive regard. Reduce the survivors initial anxieties to a level which permits them to begin talking.

Fact Stage

During the fact stage a warm-up and gathering of information occurs by recreating the event from what was heard from all sources, i.e., fact and rumor. Participants are asked to recreate the event for the facilitator. The focus of this stage is facts, not feelings.

Encourage students to engage in a moderate level of self-disclosure. The caregiver may offer statements such as "I didn't know . . . could you tell me what that was for," is facilitative in encouraging sharing.

Try to achieve an accurate sensing of the survivor's world and communicate that understanding to him/her.

Be aware of the survivors' choices of topics regarding the death to gain insight into their priorities for the moment.

Help survivors see the many factors which contributed to the death to curtail self-blaming.

Group members are asked to make a brief statement regarding their role, relationship with the deceased, how they heard about the death, and circumstances surrounding the event.

Group members take turns adding in details to make the incident come to life again.

This low initial interaction is a non-threatening warm-up and naturally leads into a discussion of feelings in the next stage. It also provides a climate to share the details about the death and to intervene to prevent secrets or rumors that may divide survivors, and lead to destructive fantasy building.

Feeling Stage

During the feeling stage the expression of feelings surrounding the event occurs. At this stage, survivors should have the opportunity to share the burden of the feelings they are experiencing in a nonjudgmental, supportive, and understanding manner. Survivors must be permitted to talk about themselves, identify and express feelings, identify their own behavioral reactions, and relate to the immediate present, i.e., the "here and now." The caregiver-as-facilitator must communicate acceptance and understanding of survivors' feelings. Acceptance of the person's feelings often helps him/her feel better immediately. It also can serve as a developmental transition to a healthier coping style in the future. Thoughtful clarification or reflection of feelings can lead to growth and change, rather than self-depreciation and self-pity.

The caregiver-as-facilitator begins by asking feeling-oriented questions. "How did you feel when that happened?" "How are you feeling now?" This is a critical component to focus on in order that adolescents acknowledge that "things do get better" with time.

Each person in the group is offered an opportunity to answer these and a variety of other questions regarding their feelings. Often survivors will confront the emotion of anger and guilt. An important step is for survivors to express thoughts of responsibility regarding the event and process the accompanying feelings of sadness.

At this stage, it is critical that no one gets left out of the discussion, and that no one dominates the discussion at the expense of others.

At times the counselor has to do very little. Survivors have a tendency to start talking and the whole process goes along with only limited guidance from the facilitator. People will most often discuss their fears, anxieties, concerns, feelings of guilt, frustration, anger, and ambivalence. All of their feelings—positive or negative, big or small—are important and need to be listened to and expressed. More importantly, however, this process allows survivors to see what subtle changes are occurring between what happened then and what is happening now.

Reactions Stage

During this stage is when an explanation of cognitive occurs and physical reactions and ramifications of the stress response is considered. This stage explores the physical and cognitive reactions to the traumatic event. Acute reactions can last from a few days to a few weeks.

Inherently, the survivor wants to move toward some form of resolution and articulates that need in terms such as: "I can't go on like this any more." "Something has got to give." "Please help me shake this feeling." Or "I feel like I'm losing my mind." Typical anxiety reactions are a sense of dread, fear of losing control, or the inability to focus or concentrate.

The caregiver-as-facilitator asks such questions as, "What reactions did you experience at the time of the incident or when you were informed of the death?" "What are you experiencing now?"

The caregiver-as-facilitator encourages students to discuss what is going on with them in their peer, school, work, and family relationships.

To help clarify reactions, the caregiver-as-facilitator may provide a model for describing reactions, such as the focus of "ownership plus description of behavior." For example, "I am afraid to go to sleep at night since this has happened," or "I feel guilty about not seeing the signs that he was considering suicide."

Learning Stage

This stage is designed to assist survivors in learning new coping skills to deal with their grief reactions. It is also therapeutic to help survivors realize that others are having similar feelings and experiences, i.e., the curative factor of universality (Yalom, 1985).

The caregiver-as-facilitator assumes the responsibility to teach the group something about their typical stress response reactions.

The emphasis is on describing how typical and natural it is for people to experience a wide variety of feelings, emotions, and physical reactions to any traumatic event. These are not unique but are universally shared reactions.

Critical to this stage is to be alert to danger signals in order to prevent negative destructive outcomes from a crisis experience; and to help survivors return to their precrisis equilibrium and interpersonal stability.

This stage also serves as a primary prevention component for future self-defeating or self-destructive behaviors by identifying the normal responses to a traumatic event in a secure, therapeutic environment with a caring, trusted adult. See Figure 5.5, Post Traumatic Stress Reactions, and Figure 5.6, Post Traumatic Stress Disorder.

Closure Stage

In the closure stage is when a wrap-up of loose ends occurs such as questions and answers are openly discussed, final reassurances are given, action planning takes place,

(Continued on Page 120)

Physical	Thinking	Emotional
Nausea	Slowed Thinking	Anxiety
Upset Stomach	Difficulty making	Fear
Tremors	decisions	Guilt
(lips, hands)	Confusion	Grief
Feeling	Disorientation	Depression
uncoordinated	(especially to	Sadness
Profuse sweating	place and time)	Feeling lost
Chills	Difficulty	Feeling abandoned
Diarrhea	calculating	Feeling isolated
Dizziness	Difficulty	Worry about
Chest pain (should	concentraing	others
be checked at	Memory problems	Wanting to hide
hospital)	Difficulty naming	Wanting to limit
Rapid heart beat	common objects	contact with
Rapid breathing	Seeing the event	others
Increased blood	over and over	Anger
pressure	Distressing dreams	Irritability
Headaches	Poor attention	Feeling numb
Muscle aches	span, etc.	Startled
Sleep disturbance,		Shocked, etc.
etc.		

Adapted from *American Psychiatric Association Diagnostic and Statistical Manual of Mental Disorders, DSM-III-R. 3rd. rev. ed.* (1987). Washington, DC: American Psychiatric Association.

Figure 5.5. Post Traumatic Stress Reactions.

Diagnostic Criteria for Post Traumatic Stress Disorder

A. Existence of a recognizable stressor that would evoke significant symptoms of distress in almost everyone.

B. Reexperiencing of the trauma as evidenced by at least one of the following:

  (1) recurrent and intrusive recollections of the event
  (2) recurrent dreams of the event
  (3) sudden acting or feeling as if the traumatic event were reoccuring because of an association with an environmental or ideational stimulus

C. Numbing of responsiveness to or reduced involvment with the external world, beginning some time after the trauma, as shown by at least one of the following:

  (1) markedly diminished interest in one or more signficant activities
  (2) feeling of detachment or estrangement from others
  (3) constricted affect

D. At least two of the following symptoms that were not present before the trauma:

  (1) hyperalterness or exaggerated startle response
  (2) sleep disturbance
  (3) guilt about surviving when others have not, or about behavior required for survival
  (4) memory impairment or trouble concentrating
  (5) avoidance of activities that arouse recollection of the traumatic event
  (6) intensification of symptoms by exposure to events that symbolize or resemble the traumatic event

Source: *American Psychaitric Association: Diagnositic and Statistical Manual of Mental Disorders, DSM-III-R. 3rd. rev. ed.* (1987). Washington, DC: American Psychiatric Associaiton. Reprinted by permission.

Figure 5.6. Post Traumatic Stress Disorder.

referrals, if needed, are made, and follow-up procedures identified. Human crises that involve post-traumatic stress often, if debriefed appropriately, serves as a catalyst for personal growth. This final stage seeks to wrap-up loose ends, answers outstanding questions, provides final assurances, and makes a plan of action that is life-centered. Groups often need direction or specific shared activity after a debriefing to bring closure to the process. Discussion surrounding memorials are often suggested and need appropriate direction.

> Survivors should be aware that closure is taking place, therefore, no new issues should be introduced or discussed at this stage of the debriefing process.

> Summary comments are offered and group members should recall thoughts and feelings regarding the debriefing experience. Specifically, the facilitator should (1) examine whether initial stress symptoms have been reduced or eliminated; (2) assess the survivors increased coping ability; and (3) determine if increased levels of relating to others and the environment has occurred, i.e., is (are) the survivor(s) genuinely hopeful regarding the immediate future?

> Make arrangements for phone calls, exchange of letters or other communication that foster follow-up contact at the time of terminating face-to-face meetings.

> The group also may close by planning a group activity together such as a "living task;" for example, going to a movie, concert, or similar activity to promote a sense of purpose and unity. Members also are advised about getting additional help, resources of interpersonal support, and social networks.

PROCESS EVALUATION

With the passage of time, and after some emotional distance has occurred between the crisis and daily routine, an objective appraisal of actions taken following the crisis could be beneficial. Death education specialists term this phase as an academic autopsy. Crisis team members, case managers, counselors, school administrators, and student leaders can candidly identify and evaluate all actions taken following a death or crisis. Questions to consider could be as follows:

Could anything have been done to prevent the death?

Were all group survivors (e.g., teachers, classmates, teammates, etc.) and subpopulations in the school, as well as at-risk persons processed?

Were school-as-community needs met?

Could any of the previous actions, steps, or interventions be eliminated in the future?

Were there enough consultants or helping professionals involved?

Is an education, identification, and intervention plan systematically incorporated within the individual school and district-wide crisis intervention plan?

SUMMARY

Children's suicidal behavior is escalating toward becoming number one mental health concern. Educating parents, teachers, and administrators should be the first step to prevention and intervention with at-risk children. Suicide intervention and prevention in the school-as-community does not end with a student's death. Public awareness and concern has grown as the number of youth lost to suicide has increased. Educators and citizens in communities throughout the nation have looked to public institutions including the school for intervention, prevention, and assistance. School counselors, administrators, and mental health professionals need to develop systematic strategies to intervene with survivors, as well as potentially at-risk students.

Young people continue to communicate and demonstrate through self-destructive behaviors that they need help with understanding their feelings of confusion, loss, alienation, loneliness, depression, anger, sadness, and guilt. Students' future coping strategies with their uncomfortable but normal feelings, their ability to adjust and maintain control over everyday life experiences, will ultimately be dependent on the assistance they obtain and the resources provided to them within the school-as-community. Counselors, administrators, and other school personnel can provide the curative environment that fosters prevention and intervention for youth risk prevention. Collective efforts to provide structured programs and secure environments to "work through" significant losses are necessary to arrest the present cycle of self-destructive behaviors of contemporary youth.

CHAPTER **6**

SCHOOL COUNSELORS AS CONSULTANTS: A BRIEF INTRODUCTION

Consultation is a function well within the competencies of school counselors. As shown in Figure 6.1, the counselor has many skills. A fundamental consultation course is required in many counselor education programs, and consultation experiences have been included in the Council for Accreditation of Counseling and Related Educational Programs (CACREP) standards for accreditation of such programs. Many states now require a course in consultation for school counselor certification. The role of consultant is one alternative to enhance counselor accountability. Adopting a counselor-as-consultant model and providing targeted services could revitalize existing school counselor programming.

Medway (1979) described consultation as collaborative problem-solving effort between the counselor-consultee and one or more persons (those receiving counseling services) who are responsible for providing some form of psychological assistance to another (the counselee). Consultation also has been called a helping process (Dinkmeyer, 1968) and an interaction between a psychological trained professional and caretaker (Meyer, Parsons, & Martin, 1979).

(Continued on Page 125)

• Collaborator	• Conceptualizer
• Stabilizer	• Facilitator
• Educator	• Inquirer
• Synthesizer	• Evaluator
• Innovator	• Energizer
• Change Agent	• Organizer
• Analyzer	• Catalyst
• Reframer	• Data Gatherer
• Advocate	• Liaison
• Negotiator	• Skilled Helper
• Conflict Manager	• Mediator
• Team Player	• Recognizer
• Transformer	• Ambassador

Figure 6.1. School counselor as consultant—an adjective checklist.

The stages of problem solving are familiar to school counselors because they parallel stage models, such as Egan (1982), for implementing a course of action in the helping process.

> Problem solving is creating change to bring actual conditions closer to conditions that are desired. A problem is a discrepancy between current conditions and desired conditions. A goal is a result that will reduce the discrepancy. There are two basic aspects of problem solving: decision making and problem analysis. Decision making consists of determining goals and choosing courses of action to reach those goals. Problem analysis consists of identifying factors that impede goal achievement and determining the forces that are on those factors. The essential elements of planning depend on accurate problem identification and shrewd decision making. These elements are: (1) determining if a particular problem is significant, (2) setting realistic goals, (3) describing the major forces that affect the problem, and (4) showing how a specific set of interventions can ameliorate the problem. (Elias & David, 1983, p. 149)

In the group process, problem solving evolves as a cyclical feedback system which is ongoing. It occurs in ten steps where each step is open to revision based on new information from the group such as

- assess the situation,

- identify the problem,

- define the goal,

- analyze the forces,

- generate strategies,

- select strategies,

- forecast potential problems,

- test strategies,

- write the work plan, and

- implement and evaluate the plan.

(Elias & David, 1983)

The counselor serves as a consultant to teachers, administrators, parents, and human service organizations. Examples of consultation activities include but are not limited to (1) assisting staff or community in creating a positive climate for the growth and development of students; (2) providing in-service or seminars for staff or parents to improve life adjustment skills; (3) helping teachers or parents to develop and use skills for coping with home/school related problems; (4) assisting teacher or parents in implementing developmental, adjustment, or remediation strategies; (5) coordinating referral or resource activities with local and community human service personnel; (6) conducting parent groups to develop parenting skills and to enhance interpersonal communication; and (7) serving as a resource in developing and enhancing human service partnerships within the community. In Figure 6.2 are listed consultation activities according to groups, administrators, teachers, parents, and students.

CONSULTATION MODELS AND HELPING ORIENTATIONS

Essentially, four major consultation models and the DIRECT technique have the potential for assimilation into school programs. The approaches are **Adlerian-based consultation, mental health consultation, behavioral consultation,** and **organizational development consultation.**

Adlerian-based Consultation

Adlerian-based consultation emphasizes psychological education. This theoretical perspective maintains that a sense of belonging is a power motivator of human behavior. Four mistaken goals for belonging which often manifest in children's behavior are the need for attention, power, revenge, and a sense of inadequacy (Dinkmeyer & Carlson, 1973).

Teachers and parents can be educated to identify children's mistaken attempts to belong and develop intervention strategies to redirect a child's behavior. The following steps are typical of the Adlerian approach:

(Continued on Page 128)

Administrators	Teachers	Parents	Students
Plan school/ community needs assessment	Implement teacher advisor program	Facilitate positive home/school partnerships	Develop peer counseling, peer tutoring, peer listening, peer mediation programs
Identify students with special needs	Identify and intervene in deficiencies in academic or personal development	Involve in volunteer program	Provide leadership training
Support instructional partnerships	Provide inservice in Life skills Crisis intervention Logical consequences Classroom management Special education Primary prevention Early intervention	Conduct parent education groups	Provide groups on Life Skills Communication Stress Management Decision Making Time Management Conflict Resolution Study Skills Self-Esteem Wellness Children of Alcoholics
Facilitate community and parent-school relations		Provide workshops on Developmental needs of children College planning Financial Aid Post-secondary training Adolescent stress Parenting skills Drug Education	
Assist in promoting a positive school climate			
Integrate the counseling program into school goals and objectives			
	Develop remedial or prescriptive program for target populations		
	Provide a team effort in home/ school partnerships		

Figure 6.2. Consultation activities.

Information about the behavior in question, including antecedents, consequences, with responses to correction through observation and/or interview is gathered.

The teacher's or parent's hypothesis regarding the misbehavior and perceptions of the student's strengths are elicited and used as the basis for an intervention plan (Dinkmeyer & Carlson, 1973).

Information about the student's perceptions and the problem is collected in a diagnostic interview with the student using a structured format called the Children's Life Style Guide (Dinkmeyer & Dinkmeyer, 1977).

An intervention plan in collaboration with the consultee is developed and implemented.

Mental Health Consultation

Mental Health Consultation is based on a community mental health approach (Caplan, 1970). Research has described application of this model in schools (Meyers et al., 1979). The mental health model uses many skills that are taught in counselor education programs.

Behavior Consultation

Behavior consultation incorporates the principles of learning and behavior modification to the consultant role. Major contributions of behavior models have been systematic methodologies, and the ability to demonstrate change in behavior (Meyers et al., 1979).

The behavioral consultant follows a systematic five-step process: (1) identification of the problem in observable terms; (2) collecting baseline data; (3) developing an intervention plan; (4) implementing the intervention; and (5) evaluating the intervention by post-baseline data collection. The development of an intervention is a collaborative effort between parent, teacher, student, and counselor.

Organizational Development Model

Organizational Development Model examines the environmental context in which the problem evolves. Student, teacher, and administrator problems are viewed as organizational, interpersonal, or climate deficiencies. The consultant's role is to improve school climate or organizational health.

Intervention strategies focus on (1) diagnosis of organizational problems, (2) open communication, (3) goal establishment, (4) conflict resolution, (5) effective staff meetings, (6) problem solving, and (7) decision-making (Schunk & Miles, 1971).

DIRECT-Technique

Perhaps one of the most applicable models for consultation in the school, which incorporates many of the principles discussed thus far, is the systematic training model entitled the Direct Individual Response Educational Consulting Technique (DIRECT).

DIRECT was developed to meet the identified need for a training model (Strum, 1982). The model delineates seven steps in the consulting process and further specifies four levels of appropriate consultation "leads" to facilitate the development of each step. The DIRECT model is specially designed to promote development of consulting interview skills. DIRECT represents a synthesis of previous approaches and further clarifies consulting steps in order to present a technique for training. The seven steps in the DIRECT consulting session are listed in Steps A through G that follow.

Step A: Establishing A Consulting Relationship. Establishing rapport, gaining an understanding of the consultee and the problem-situation, and setting direction of the session are goals of the first step. The consultant's accurate empathetic response sets the tone for the helping relationship. The consultant assumes responsibility for systematic problem analysis and action planning process by using leads that give structure to the opening dialogue.

Step B: Identify-Clarify the Problem Situation. The consultant must be able to hear the "real" problem as well as the "presenting problem." The problem may be redefined, enlarged, or narrowed in scope. The consultant must not allow a problem too global or general to be identified for action planning.

Step C: Determine Desired Outcome. The goal is to restate problem-situation negatives as desired outcomes or behaviors that can be worked toward. Specific behaviors or goals must be set by the consultee. By specifying these goals, a final understanding of the problem is solidified. The consultant helps the consultee state the goals in measurable or observable terms.

Step D: Developing Ideas and Strategies. Brainstorming ideas that lead to the desired outcomes is the goal of this step. The consultant is supportive of new ideas presented and may offer further strategies. The consultant's ideas are not imposed on the consultees, however.

Step E: Develop a Plan. Ideas or a combination of strategies must be put into a plan-of-action statement. Each idea must be weighed regarding its potential to promote the desired outcome. The consultee must understand that the elements of any new plan will call for new behaviors. The initial "change" in the problem situation must necessarily be changed by the consultee. A final plan is selected by consensus, indicating the collaboration of consultant and consultee as equals in the process of the plan formation.

Step F: Specify the Plan. The goal of this step is to work out the important details necessary for successful plan implementation. The consultant helps the consultee break down the plan into sequential steps, establish a time line, and determine an evaluation format. The consultant encourages immediate consultee action on the first step of the plan.

Step G: Confirm Consulting Relationship. During the concluding step, an ongoing relationship is affirmed, and a discussion of the problem-solving (DIRECT) process is initiated. The consultee thus begins to learn the sequence of problem-solving steps. A follow-up meeting is proposed to monitor the progress of the agreed upon plan and to continue consultee growth in problem solving (Strum, 1982, p. 279).

BENEFITS OF CONSULTATION

A number of benefits are received through employing a systematic consultation model. In addition to gaining increased assistance from families and school personnel, it provides the following:

Improved relationships among teachers, administrators, and support personnel.

Better relationships between parents and the school.

Improved referral linkages with human service organizations.

Concrete strategies to enhance the personal development of the child/adolescent at home and in school.

Families with a means to understand the school's and the counselor's role in assisting the child/adolescent.

Important credibility for the school counselor as resources for parents and school personnel.

Reinforcement of the value of the school counselor to administrators in the realm of primary prevention by reducing such things as the number of parent conferences.

Systematic consultation which serves to provide accountability in light of large counselor-student-ratios and more diverse student populations.

A developmental guidance and counseling program with a primary prevention perspective. If the counselor assists more parents and teachers in relating to youth, more students in school will overcome academic or interpersonal difficulties.

A model of effective communication, collective decision-making, and facilitative group techniques enables the counselor to improve participants' commitment and involvement in the consultation process. This is a direct service to the school. Indirectly, the counselor also can promote the concept of **pyramiding** (Casner-Lotto, 1988) which when properly done, increases the number of people who have input into decision-making and therefore increases the acceptance of new programs and policies. Pyramiding requires each member of a group to interact with five to seven peers. This interaction consists of communicating information about the group's work or about a specific project and gathering feedback from interested colleagues who are not members of the group. Each member of the initial group of five to seven individuals is then expected to reach a similar number of people, who, in turn, contact others. In this way, a significant portion of the school population can be reached in a relatively short time (Casner-Lotto, 1988, p. 351).

A continuity of programs and linkages of services is maintained by the counselor through effective consultation and collaboration with administrators, teachers, and parents. Whenever a counselor helps parents and teachers develop new skills or strategies and gain insight into the behavior of children, consultation is considered an "indirect service to children."

A more efficient use of specific skills and generic resources. Consultation has generally been defined as an "indirect service to teachers, parents, and the school community" (Reschly, 1976). Through consultation, a teacher or parent can learn skills and strategies to solve a problem and apply those skills to future problems (Mayer, 1972). Thus, the work with one teacher can effect 25 to 30 students in one year and potentially thousands of students during one teacher's career. Working with parents can have a similar effect.

CHAPTER **7**

CONSULTING WITH TEACHERS AND OTHER SUPPORT PERSONNEL

Teaching may be defined as the art and craft of persuading, coercing, cajoling, threatening, enticing, entertaining, outwitting, and disciplining others, usually younger, into the dawning of a suspicion that knowledge may be preferable to ignorance.

Wilson O. Clough

CONSULTATION AS PROBLEM SOLVING

Fostering intellectual, interpersonal, and affective growth of youth, especially through consultation with teachers, has long been considered one of the primary roles of the school counselor. Because of its efficiency and efficacy, teacher consultation has become increasingly desirable. Effective consultation with parents, teachers, and other helping professionals is an important step in developing a proactive counseling program. School counselors represent a wealth of resources and skills that can enhance any staff development program. An added dimension occurs when staff development goals are school-based rather than division-based. Division-based goals tend to be generic in nature, reflecting broad spectrum of needs. School-based staff development reflects the targeted needs of the school and community. Selected examples of staff development topics could include

- maximizing achievement of the marginal student,

- developing positive student-teacher relationships,

- "carefronting" the parent of a student in academic trouble,

- enhancing student self-esteem,

- creating a more nurturing school climate,

- managing stress and information overload,

- communicating more effectively to the single-parent family, and

- uncloseting the cumulative record.

With increasing demands upon teacher's management and therapeutic skills, they often welcome the counselor's skills especially in areas that increase cooperative efforts between teacher and parent. Relationships among parent, teacher, student, and counselor can benefit from consultation that focuses on problem solving. In Figure 7.1 is outlined a consultation model that follows a problem-solving approach which focuses on three stages: (1) establishing the relationship, (2) identifying the problem, and (3) facilitating change. Counselor skills which focus on areas such as active listening, feedback, empathy, genuineness, concreteness, and action planning help facilitate remediation of the problem. This approach promotes a more facilitative attitude on the part of the teacher which in turn promotes the greatest gains in learning.

Inherently, the teacher is in a unique position to alter a child's behavior problem more expediently in the natural environment of the classroom. Joint decision making and

(Continued on Page 136)

Stage	Skill	Functions
	Acceptance	Consultant expresses concern.
Establishing the Relationship	Active Listening	Teacher presents more data.
	Acknowledging Strengths	Teacher has had success in the past and the counselor recognizes that the setback is temporary.
	Active Listening	Consultant is beginning to grasp the magnitude of the problem by the teacher.
	Feedback	Based on information obtained from the classroom.
Identifying the Problem	Active Listening and Feedback	
	Concreteness	The consultant wants the teacher to be more specific.
	Commitment	The teacher has stated readiness to do something and a specific behavior has been identified.
	Active Listening	Clarification of the problem.
	Test Alternatives	The consultant and teacher together develop a list of strategies that might work.
	Support	The consultant agrees and reinforces what the teacher has been saying.
Facilitating Change	Developing a Plan of Action	Summary of what the teacher is going to do.

Source: Mickelson, D.J., & Davis, J.L. (1977). A consultation model for the school Counselor. *The School Counselor, 40,* 3, p. 101.

Figure 7.1. Consultation model that follows a problem-solving approach.

collaboration among administrators, teachers, counselors, parents, and students clarifies educational goals, reduces conflicts, and identifies resources. The ultimate outcomes are interpersonal adjustment and intellectual and emotional well-being.

COUNSELORS AND TEACHERS AS PARTNERS
Implementing A Teacher Advisor (T A.) System

Teacher advisor-advisee programs integrate the school counseling program into the total school arena. Teachers and counselors working together as team members is an investment with multiple returns for student-centered environments. By having both a teacher and counselor as an advisor, students can be encouraged to perform to their fullest potential.

Selection of Advisors

Each spring, all students list five members of the professional staff, in order of preference, whom they wish to act as their advisor. After review by the professional staff or advisor selection committee, each student is assigned an advisor. (This can be accomplished effectively and efficiently on the computer.) Students who wish to remain with their current advisor are encouraged to do so, and are assured of assignment to the same advisor for the following year. During the school year, if a student desires to change advisors, a formal request must be made.

Advisee groups are composed of 8 to 15 students from all grade levels, and meet each morning during the school year. The teacher advisor (T A.) system is designed to augment the guidance services available to students by (1) providing regular individual attention to every student, and (2) increasing communication between the home and the school. During TA period, time is allotted for communication: (1) general school communication: student activities, guidance information; and (2) personal communication: academic progress, school/ community activities, special recognition, and problem solving.

Teacher Advisor's Role

The purpose of the teacher advisor program is to provide a comfortable non-teaching arena for the student and the teacher. The advisor serves a variety of functions such as

- orienting new students,

- assisting students with school adjustment,

- serving as a central staff member with whom students can discuss their adjustment concerns,

- settling misunderstandings between students or other staff members,

- organizing and participating in group discussions,

- knowing the students better academically,

- identifying students who need help and assisting them in getting help,

- providing an opportunity for students to work in groups with different grade levels,

- helping students recognize and accept individual differences, and

- helping students learn skills in communication and cooperation.

Student Advisor: An Advocate for the Student

Serves as a buffer between student, general faculty, administration, parent, and community;

contributes to the understanding of other staff members of the academic strengths, weaknesses, problems, and interests of each student;

controls the student's overall academic schedule, assisting in the decisions and selection based on needs and strengths;

assists the student in the planning of exploratory, extracurricular, independent study, and other academic choice activities; and

communicates information about facilities, materials, and personnel to students and parents.

Benefits of a Teacher-Advisor

Another significant adult builds a relationship with students characterized by caring, trust, honesty, and communication;

teachers and coaches can interact with students without having to worry about winning or grading;

it fosters a sense of belonging and responsibility through participation in home-based activities;

it provides an arena to conduct activities which focus on increasing social skills of advisees, and on growth in personal and interpersonal understanding;

it places increased emphasis on the prevention of problems in the lives of students; and

students learn to work in a group and to realize the need for getting along with others in order to meet individual group needs.

In Figure 7.2 is a more detailed Student Assistance Program Behavior Report that also can be used for feedback, monitoring, or identifying potential problems in student performance.

(Continued on Page 140)

STUDENT ASSISTANCE PROGRAM
BEHAVIOR REPORT

Student: _____   Date: _____

Grade: _____   Observer: _____

Return To: _____   Please Return By: _____

Bell of day you have student: _____

Please mark the appropriate areas that you have observed about this student in or out of the classroom. After completing this report, please return to a member of the **Student Assistance Core Team**. By marking those areas you have actually observed, you may be providing a student with needed assistance. This information is confidential. Please take the necessary measures to insure confidentiality.

Grades
☐ Lower Grades - Change in Achievement
☐ Academic Failure
☐ Always Behind in Class
☐ Lack of Motivation-Apathy
☐ Cheating

School Attendance
☐ Absenteeism
☐ Frequently Tardy
☐ On Absentee List But Seen In School
☐ Frequently Requesting to be Out of Class (Trips to Restroom, to Nurse, to Counselor)

Physical Symptoms
☐ Sleeping in Class
☐ Physical Complaints
☐ Physical Injuries
☐ Staggering or Stumbling
☐ Smelling of Alcohol or Marijuana
☐ Poor Coordination
☐ Glassy, Bloodshot Eyes
☐ Slurred Speech
☐ Continuous, cold-like symptoms (runny nose, sniffles, nosebleeds)

Behavior
☐ Constant Defiance of Rules
☐ Frequent Discipline Referrals/Action
☐ Fighting or Provoking Conflicts
☐ Excessive Nervousness
☐ Withdrawn
☐ Verbal Abuse
☐ Frequently Crying
☐ Excessive Forgetfulness
☐ Frequently Tired
☐ Talks Freely About Drug/Alcohol Use
☐ Erratic Behavior/Mood Swings
☐ Change in Friends
☐ Change in Appearance
☐ Sudden Popularity
☐ Older Social Group
☐ Disoriented Sense of Time
☐ Carries Large Amounts of Money
☐ Depression
☐ Defensiveness
☐ Increasing Non-Involvement
☐ Complaints of Family Problems

Alcohol or Drug Abuse Behaviors (Check Appropriate Column)

Witnessed	Suspected	Behavior
_____	_____	Selling, Distributing Alcohol or Other Drugs
_____	_____	Possession of Alcohol or Other Drugs
_____	_____	Possession of drug paraphenalia
_____	_____	Use of Alcohol or Other Drugs
_____	_____	Intoxication
_____	_____	Exchanging Large Sums of Money
_____	_____	Other (Please elaborate): _____

_____

_____

Drug Free Schools and Communities/Student Assistance Programs
Chesapeake Public Schools ● P.O. Box 15204
Chesapeake, VA 23320 ● 804-547-0153

Figure 7.2. Student Assistance Program Behavior Report.

Figure 7.2. Continued.

Student Assistance Program
Behavior Report
For Parents

A Combination of several of these behaviors may signal that your child is in need of assistance. The following changes often occur. Please check appropriate items.

School/Family Behavior Changes
- ☐ Gradual withdrawal from school and activities
- ☐ Drop in school work quality and drop in grades
- ☐ Rejection of family standards and values
- ☐ Stays in room, isolates self
- ☐ Radical change in friendships
- ☐ Phone calls at odd hours
- ☐ Disappearance of money and valuables from home
- ☐ Has run away or taken unannounced stays with friends
- ☐ Guards clothes like jacket closely, wears it consistently
- ☐ Older social group, adult contacts
- ☐ Increased secretiveness, especially about friends
- ☐ Misrepresentation of facts, lying, excuses
- ☐ Conversations about alcohol or other drug abuse
- ☐ Sudden popularity, sought out by others

Legal/Law Violations
- ☐ Incidents of violence/frequent fights
- ☐ Shoplifting
- ☐ DUI
- ☐ Trespassing
- ☐ Breaking and entering

Emotional Changes
- ☐ Overreaction to criticism from any source
- ☐ Erratic mood changes - sudden outbursts
- ☐ Anxious, overstimulated, very tense
- ☐ Extreme negativism toward self and others
- ☐ Withdrawan
- ☐ Talks of suicide
- ☐ Unusually suspicious, paranoid
- ☐ Abandoning of goals/reduction of ambitions

Physical Changes
- ☐ Increase in minor illness
- ☐ Apathy, lethargy, stares, lack of response
- ☐ Neglect of personal appearance/hygiene
- ☐ Has physical injuries
- ☐ Smells of alcohol or pot
- ☐ Lack of usual coordination
- ☐ Glassy, bloodshot eyes, wears sunglasses
- ☐ Slurred speech
- ☐ Runny nose, watery eyes/inflammed nose and eyelids
- ☐ Muscle jerking or rigidity
- ☐ Unusually poor appetite
- ☐ Falls asleep easily for a long period of time

When were these behaviors first noticed? _____

_____

How long did the behaviors continue? _____

_____

MOTIVATION AND ENCOURAGEMENT

The Average Child

I don't cause teachers trouble
My grades have been okay.
I listen in my classes
and I'm in school every day.
My teachers think I'm average
My parents think so too.
I wish I didn't know that
'Cause there's lots I'd like to do.
I'd like to build a rocket

I have a book that tells you how.
Or start a stamp collection
Well, no use trying now.
'Cause since I found out I'm average
I'm just smart enough to see
To know there's nothing special
That I should expect of me.
I'm part of that majority
That hump part of the bell.
Who spends his life unnoticed
In my "only average" shell.

Anonymous

Parents, teachers, administrators, and counselors frequently reflect on how to motivate students more effectively. The theory and techniques of encouragement increases motivation among recipients and lessens feelings of inadequacy. It communicates trust, respect, competence, and ability. Dinkmeyer and Dreikur (1963) maintained that the proper use of encouragement involves the following:

Valuing individuals as they are, not as their reputation indicates, or as one hopes they will be. Believing in individuals as good and worthwhile will facilitate acting toward them in this manner.

Having faith in the abilities of others. This enables the helper to win confidence while building the self-respect of the other person.

Showing faith in others. This will help them to believe in themselves.

Giving recognition for effort, as well as for a job well done.

Using a group to help the person develop. This makes practical use of the assumption that, for social beings, the need to belong is basic.

Integrating the group so that the individual can discover his or her place and begin working positively from that point.

Planning for success, and assisting in the development of skills that are sequentially and psychologically paced.

Identifying and focusing on strengths and assets rather than on mistakes.

Using the interests of the individual in order to motivate learning and instruction.

Skills to Foster Affective Growth

In a survey of expert opinion, Stein and French (1984) identified "the key skills, concepts, and attitudes" necessary for teachers to foster the affective growth of their students. The following skills were identified as being essential to foster students' affective growth:

- having general teacher/learner communication skills;
- using reflective listening;
- using "I" messages;
- using problem-solving and decision-making techniques;
- helping learners to increase their own ability to make decisions;
- increasing learners' involvement with making rules in the classroom;
- using effective discipline methods;
- using nonpunitive discipline methods;
- using classroom activities designed to increase learner's self-esteem;
- increasing learner's acceptance of other children and adults;
- helping learners accept themselves, their families, and their own cultures;
- helping learners to increase self-control;
- increasing cooperation and cooperative work among learners in the classroom;
- helping learners to learn acceptable outlets for strong emotions;
- structuring learners' work so as to ensure an adequate amount of success;
- integrating cognitive and affective learning goals;

- having a general group discussion and group leadership skills;
- having a general skill in at least one method of counseling;
- having skill in crisis counseling and intervention;
- using creative writing for affective development;
- using children's literature as a resource for affective development;
- using role playing in the classroom;
- establishing trust between the teacher and the learner;
- knowing teacher's own self-awareness;
- having ability to deal with teacher's own emotions as they arise in the classroom;
- having skills at the deliberate modeling of acceptable behavior;
- having awareness of own philosophy of education and skill at using it as a daily guide; and
- having the ability to laugh at one's self and one's dilemmas.

Six Essential Concepts

To encourage affective growth the following six concepts are considered essential:

understanding the special needs and psychological development of adolescents;

having knowledge of the typical emotional problems of normal development;

having knowledge of the development and self-esteem in children and adolescents;

understanding the positive and negative effects of praise on emotional growth; and

understanding emotional, academic, and intellectual readiness factors.

Fourteen Attitudes

The importance of teacher attitude has been stressed by many researchers. The power of teachers' expectations to bring about a self-fulfilling prophesy is a classic focus topic in most education courses. From a list of twenty-five attitudes the following are essential:

> preference for long-term goals as well as immediate gains;
>
> belief that teachers can and should have an impact on the development of emotional well-being of their learners;
>
> belief that the teacher/learner relationship should be one of mutual trust;
>
> belief that facilitating the development of emotional well-being should be a part of the school's objectives;
>
> belief that affective learnings are at least as important as cognitive learnings;
>
> attitude of great respect for the confidentiality of a learner's personal communication;
>
> belief that children should be treated differently according to their individual needs;
>
> commitment to avoidance of unnecessary failure;
>
> decreased accent on rigid grading systems;
>
> willingness to genuinely listen to learner's ideas and feelings;
>
> attitude of positive expectation;
>
> acceptance of learners as unique, worthy, and diverse
>
> acceptance that no teacher can help all learners; and
>
> commitment to own emotional growth, self-worth, and self-confidence.

CHAPTER 8

CONSULTING WITH FAMILIES

Memorandum

To: Parents

From: Your loving Child

Don't spoil me. I know quite well that I shouldn't have all I ask for—I'm only testing you.

Don't tease me, or make me feel smaller than I am. It only makes be behave stupidly "big."

Don't correct me in front of people if you can help it. I'll take much more notice if you talk quietly with me in private.

Don't ridicule me or make me feel that my mistakes are sins. It upsets my sense of values.

Don't be too upset when I say "I hate you." It isn't you I hate, but your power to thwart me.

Don't be taking too much notice of my small ailments. Sometimes they get me the attention I need.

Don't nag. If you do, I shall have to protect myself by appearing deaf.

Don't bribe me or make rash promises. Remember that I feel badly let down when promises are broken.

Don't be inconsistent. That completely confuses me and makes me lose faith in you.

Don't tell me my fears are silly. They are terribly real to me and you can do so much to reassure me if you try to understand.

Don't think it's beneath your dignity to apologize to me. An honest apology makes me feel warm towards you.

Don't forget how quickly I am growing up. It must be very difficult for you to keep pace with me, but please try.

Don't forget. I love experimenting. I couldn't get along without it so please put up with it.

Don't compare me with anyone else. Like me for what I am.

Don't ask me, "What is it?" when I bring home something I created in school. I can give you a better idea if you say, "Tell me about it."

Don't tell me I'm bad when it's my behavior you disapprove of. Try to arrange situations so that my behavior is socially acceptable.

Don't forget that I can't thrive without a lot of understanding and love. But I don't need to tell you, do I?

Author: Unknown

HOME-SCHOOL PARTNERSHIPS

Various proponents such as Amatac and Fabrick (1984), Downing (1983), and Nicoll (1984) have maintained that family counseling is a legitimate extension of the school counseling program. Home-school partnerships have repeatedly shown positive results in children's affective and cognitive development.

Duncan and Fitzgerald (1969) found that individual counselor-parent conferences at the beginning of the school year were effective in preventing problems of absenteeism, discipline, and dropouts. Therrium (1979), Cox and Matthews (1977), and O'Dell (1974) are among numerous researchers who found parent education to have lasting benefit. Furthermore, Lombana and Lombana (1982) maintained that a home/school collaboration model should differentiate between parent involvement, parent conferences, parent education, and parent counseling, illustrating an inverse relationship between parental needs and counselor time and skills. In Figure 8.1, The Home-

(Continued on Page 148)

The Home-School Partnership

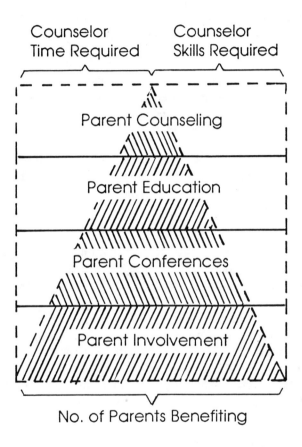

Figure 8.1. The home-school partnership: A model for counselors.

Source: Lombana, J.H., & Lombana, A.E. .(1982). The home-school partnership: A model for counselors. *Personnel & Guidance Journal, 61,* 1, p. 36. Reprinted by permission.

Figure 8.1. The home-school partnership: A model for counselors.

School Partnership: A Model for Counselors, illustrates the extent of parent involvement in relation to counselor's time and skill requirements.

In reference to parent involvement strategies, Karnes (1979) provides some guidelines which can enhance parent participation:

> Plan activities that make sense to parents. Parents should be able to understand the value of the counseling program, not only in general terms but also in relation to his or her own needs and interests.

> Provide parents with the information they need. Recommendations and directions are more likely to be followed if they are specific and suited to an individual situation.

> Encourage parents to become involved in the classroom. For parents who are uncomfortable tutoring or grading papers, assisting with field trips also helps develop an understanding of the educational process.

> Plan activities in which parents can work cooperatively with other parents. Often parents can learn more from each other than they can from the counselor or teacher.

> Give parents adequate feedback on their contributions. Positive feedback encourages greater involvement and commitment; in addition, it carries over into parent-child interaction. See Figure 8.2, How Welcome Are Parents In Our School, is a survey used by PTA. The items listed suggest means for making parents feel welcome in our schools.

VALUE OF PARENT CONFERENCES

The counselor-parent-teacher-student conference has the potential to be one of the most effective means of strengthening the home-school relationship while serving to exchange

(Continued on Page 150)

How welcome are parents in our school?

Directions: Think about the experiences you have had when you have visited your child's school. Your PTA and the school staff want to make parents feel comfortable and a part of the school.

Please take a few minutes to fill out the following brief survey. Be honest. All answers will be anonymous—please don't write your name on the sheet. Your PTA leader will collect the surveys.

After the PTA has analyzed the results, a committee composed of PTA leaders and other parents, the principal and teacher representatives will decide how best to use the information and make recommendations, if necessary, for helping parents feel more welcome in our school.

	(Circle One)		
Am I always greeted in a friendly, courteous way when I contact the school either on the phone or in person?	Yes	No	Do Not Know
Does the school have a special area to greet visitors, equipped with information about the school and directions so that I can find my way around the building?	Yes	No	Do Not Know
Did the school conduct some kind of orientation program for my family when I first enrolled my child?	Yes	No	Do Not Know
Do school staff and parents have informal occasions where we can get to know each other during the school year?	Yes	No	Do Not Know
Does the principal have regular office hours when parents and students can stop in?	Yes	No	Do Not Know
(If "Yes" to the above question) Are those hours convenient for me?	Yes	No	Do Not Know
Is there a school suggestion box where teachers', students', and parents' ideas are encouraged and are ideas implemented when possible?	Yes	No	Do Not Know
Does the school encourage me to visit my child's classroom outside of planned occasions (after checking first with the teacher involved)?	Yes	No	Do Not Know
Am I (and other parents) welcome to use the building after hours for community purposes?	Yes	No	Do Not Know
Does the principal ask for parents' suggestions when making decisions that will affect the running of the school?	Yes	No	Do Not Know
Does the school provide a variety of means (written and verbal) so all parents (including illiterate and limited English-speaking parents) can understand the curriculum and participate in the school's activities?	Yes	No	Do Not Know
Does the school provide written information to parents about school rules, parent-teacher conferences and other important items?	Yes	No	Do Not Know

Feel free to write any comments and suggestions:

_____

_____

_____

Source: *1988 National PTA is What WE Make It! Planning Kit.* Copyright 1988 National PTA, 700 N. Rush Street, Chicago, IL 60611-2571. Permission to reprint has been granted by the National PTA. Credit the National PTA.

Figure 8.2. How welcome are parents in our school.

information, solve problems, and make educational plans for an individual student or the entire family (Lombana & Lombana, 1982). Yet, very few studies contain empirical data about parent conferences. One of the few studies measured the effects of establishing a parent-counselor conference relationship prior to the student's entry into junior high school (Wise & Ginther, 1981). Significant findings included increased student attendance, increased grade point averages, and additional parent contact with the school. Dropout rate and disciplinary referrals significantly decreased, and parent-child communication tended to increase for those who participated in the conferences. In Figure 8.3 is a sample of a conference planning sheet.

Strother and Jacobs (1986) provided a systematic step-by-step procedure for an effective conference if parents are willing to come to school at least once.

> *Initial contact:* Set the tone with the initial contact to the home. Convey a message of cooperation and indicate that as the counselor you value their input. A statement like "we need your opinion" or "the information you could provide us would be valuable" demonstrates a spirit of equality and openness.
>
> *Perception check:* Assess the parents' initial feelings about coming to school. Engage them in a dialogue that covers questions such as the following:
>
> * Have parents had previous contact with the school?
> * Was the contact positive or negative?
> * Do the parents understand the role of the school counselor?
> * What are the parents' feelings toward the school and their child's school experiences?
> * Are they willing to be part of the helping process?
>
> *Information delivery:* Introduce the critical information concerning the child such as academic, behavioral, or social difficulties. Explanation should be simple and concrete. Cooperation and encouragement should be the mutual goal. The focus should be on the problem not on personalities which may be involved. The focus should be in the "here-and-now."

(Continued on Page 152)

Student: _____ Grade: _____ Date: _____

Teacher: _____ Parent(s), Guardian: _____

	Steady Growth	Needs Improvement	Needs Immediate Attention

Statements by Teacher:

Social Attitides and Behaviors:
1. Accepts responsibilities
2. Is thoughtful of rights of others
3. Cooperates in work and play
4. Receives and gives criticism in a friendly way
5. Is dependable
6. Shows self-control
7. Is courteous
8. Appears to make friends easily
9. _____
10. _____

Work, Play, and Personal Habits:
1. Alertness: listens attentively and follows directions
2. Uses time to good advantage
3. Takes care of materials
4. Completes work neatly
5. Begins and completes work in reasonable length of time
6. Obeys safety rules
7. Is careful of personal appearance
8. Participates in games
9. Shows good sportsmanship
10. _____

Other Observations:
1. Profits from use of individualized instructional materials
2. Uses problem solving techniques
3. Participates in class meetings
4. _____
5. _____

Data From File:
Norm-referenced test data
   Test: _____
   Composite: _____
   Reading: _____   Other test data: _____
   Math: _____
   Language Arts: _____

   _____   _____
   _____   _____

Source: Canady, R.L., & Seyfarth, J.T. (1979). How parent-teacher conferences build partnerships. *Phi Delta Kappan.* Bloomington, IN. Reprinted by permission.

Figure 8.3. Conference planning sheet.

Reception check: Respond to feelings, understanding, and reaction of parents. Ask, "How are you feeling about what I've told you?" Assess their commitment and understanding. Have alternative methods of presenting information since parents differ in their knowledge, their level of understanding, and their school experiences. Elicit suggestions from them about potential strategies to explore.

Assess the family dynamics: Explore relationships in the family in a nonthreatening way to assess if strategies can be realistically carried out by the parent(s). For example, "Are there any problems that the parents are aware of in the family regarding other children?" "Is the home atmosphere calm or tense?" "Are work schedules erratic, is supervision reliable and consistent?" and "Do other family members get along?"

Education and strategy implementation: Assess if the parent(s) is(are) willing to work cooperatively to help the child. Involve the child at this stage of the process.

Summarize, confirm, clarify: The counselor should summarize the information discussed and presented, repeat strategies to be used to help the child, and restate what each person has agreed to do in terms of behavior changes, homework assignments, and family/ school responsibilities. This may also be reinforced with a written contract signed by all parties involved. This helps solidify the agreement. Also include your name and telephone number, as well as the best time to reach you in the event the family needs some reinforcement or needs to amend the contract. Check for final questions and set a time for a follow-up meeting.

Follow-up for follow-through: Follow-up on plans discussed in the conference 48 to 72 hours later. Express positive feelings about the conference; offer support and encouragement. Confirm a date and time for the next meeting.

In Figure 8.4 are listed elements of effective parent teacher conferences and in Figure 8.5 is an effective conference continuum. These two figures may suggest means for making the conference more effective.

Student Led Conferences

Little and Allen (1989) maintained that school counselors can demonstrate support for teachers by initiating and implementing student-led conferences, especially at the elementary or middle school level. Guyton and Fielstein (1989) further outlined the educational objectives of the student-led conference: (1) to foster a sense of accountability within the student for academic progress, (2) to encourage students to take pride in their work, (3) to allow for more time for each conference, and (4) to encourage student-parent communication with regard to school performance.

A schedule of events prior to the parent conference could involve developing mini-lessons to prepare the student to handle his/her conference. Topics for the lessons could be explaining the report card and grading system, selecting examples of classroom work to support the letter grade, making subject folders for displaying daily work, identifying strengths and weaknesses, keeping a log of homework assignments and time spent on task, using effective communication for leading a conference, and discussing appropriate social conduct.

Guyton and Fielstein (1989) maintained that student-led conferences have the potential to

- improve student/parent communication and foster greater understanding of the child's progress and academic record;
- encourage students to assume greater ownership and responsibility for grades and academic progress;
- increase student accountability for daily work as well as homework prior to, and in preparation for, the conference; and
- eliminate the negative connotation that parent/teacher conferences often project.

(Continued on Page 156)

Teacher Initiated	Common Elements	Parent Initiated
Prepare for conference in advance.	Allow enough time.	Positively identify parent requesting meeting.
Give parent(s) some idea of topic.	Determine whether student should be present.	If parent shares topic, collect necessary background information.
Specify points to be made.	Do not become defensive; maintain open mind.	Have pertinent student records accessible for conference.
Prepare written progress report to include: 1. survey of student 2. areas of concern 3. areas of strength.	Listen to what parent is saying, specifically and implied.	Do not make assumptions; ask teacher(s) or administrator(s) to express concern.
Don't wait for regularly scheduled conference if a matter arises; deal with it.	Seek clarification when necessary.	Get complete story before suggesting actions or solutions.
Structure conference for parent(s): why, what, when; explain purpose.	Avoid overwhelming parent with irrelevant material or use of jargon; be thorough.	
Allow parent(s) time to read and/or discuss written summary.	Meet parent(s) at building entry point if possible.	
	Show parent concern and respect—respect as person, concern as patron of school; maintain positive, professional demeanor.	
	Make environment for conference conducive to open communication; avoid physical barriers.	
	Attempt to part on positive note; set up future conference or referral procedures before parent leaves.	
	Be sure to carry out any promised follow-up.	

Sources: Rotter, J.C., & Robinson, E.H. (1982). Parent-teacher conferencing. The National Education Association. Washinton, DC. Reprinted by permission.

Figure 8.4. Elements of effective parent-teacher conferences.

		A	S	N
A = Always	S = Sometimes	N = Never		

		A	S	N
1.	Was the tone and "opening" of the conference designed to help all members feel comfortable?	___	___	___
2.	Were parents given some idea in advance of the topic to be discussed . . . ?	___	___	___
3.	Was enough time allowed for the conference?	___	___	___
4.	Was the emotional climate of the conference positive?	___	___	___
5.	Was problem solving directed at personalities or behavior?	___	___	___
6.	Was there a balance between positive and negative remarks?	___	___	___
7.	Did colleagues avoid becoming defensive when parents question judgment or procedures?	___	___	___
8.	Did colleagues and parents maintain an open mind to problem solving ideas?	___	___	___
9.	Were the goals of the conference understood by all persons present?	___	___	___
10.	Were the goals of the conference met?	___	___	___
11.	Were efforts made to include the student in the conference to establish goals and to reinforce resolutions?	___	___	___
12.	Were efforts made to avoid overwhelming parent(s) with the presence of other school personnel?	___	___	___
13.	Were efforts made to avoid overwhelming parent(s) with irrelevant material or use of "educanese?"	___	___	___
14.	Was the closure of the conference appropriate?	___	___	___
15.	Were there provisions made to follow up on commitments?	___	___	___

Figure 8.5. Effective Conference Continuum.

INVOLVING PARENTS IN THEIR
CHILD'S ACADEMIC PERFORMANCE
AND CAREER DEVELOPMENT

Counselors, by themselves, cannot bring about students' academic achievement or career development. However, the counselor can capitalize on the existing interest and commitment that parents have for their offsprings. Although may parents may have unrealistically high expectations for their child, career guidance and academic achievement are top priorities for students and their families. Many times all families want is a structured arena to discuss some of their anxieties about academic preparation and post-secondary opportunities.

Parents want validation that the course their child has chosen to follow is appropriate and congruent in terms of ability, aptitude, and interest. The following suggestions are provided as interventions for counselor involvement with academic performance and career development. Building parent involvement in their child's academic achievement include

> programs using the model of parents as tutors or home-teachers increase academic performance;

> opportunities for families to supplement and reinforce their child's academic performance; and

> a systematic communication network for parents, particularly on the high school level with a dual accountability strategy: (1) regular and timely newsletter communication of important dates, programs, and enrichment opportunities; and (2) early notification whenever possible when academic or interpersonal problems arise.

In addition, Roberts (1984) advocated "uncloseting the cumulative record" with parent-student-counselor conference groups with discussion of the following:

Generally,

> explanation of a cumulative record and what it contains;

discussion of ability as measured by standardized tests and given by category; and

discussion of achievement as measured by standardized tests and interpreted by national and/ or local percentile rank.

More specifically,

process past and present report cards with question number one—"Is my child/Am I performing in school as well as the indicators (test scores) predict he/ she/I might?" And Question number two—"If not, why not?" What steps are needed to improve school?; and

examine interests and tentative career choices— give the student and parent an opportunity to share expectations and interests. Provide fact sheets with general information on (1) occupational job clusters and (2) differentiated preparation programs offered at the district's high schools (honors, academic, vocational, or technical) with prerequisite grade point averages and percentile ranks for each program and student's potential eligibility.

STRATEGIES TO IMPROVE
ACADEMIC PERFORMANCE

Sometimes some very simple things can be implemented to improve student performance. Some suggestions include

systematically attending to homework at a specific time of day, every day;

doing homework in a specific study area;

having a study partner for difficult subjects;

re-copying notes in an organized manner for systematic memorization;

following a daily schedule for the completion of work;

following a weekly schedule for the completion of assignments;

following a semi-quarterly schedule for the completion of work;

implementing a contract between teacher, student, and parent (A homework contract encourages young people to accept responsibility for an agreement made between parent and child contingent upon the completion of teacher requirements. Complying to academic requirements and performing appropriately provides certain rewards agreed upon prior to the goal.);

incorporating time-management strategies between school, family, extracurricular, and leisure activities often creates insight in itself (Time-management skills are often a critical component of anyone's maximum performance.);

implementing a weekly "progress report" from the teacher, whose subject is most difficult for the student, helps to align goals, objectives, and expected performance; and

identify specific academic study skill problems that a student may have and as a team focus on specific strategies that may remedy the problem.

INVOLVING PARENTS
AS CAREER COUNSELORS

Parents play a primary role in their child's career development and school counseling can benefit significantly by tapping into this resource (Birk & Blimline, 1984; Daniels, Karmos, & Presley, 1983; Noeth, Engen, & Noeth, 1984; Otto & Call, 1985; Prediger & Sawyer, 1985). The following activities have a direct and indirect influence on families.

Provide parent study groups to share current information about emerging careers, nontraditional careers, income projections, occupational outlook, and local training opportunities. These study groups could be provided through the community employment services, or by local colleges on a quarterly basis on the school premises. School counselors merely need to coordinate the activity and "get the word out" to parents. Many agencies in the community would welcome the chance to participate because it also increases their visibility.

Use parents as career resource people in parent/student workshops to facilitate discussion and understanding of a particular career choice.

Conduct student sessions of family influence on their careers to process issues such as independence and family differentiation. Techniques which can facilitate this process include family systems review, paradigms of family interaction, family sculpting, family constellation diagrams, occupational family trees, and exploration of family work values (Splete & Freeman-George, 1985).

PRIMARY PREVENTION AND EARLY INTERVENTION FOR FAMILIES

In the past, children and adolescents with school related problems were often understood to be anxious, acting-out, depressed, immature, passive-aggressive, or emotionally disturbed. Today, however, children and adolescents' classroom behaviors have been explained as a function of the levels of health and stress in their family systems. Boyer and Horne (1988) offer the following differences between functional and dysfunctional families:

Functional Families' Behaviors

- Use humor, praise, and encouragement;
- respect and prize each other;
- communicate clearly;
- solve family problems effectively and democratically;

- perform fairly and consistently;
- use effective disciplinary methods, and
- touch affectionately.

Dysfunctional Families' Behaviors

- Use criticism, put-downs, and sarcasm;
- devalue or envy each other;
- communicate poorly and infrequently;
- cannot solve family problems without resorting to power and autocratic decisions;
- perform autocratically and inconsistently;
- use ineffective corporal punishment methods; and
- use touch as a control method.

The level of stress and family dysfunction has increased in proportion to the number of school-age youth from single-parent and disrupted families. Primary prevention strategies need to focus on education through parent support or parent student groups. Concurrently, early intervention strategies should focus on counselor assisted procedures to empower parents in caring for their offspring. Baruth and Burggraf (1983) have suggested that parent study groups be developed for the purpose of helping families. They have developed the following guidelines for helping professionals starting such study groups:

inform parents about study groups by providing basic information such as the time and place for the group's meeting. (Letters sent home with children or public announcements in local media can be helpful in keeping parents informed.);

limit the size of the group from 8 to 12 parents to foster better parental communication;

set the time and place for the meetings, preferably around the parents' schedule;

plan meetings to last two hours on a weekly basis for ten sessions;

establish a deadline when parents can enter the study group with no new members added after two sessions have been completed; and

before one teaches a parent study group, one should participate first as a group member, then co-lead a group with supervision.

Parent networks and support groups aimed at restoring supportive family interactions by promoting positive communication are gaining momentum in every community across the nation. Small grass roots groups of parents have generated enormous attention as they empower parents to intervene in their child's life. Combatting peer pressure and it's lure toward alcohol and drug abuse is one example.

The role of the school and counselor should focus on extending the parent groups' potential to operate independently. Definition of community goals and activities should be parent generated. The school counselor should lend support and resources such as

speaking or assisting with arrangements for other speakers;

providing films, articles, brochures, and resources lists of materials and curricula;

training groups in planning, evaluating, and prevention of self-destructive behaviors among adolescents;

assisting in the design and implementation of community needs assessment;

facilitating interagency cooperation;

maintaining a community calendar and mailing list; and

coordinating information in the community newspaper.

SCHOOL COUNSELORS AS PROMOTERS OF A MORE POSITIVE SCHOOL CLIMATE

On School Climate . . .

What I am asking for is that we suspend for a time as a matter of policy our pathological preoccupation with pupil effects as defined in statements of objectives or norm-based achievement tests. What I am asking for is that we concentrate, as an alternative, on the quality of life in the schools—not just for pupils but for all who live there each day.

John Goodlad

ORGANIZATIONS AND CHANGE

Change is a fact of contemporary life. The notion of slowing the pace of change is almost nonexistent. In the role of potential change agent, the school counselor is in the position to understand the school-as-institution within the context of the school-as-community. The counselor can assist in developing strategies of plan changed through influencing informal systems within both environmental contexts.

A caveat—it is not unusual for people to resist change and to want to keep things as they are. Odiorne (1981) asserted that "the best minds of our society often seem bent upon criticism and resistance rather than on creation." Perhaps, the best summary of factors that affect resistance was compiled by Zaltman, Duncan, and Holbek (1973). Among the possible determinants of resistance are the need for stability, the use of foreign jargon, the impact on existing social relationships, personal threat, local pride, felt needs, and economic factors. Structural factors affecting resistance include: stratification, division of labor, and hierarchical and status differences. Individual resistance factors include perception, motivation, attitude, legitimization, accompaniments of trial, results of evaluation, and actual adoption or rejection.

Counselors have the unique training and skills to decompress resistance to programs and services. Various leaders in the counseling profession have encouraged school counselors to view themselves as agents of change in organizational behavior. With emerging management orientations that are based on organizational development and improvement, this seems to be a logical extension of counselor skills. When the five change agent roles (Figure 9.1) are functionally related to the problem-solving process, the result is a dynamic process for effectively accomplishing change within an organization (Chartier, 1985).

ROLES OF CHANGE AGENT

The process of change involves five modes which provide functional roles for facilitating organizational change. They are (Figure 9.1)

- catalyzer,
- process helper,
- solution giver,
- resource linker, and
- stabilizer.

Change agents evolve in open organizations to overcome inertia and to activate initial work on serious problems.

(Continued on Page 166)

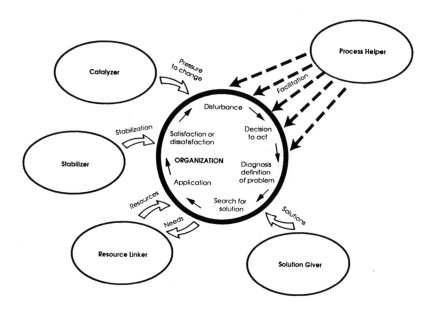

Source: Chartier, M.R. (1985). Functional roles for facilitating change. The 1985 annual: Developing human resources. San Diego, CA: University Associates. Reprinted by permission.

Figure 9.1. Five roles of change agents.

The **catalyst** energizes the school-as-institution to come to terms with it's problems and he/she draws attention to the need for change. For example, the catalyst may focus on such problems as failure, retention, or discipline procedures that alienate students rather than engage them to the school community.

The **process helper** is knowledgeable in how to facilitate change in individuals or departments. Process helpers utilize problem-solving skills such as

- recognizing needs,
- analyzing problems,
- setting goals,
- obtaining needed resources, and/or
- generating and evaluating solutions in order to facilitate change. Analyzing the relationship between test scores, curriculum, and student achievement indicators would be a comfortable role for a process helper.

The **solution giver** requires more than generating solutions. It involves a sense of timing and effective communication to create awareness of the solution's value and to gain it's ultimate acceptance. The change agent as solution giver also can assist the school-as-community in adapting to it's goals. The solution giver might review potential interventions that could solve the problem of underachievement such as more small group counseling, having less classroom interruptions, or implementing an "adopt-a-student" program.

Effective change also requires the interlinking of needs to resources. Resources can consist of money, or a means to money; special knowledge; skills in analyzing problems; knowledge of solutions; and the ability to formulate, adapt, and adopt solutions or expertise in the process of change. The **resource linker** can bring this process to fruition. The resource linker could be someone who can write grants and work with business, industry, and the Chamber of Commerce.

Change agent as **stabilizer** focuses on the school-as-community's need for stability, especially after a successful change has been implemented. He/she shows the school how to

build and maintain organizational boundaries;

build interdependency and cohesiveness between departments and across the curriculum;

maintain openness, feedback, and stability; and

keep the school focused on the goals. Someone who can envision the school into the twenty-first century would function well in this capacity.

Organizational development is an educational process by which human resources are continuously identified, allocated, and expanded in ways that make these resources more available to the organization and, therefore, improve the organization's problem solving abilities (Sherwood, 1972, p. 153). Many conceptual models, primarily based on open-system theory depict organizations as systems of interacting elements, and identify both the explicit and implicit structures of organizational life. A complete model is offered by Jones (1981) in his "Organizational Universe Model" (Figure 9.2). Typical organizational values, including respect and dignity in the treatment of people, cooperation, functional openness, interdependence, authenticity, and profitability, are placed at the core of a set of concentric circles. The next ring, goals, considers how the values are articulated or operationalized. For example, if one of the values is respect for people, courtesy in all interpersonal interactions might be the operational goal. When people are treated discourteously, it can be assumed either that the value of respect is not authentic, or that the relationship between courteous behavior and respect is not clear to members of the organization or not explicit enough in policy to guide their behaviors.

At the core of the school or school division is a set of values, a raison d'etre or shared belief system. Annual school goals are best understood in terms of the values on which they are based. Objectives are targeted needs that are assessed

(Continued on Page 169)

ENVIRONMENT

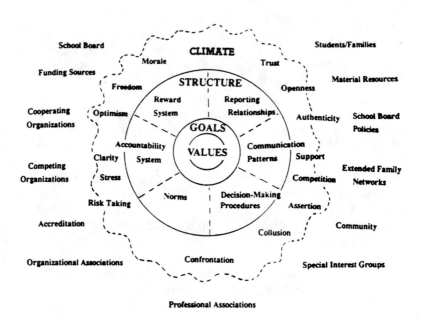

Source: Jones, J.E. (1981). The organziational universe model. In J.E. Jones and J.W. Pfeiffer (Eds.), *The annual handbook for group facilitators*. San Diego, CA: University Associates. Reprinted by permission.

Figure 9.2. The organizational universe model.

from the school-as-community. The structure for implementing changes within the organization consists of the variables depicted in the organizational universe model. The six interdependent systems (Figure 9.2)—reporting relationship, communication patterns, decision-making procedures, norms, accountability systems, and reward systems—are the locus of organizational change. Problems that arise among the units of the organization can be traced to deficiencies in these six systems.

Many of us know the feeling well, information overload, the malady which accompanies our participation in an information age. Something beyond communication is required of all of us who try to provide our counselees or colleagues with information to make wise decisions. The key concept according to behavioral science studies are flow, information, and influence. Attention to the diffusion of information process (Figure 9.3) provides an understanding of how new ideas are accepted. Since public decisions are aggregated individual decisions, it also is a map to the public adoption of ideas and positions helpful to counseling and education.

Jackson (1986) stated the public relations experts call diffusion process the two-step flow. In Phases A and B (Figure 9.3), information is key to gain awareness and understanding of the situation. Mass impersonal media are most efficient avenues for this since they can reach thousands with the same message at the same time.

Thereafter, information loses it's clout. Peer pressure and social acceptability take over in Phases C, D, and E (Figure 9.3). Until the idea is assimilated by people whose opinion we value, the great majority of Americans—at least 98% on most topics—will not adopt an idea. Despite our bravado about being independent, the fact is we are very sensitive to what others think about us.

So strong is our need for human verification of our tentative decisions that in Phase D, the highest influence is held by advocates who are rarely uninterested parties. Psychologically, we require another human voice to push us to accept our own emerging decision or to turn us away from it. We need and welcome opinion leaders in our often confusing, over-communicated world (Jackson, 1986, p. 28).

(Continued on Page 171)

The Diffusion Process: The Flow of Information and Influence Toward Decision Making

	A. Awareness	B. Information	C. Evaluation	D. Trial	E. Adoption	F. Reinforcement
PHASES	Learns about an idea or practice but lacks detail	Gets facts, develops interest, sees possibilities	Tries it mentally, weighs alternatives	Social acceptability, experimentation	Full-scale use, adopts it	Continued commitment
INFLUENCES BY PRIORITY	1. Mass media and impersonal and message forms	1. Mass media and impersonal message forms	1. Friends and neighbors	1. Opinion leaders and advocates	1. Friends and neighbors	1. Appropriate mix of mass media and interactive techniques
	2. Experts and agencies	2. Opinion leaders and advocates	2. Opinion leaders and advocates	2. Friends and neighbors	2. Opinion leaders and advocates	
	3. Friends and neighbors	3. Experts and neighbors	3. Experts and agencies	3. Experts and agencies	3. Experts and agencies	
	4. Opinion leaders and advocates	4. Friends and neighbors	4. Mass media and impersonal message forms	4. Mass media and impersonal message forms	4. Mass media and impersonal message forms	

Significance: Note that *impersonal media* (print, broadcast) cease being effective after Phase B, when *personal media* (people, experts, opinion leaders) take over as the need for psychological support and social acceptability replace the need for information.

Source: Jackson, P. (1986). *How to build public relationships that motivate real support.* NASSP Bulletin, 70, 494, 25-34. Reprinted by permission.

Figure 9.3. The diffusion process: The flow of information and influence toward decision making.

Fundamentally, the most basic principle to be observed by the counselor as change agent is that people who are to be affected by change should be involved in planning, implementing, and carrying out our innovation. When people feel ownership, the goals of change will be more readily accepted, internalized, implemented, and evaluated. Mann (1978) outlined the characteristics that are needed to enhance the interpersonal relationships within an organization:

- agreement on goals,
- open systems of communication,
- support characterized by mutual respect and trust,
- extensive use of member skills, and
- productive management of conflict.

Organization health promotes these individual and group interactions. As a consultant, and change agent, the counselor will want to use counseling skills to facilitate the organizational improvements or change process. The counselor also manifests other comfortable roles in their repertoire such as advocate, role model, skill resource person, facilitator, trainer, and helping professional. Within these dimensions, inviting skills such as acceptance, understanding, empathetic listening, constructive feedback and genuineness are second nature to most counselors.

POWER OR INFLUENCE:
HOW TO INFLUENCE CHANGE

"Power" is employed in the schools to determine curricula, to establish instructional parameters, to allocate human and fiscal resources, and a myriad of administrative decisions. The school-as-institution manifests the general characteristics of bureaucracies. These characteristics tend to foster impersonal behavior on the part of the members, with a structure of hierarchical interpersonal relationships, and a division of labor which often disenfranchises others from participating in decision making. It also increases stress among participants. All of these characteristics tend to distance professional interactions and thwart personal and institutional growth.

From the perspective of school-as-community, counselors can position themselves within the school setting as catalyst for constructive change. Access to data, for example, increases the school counselor's ability to "influence" the school's policy and structure. Podemski and Childers (1980) maintained that (1) counselors have access to many forms of school-based data (such as attendance figures, opinions of graduates, figures related to types and frequency of discipline, failure rates, standardized test scores, and information on service usage.) Hence counselor's recommendations are data based, and thus carry additional weight over more subjective perceptions or recommendations; and (2) the counselor has a data-related advantage to "collect and frame" new information in areas that the counselor perceives as important. Through data collection and analysis, the counselor can assess organizational needs, sense problems, and facilitate change (Podemski & Childers, 1980, p. 172). After gathering significant data, the next hurdle is to present a convincing argument to administrators or policy makers.

SCHOOL COUNSELOR AS
FACILITATOR OF ORGANIZATIONAL HEALTH

Miles (1971) is perhaps the first proponent who isolated the concept of organizational health as "the ability of an organization to function effectively, to cope adequately, to change appropriately, and to grow from within" (p. 335). Organizational health is composed of the following ten dimensions: goal focus, communication, adequacy, optimal power equalization, resource utilization, cohesiveness, morale, innovativeness, autonomy, adaptation, and problem-solving adequacy.

In school-as-community, the level of organizational health is positively related to teacher's attitudes toward student discipline (Fairman & Haddock, 1981), student's attitudes toward school (Haddock, 1980), and student's level of achievement (Fairman, 1983). The school-as-community also is a social unit. Collectively, all individuals who interact with the school should strive for an environment that possesses the twenty-one characteristics of organizational health and climate factors as illustrated in Figure 9.4, Characteristics of Healthy Organizations, and Figure 9.5, Organizational Climate Questionnaire.

The increased attention of the role of the counselor as consultant and facilitator of organizational climate is supported by a contemporary cluster of researchers (Avis & Bigelow, 1984; Blocker & Rapoza, 1972; Steward & Avis, 1984). Avis and Bigelow maintained that counselor skills can

> "Improve the Human Environment of Schools" (IHES—pronounced 'eyes') with positive climate groups composed of students, teachers, parents, support staff, administrators, and community members who organize with the purpose to address issues related to the human environment of the school that affect learning and the quality of life. The IHES meetings are conducted by a facilitator whose role is to manage the process of problem solving in a climate of mutual respect, collaboration, order, and optimism. (Avis, 1987, p. 297)

Counselors are excellent facilitators of IHES groups because of their well-developed skills in attending, paraphrasing, reflecting, and summarizing (Carkhuff, Pierce, & Cannon, 1977; Ivey & Authier, 1978). More specifically, counselors can model, reinforce, and facilitate the following skills:

Empathy: communicating an understanding of several perspectives of what is said among group members.

Genuineness: being spontaneous, nondefensive, consistent, and self-sharing of both feelings and thoughts.

Concreteness: helping members of the group to be specific rather than ambiguous or abstract in problem identification.

Interpretation and Reflection: reflecting feeling and offering hypotheses and hunches to clarify goals; provide direction, awareness and integration.

Self-disclosure: sharing something about personal experience to increase the ability to work with others;

(Continued on Page 176)

1. Objectives are widely shared and there is a strong and consistent flow of energy and time spent working toward these objectives.

2. People feel free to signal their awareness of difficulties because they expect the problem to be dealt with and they are optimistic they can be solved.

3. Problem solving is highly pragmatic.

4. Organizational level as such is not considered a factor in determining the points of decision making.

5. There is a noticeable sense of team work in performance, planning, and discipline (i.e., a shared responsibility).

6. The judgment of people lower down in the organization is respected.

7. The range of problems tackled includes personal needs and human relations.

8. Collaboration is freely entered into.

9. Conflicts are considered important to decision making and personal growth. They are dealt with in the open.

10. When there is a crisis, the people quickly band together to work until the crisis departs.

11. Joint critique of progress is routine.

12. Relationships are honest.

13. Leadership is flexible, shifting in style and purpose to suit the situation.

14. There is a high degree of trust in style and purpose to suit the situation.

15. Risk is accepted as a condition of growth and change.

16. Poor performance is confronted and a joint resolution sought.

17. Organizational structure, procedures, and policies are fashioned to help people get the job done and to protect the long-term health of the organization, not to give each bureaucrat his or her due.

18. There is a sense of order, and yet a high rate of innovation. Old methods are questioned and often give way to newer ones.

19. The organization itself adapts swiftly to opportunities or other changes because every pair of eyes is watching and every head is anticipating the future.

20. Frustrations are the call to action. "It's our responsibility to save the ship."

21. There is a consistency between what is said and what is done.

Source: Shipman, N.J., Martin, J.B., McKay, A.B., & Anatiasi, R.E. (1983). *Effective time management techniques for school administrators.* Englewood Cliffs, NJ: Prentice-Hall, p. 36. Reprinted by permission.

Figure 9.4. Characteristics of a healthy organization.

For each of the seven organizational climate dimensions described below, place an (A) above the number that indicates your assessment of the organization's current position on that dimension and an (I) above the number that indicates your choice of where the organization should ideally be on this dimension.

1 **Conformity.** The feeling that there are many externally imposed constraints in the organization; the degree to which members feel that there are many rules, procedures, policies, and practices to which they have to conform rather than being able to do their work as they see fit.

Conformity is not characteristic   1 2 3 4 5 6 7 8 9 10   Conformity is very characteristic
of this organization.   of this organization.

2 **Responsibility.** Members of the organization are given personal responsibility to achieve their part of the organization's goals; the degree to which members feel that they can make decisions and solve problems without checking with superiors each step of the way.

No responsibility is given in the   1 2 3 4 5 6 7 8 9 10   There is a great emphasis on
organization.   personal responsibility in the organization.

3 **Standards.** The emphasis the organization places on quality performance and outstanding production, including the degree to which the member feels the organization is setting challenging goals for itself and communicating these goal commitments to members.

Standards are very low or   1 2 3 4 5 6 7 8 9 10   High, challenging standards are
nonexistent in the organization.   set in the organization.

4 **Rewards.** The degree to which members feel that they are being recognized and rewarded for good work rather than being ignored, criticized, or punished when something goes wrong.

Members are ignored, punished   1 2 3 4 5 6 7 8 9 10   Members are recognized and
or criticized.   rewarded positively.

5 **Organizational Clarity.** The feeling among members that things are well organized and that goals are clearly defined rather than being disorderly, confused, or chaotic.

The organization is disorderly,   1 2 3 4 5 6 7 8 9 10   The organization is well
confused, and chaotic.   organized with clearly defined goals.

6 **Warmth and Support.** The feeling that friendliness is a valued norm in the organization, that members trust one another and offer support to one another. The feeling that good relationships prevail in the work environment.

There is no warmth and support   1 2 3 4 5 6 7 8 9 10   Warmth and support are
in the organization.   characteristic of the organization.

7 **Leadership.** The willingness of organization members to accept leadership and direction from qualified others. As needs for leadership arise, members feel free to take leadership roles and are rewarded for successful leadership. Leadership is based on expertise. The organization is not dominated by, or dependent on, one or two individuals.

Leadership is not rewarded;   1 2 3 4 5 6 7 8 9 10   Members accept and reward
members are dominated or   leadership based on expertise.
dependent and resist leadership.

Source: Kolb, D.A., Rubin, I.M., & McIntyre, J.M. (1984). *Organizational psychology: An experimental approach to organizational behavior.* Englewood Cliffs, NJ: Prentice-Hall. Reprinted by permission.

Figure 9.5. Organizational climate questionnaire.

though mutual sharing problems are no longer unique they are universal and shared by colleagues.

Direct, Mutual Talk: facilitating in others the ability to discuss directly and openly about what is happening in the "here-and-now" in their working relationships.

Summarizing: summing up progress with the purpose of providing feedback and integration of goals and objectives.

Awareness of Transference: understanding when others transfer to the group "unfinished business" from past relationships with significant people; or from counter transference—when a counselor's own needs or unresolved personal conflicts become entangled in the organizational relationship.

Factors that are consistently in the forefront of curative, creative, positive organizations are as follows:

- high morale among faculty, staff, and students;
- respect and trust;
- genuine positive regard;
- a we-spirit/a collective vision;
- activities nurturing positive social and interpersonal relationships;
- emphasis on excellence;
- cohesiveness between and among others;
- many opportunities for recognition;
- trust;
- warmth and acceptance;
- involvement of all students, faculty, and staff;
- accessibility and open communication; and
- attractive physical environment.

IMPROVING SCHOOL CLIMATE AND STUDENT MORALE

The school community develops distinctive normative patterns that draw students toward or away from particular activities and domains of development (social, academic, and physical). These normative patterns often have a profound and long-term effect on self-concepts, values, and coping skills. Personalities tend to interact within the social system productively or unproductively with subtle influences on motivation and learning style (Joyce, Hersh, & McKibbin, 1983, p. 114).

Lightfoot (1983), further delineates the effects of a diminishing sense of belonging within the school-as-institution. He maintained that many students feel isolated and alone as they move through their day. Many communities also are exclusionary. The tone of the school is dominated by a superficial sophistication where the primary preoccupations are in finding the right clothes, the right friends, and the right kind of car. The troubles inside the school reflect a "depressive core in the community." Without goals or traditions to unite energies, hostility is directed inward and divisions intensify across race, class, and ethnic lines. Major cliques within these divisions also create a highly stratified culture where differences are exaggerated—the "Brains," the "Jocks," the "Hicks," the "Heads," the "Skaters and Surfers," are some examples. The emphasis on community is not particularly strong, as reflected by the presence of student cliques, and the lack of tolerance for different values (Lightfoot, 1983, p. 50).

Rogers (1980) further asserted, "If we are truly aware, we can hear the silent screams of denied feelings echoing off every classroom wall" (p. 251). He added,

> I deplore the manner in which, from early years, the child's education splits him or her: the mind can come to school, and the body is permitted peripherally to tail along, but the feelings and emotions can live freely and expressively only outside the school . . . I am deeply concerned with what is going on in American educational institutions. They have focused so intently on ideas, have limited themselves so completely to educating from the neck up that the resulting narrowness is having serious social consequences. (p. 263)

Indeed, many young people come to school alienated and depersonalized and find little assistance there to help them cope with isolation and loneliness. Many high schools, for example, can be repressive places and control oriented. Students feel they have little power to change things. Collective intervention strategies should focus on

- diagnosis of school/community needs and problems;
- open communication;
- identified goals;
- conflict resolution;
- effective staff, student, and parent conferencing; and
- problem solving and decision making.

The characteristics that define communities as having a strong sense of wellness are caring, commitment, and trust. This allows for strong bonds between individuals to risk, succeed, and grow.

The following nine sets of ideas are reprinted by permission from ERIC Counseling and Personnel Services Clearinghouse (1983). These activities are offered with the understanding variations will be needed to (1) meet the various maturity and developmental needs of student populations, and (2) meet the the various needs of the school and community. These activities could be a viable catalyst for open communication and shared responsibility by providing a more nurturing, responsive school environment.

To Improve Attitude and Attendance (25 Ideas):

Establish a guidance curriculum and courses that emphasize pupil achievement.

Provide realistic academic experiences for the non-college bound.

Dismantle class, ethnic, or racial cliques.

Use more small group counseling and instruction.

Promote school activities that give the student a sense of belonging.

Have monthly cultural or fine arts festivals in the school commons featuring performances of students or community groups. Performance from a variety of ethnic groups represented in the school and community could be featured.

Replace the mass-feeding-mess-hall cafeteria with small round tables to encourage more small group interaction.

Involve the uninvolved. Seek out the students who are not involved in school and provide low risk opportunities to involve and recognize them.

Expand counseling programs to include more peer and group activities.

Increase communication among students of different backgrounds.

Provide more activities that enhance intergroup relations.

Include more adults in all school activities.

Implement a positive school-wide staff development program to improve school and classroom climate.

Remove or reduce student participation fees.

Reevaluate or change punitive attendance policies.

Improve the physical appearance of the school campus.

Reduce the pupil/teacher ratio.

Make high school courses more relevant for students not planning to go to college.

Increase counseling for students with learning disabilities.

Use more adults in the school as volunteers, aides, paraprofessionals, and resource persons.

Emphasize higher expectations for learning, especially among minority groups.

Make it possible for qualified students to take college courses while still in high school.

Provide appropriate counseling for truant students.

Intervene with parents of students who have serious truancy problems.

Work closer with city agencies such as the courts, probation, social services, and the health department so that appointments are scheduled around school time.

To Have Fewer Student Suspensions, Expulsions, and Dropouts (13 Ideas):

Change unfair and authoritarian administrative practices.

Abolish oppressive school policies such as the dress code.

Reevaluate relationships between truancy and suspension practices; avoid using suspension as a punishment for truancy.

Substitute in-school detention as a means of discipline, rather than out-of-school suspension.

Reserve suspensions for only the most serious troublemakers.

Require a parent conference prior to any suspension.

Examine district suspension policies regarding penalties for minor offenses such as tardiness, student-to-student or student-to-teacher conflicts, eating in class, or discourteous conduct.

Establish a specific reinstatement program to accompany every student expulsion before it is initiated.

Review district expulsion policies regarding penalties for major offenses such as personal threats, vandalism, assault, battery, drug or alcohol possession, or distribution.

Increase the counseling and guidance services available to all students.

Reorganize or structure the horizontal and vertical curriculum, i.e., the tracking system used in grouping students for instruction.

Eliminate the assessment of fees for participation in school activities, and advanced placement testing programs.

Amend school or club rules or procedures that segregate or isolate minority or low income students within the school program.

To Involve Teachers, Administrators, and Other Support Personnel in Decision Making (10 Ideas):

Give school principals more autonomy to manage their own school.

Improve communications between administration, superintendent, and school board.

Encourage school administrators to become more actively and directly involved with students and their programs.

Include entire school staff input in decision making and goal setting.

Give teachers a bigger voice in governing their schools.

Create a faculty advisory committee which will take suggestions for overall school improvement projects.

Include more classified personnel (secretary, nurse, in-school suspension coordinator, cafeteria manager, or other paraprofessionals) in staff meetings.

Provide more direct contact between counselors, school social workers, and psychologists.

Involve more school personnel in working directly with students on a non-graded basis.

**To Involve Students and Parents
in Decision Making (5 Ideas):**

Make better use of school advisory boards and support groups.

Encourage parents to share their views on home and cultural values.

Provide a means for parents to be more involved with student activities.

Provide a regular means for students to express their concerns to district administrators and parent groups.

Develop and publish policy statements regarding "Students' Rights and Responsibilities."

To Promote Better Student Self-concept (15 Ideas):

Expand group counseling activities that develop students' self-esteem and positive attitudes.

Develop altruistic service projects for students to participate in under the auspices that "we feel better about ourselves when we make others feel better."

Provide in-service for teachers and other support personnel in methods of developing positive self-images in students.

Provide activities that give students recognition and affirmation.

Insist on broad community involvement in school policy-making and governing.

Consider parents' opinions and advice in deciding such issues as student activities, use of volunteers, implementing curriculum changes, using community resources, and parent involvement in the classroom.

Use students as advisors to the superintendent; establish a Youth Forum or similar advisory group.

Use students' suggestions for making the curriculum more responsive to students' needs.

Include students in all major aspects of school operation, beginning in the primary grades.

Expand students' lines of communication to the school faculty and administration.

Set up a monthly program in which teachers recommend students who do not usually receive recognition to eat lunch with the principal, a coach, or other significant adult in the student's life.

Invite helping professionals in the community to serve as a resource people for 6 to 8 week group counseling sessions on self-esteem, dealing with loss, or personal development.

Implement a "student adoption program" and entitle it "Each One Reach One" where each member of the instructional staff adopts an at-risk student (with behavioral problems, adjustment problems, attendance problems, or family problems) to meet with them on a daily basis to discuss problems, progress, or barriers to success and to develop short-term strategies to enhance success rather than failure.

Have the parent newsletter or school newspaper recognize as many students as possible for contributions to the school. Try to find students who are seldom identified but contribute to the school program in a unique way. Identify and recognize other areas in which students excel such as vocational/technical areas; student volunteers in local activities such as the hospital auxiliary, fire department, and other volunteer service projects and student employees of the month, through school work programs.

Promote clubs and service organizations that are altruistic and other centered with community service contributions. To invest energy in another person or worthwhile cause provides a purpose and a reliable goal for our youth. Students often rediscover their self-importance by learning their value to others. Participation in such activities as Students Against Drunk Drivers (SADD), Students Organized for Developing Attitudes (SODA), "Just Say NO" Clubs, Responsible Educated Adolescents Can Help America (REACH), or the Special Olympics are selected examples.

To Improve Services to Students and Their Families (16 Ideas):

Increase the counseling and guidance services available to all students; make guidance and counseling programs more visible and accessible; establish a guidance curriculum and classroom courses that emphasize pupil services to specific needs.

Expand career guidance activities K through 12.

Provide more effective counseling programs, including specialized counselors, student assistance counselors, bilingual and minority counselors, or education for employment counselors.

Provide more personal counseling for such problems as drugs, alcohol, smoking; anorexia, and bulimia.

Train volunteer teachers or support personnel to serve as positive role models and to lead support groups and discussions on subjects such as time management, stress, and academic problem-solving strategies. Many caring educators welcome an opportunity to interact with students on a more affective domain.

Implement a student stress reduction program for students and/or their families.

Implement a routine system in which each teacher telephones the home of four or five students a week to relate some positive aspect of the students' role in the classroom, on the team, or in the club.

Improve written and oral communication to students and their families.

Increase the number of parent conferences, open house programs, and home visits.

Offer appropriate parent education courses in such areas as preventing drug and alcohol abuse, setting achievement goals, setting limits, and improving academic achievement.

Establish multicultural education programs for parents.

Send regular reports to parents on school activities.

Reserve a telephone line and an answering machine for after hours so parents can dial and hear activities, programs, or important dates on a daily basis.

Recognize parents for their interest and involvement in school activities.

Invite parents to school for more informal visits.

Establish school site advisory councils that are broadly representative of each school community.

To Improve Services to Faculty, Staff, and Administrators (7 Ideas):

Establish procedures that enable teacher to be more creative and innovative.

Arrange for teachers to receive mini-grants or internships from local community businesses.

Use advisory groups to provide community feedback on administrator's performance.

Involve the Chamber of Commerce and school division in the adopt-a-school program.

Expand pupil personnel services to include more consultation to administrators and faculty from school psychologists, counselors, nurses, school social workers, and child welfare or attendance workers.

Establish regular and continuous inservice training programs for the school staff in such areas as classroom management, the use of positive reinforcement, learning styles, and the identification of students in need of support or supervision.

Provide for adequate needs assessment, program development, research, and evaluation.

To Decrease Staff Absenteeism, Requests for Transfer, and Resignations (24 Ideas):

Conduct a survey of staff needs, concerns, and interests.

Assign staff members to work in areas in which they are most interested and qualified.

Increase the "ownership" that teachers have over school programs.

Require staff input and cooperation, on such issues as student discipline policies, ordering and sharing supplies, articulation between grade levels and departments, homework, report cards, grading, reports to parents, and supervision of students outside of class.

Give school personnel more control over their use of time.

Establish cooperative staff approaches to solving school problems.

Focus on attainable short-range objectives rather than broad long-range goals.

Recognize success immediately; publicize positive results in discipline, attendance, and learning activities.

Include announcements of progress in each staff or advisory board meeting.

Share staff experiences that are producing success with students.

Emphasize activities that bring staff members closer together and help them work more effectively with one another.

Develop a mutual "support system" that allows staff members to help each other get what they want.

Arrange activities so that teachers and others can meet to plan on school time.

Initiate a positive systematic program to improve school morale, health, and well-being.

Attend to the "little things" that affect staff morale such as clerical help, time for planning, fewer interruptions, adequate supplies, work space, and an unencumbered lunch bell.

Recognize outstanding teachers for their skills, interest, and enthusiasm.

Allow teachers to be creative regarding school and classroom management.

Recognize the entire staff publicly for positive performance.

Keep the staff well-informed at all times.

Emphasize the need for teachers who understand and care about students.

Create a sense of belonging within the school staff.

Recognize the contributions of staff members who are sensitive to the needs of students.

Work for administrators who possess good counseling skills.

Provide structured activities, such as implementing a "secret pal program," for staff personnel to get to know one another better.

To Decrease Vandalism and Violence (7 Ideas):

Clean up school buildings, maintain adequate facilities, and replace obsolete equipment.

Improve the form and function of the school building by such things as adding a student lounge or benches, removing fences, using student designed murals, and displays, and providing continuous message centers for extracurricular activities and important dates.

Increase the psychological services to students with learning disabilities, emotional disabilities, or attention deficit disorder.

Establish a positive, preventive program to counteract conflict and violence, including provisions for isolating troublemakers, negotiating, and using parents, police, and community leaders.

Adopt a practical means of keeping "outsiders" and non-students off school grounds, especially on the middle and secondary level.

Keep overcrowding to a minimum; schedule student activities to avoid long lines to use cafeteria, restrooms, or lockers.

Provide more opportunities for minority groups and disadvantaged students to participate in all school programs.

SCHOOL CLIMATE BASELINE DATA

School climate improvement projects require a long-term commitment to organizational and institutional change. Baseline data needs to be collected in the following areas: student/teacher absences, failure rate, test performance, grade point average, dropouts, etc.

A profile of school climate assets or deficits can be gathered from data that is readily available from different sources inside and outside the school. The format in Figure 9.6 provides important baseline data so that the impact of improvement can be measured.

Many educators have become classically conditioned to do anything but pay attention during long, mundane faculty meetings. Like their students, they also have developed the unique ability to do two things at one time; listen to the speaker, and grade papers, make out a grocery list, sketch out game plays, pass a note to a colleague, fill out failure notice, or any combination of the above.

(Continued on Page 192)

Target Data	Present Status	Intervention	Post Intervention
Student Absences by Grade			
Student Grade Point Averages Above 2.00 Below 2.00			
Profile Achievement Scores			
Expulsions			
Vandalism			
Percent of Dropouts			
Percent Single Parent Families			
Attendance: Athletic Events			
Attendance: Other Extracurricular Activities			
Visitation: School Clinic			
Visitation: Counseling Department			
Visitation: Library			
Visitation: Career Resource Center			
Parent Involvement in School Activities			
Teacher Absences			
Number of Teacher Sponsored Activities			
Enrollment: Honors by Grade			
Enrollment: Advanced Placement By Grade			
Enrollment: Remedial Classes By Grade			
Enrollment: Special Education by Program			
Attendance: 4 year Colleges			
Attendance: 2 year Colleges			
Attendance: Vocational Technical Programs			
Attendance: Armed Services			
Attendance: Immediate Job Entry			
Disciplinary Referrals			
Suspensions			

Figure 9.6. School climate profile baseline data.

PRODUCTIVE MEETINGS PROMOTE
A SHARED COMMITMENT

Faculty Meeting (As Seen by the Principal)

Some adore me,
    some deplore me
Many obviously ignore me
Plagued by fictional fears
    or factual
Bound by promises
    contractual
Gathered here at half-past
    three
My eyes sweep o'er the
    faculty.

In mid-row sitting,
    needles flitting
The home ec. teacher and
    her knitting
Fill the room with clicks
    and clashes
Colored yarn and needle
    flashes
Nor does my ever-
    impassioned pitch
Ever make her drop a stitch.

Slashing, mangling, red ink
    strangling
Every participle dangling,
Gorge as well as hot tears
    welling
Over his students' novel
    spelling
Unrefining these refinements
An English teacher grades
    assignments.

Wild eyes flashing,
    sharp teeth gnashing
All the classic gripes
    rehashing
Seeking further ammunition
For the loyal opposition
Slouches with scorn
    and anger vast
The resident iconoclast.

The head coach vexes both the sexes
With his little "O's" and "X's"
Fighting to suppress his
    cackles
Pulling guards and trapping
    tackles
Breaking bones and jarring
    marrows
With dotted lines and solid
    arrows.

Hot breath heaving,
    fantasy weaving,
Lost blonde hair and
    lost youth grieving
Caught in tides of passion's
    floods
Sits of the last of the
    super studs.
Quietly sits 'twixt awe and
    lust
Over the drill team sponsor's
    looks.

Then I spied him,
    none could hide him
Though they scorned and
    vilified him
There amid the ghastly
    horrors
Of the snoozers and
    the snorers
Sat, awake with wide eyes
    glistening
A first year teacher who was
    listening.

Oh the Glory, transitory
Must I tell the awful story?
He whose wide-eyed
    innocence
Offered fleeting recompense
For the universal scoff
Had his hearing aid
    turned off.

Robert J. Welch, Associate Principal
Shawnee Mission South High School
Shawnee Mission, Kansas

Meetings are perceived as a waste of time and something to avoid unless absolutely necessary. Even the most well-meaning speaker is guilty by association to the long rhetoric of school administrators.

Everyone complains that meetings are time wasters with frequently no value or purpose. Counselors invariably become members or chairpersons of committees as part of advisory, task force, or police groups. Some time-saving strategies can improve the quality of meetings and the meaning for participants. Fundamentally, leadership introduces issues, asks others for input, and contributes personally to issues. Other characteristics include the following:

> A preplanned action agenda which outlines the objectives of the meeting and participant's expectations. The agenda projects order, and has a designated beginning and ending time that is strictly enforced. Time estimates of each item are designated. A recorder keeps a written outline of decisions and issues.

> A meeting is a catalyst for a commitment to pursue matters further. The group is inspired with a sense of purpose and direction as well as motivation to bring the process to fruition.

> A meeting encourages open discussion of all issues. Disagreement is perceived as an opportunity rather than a threat. Respect for differences of opinion are accepted as part of the problem solving and consensus building. Disagreements can help the group decide from a wide range of information with a potential for more effective solutions.

> A meeting provides timely and relevant information for collective decision making, problem solving, and solutions.

> A meeting should never be spent on hearing announcements about future events, dates, or clarification of policy directives. These should be disseminated through a memorandum posted on department chairs' bulletin boards.

The following guidelines can improve the content and quality of meetings:

> Distribute the agenda ahead of time so that faculty and staff can anticipate focus topics.

> Ask for contributions from the staff or assign areas of responsibility. Don't be afraid to delegate. When we attempt to attend to every single detail, we lose sight of the "big picture."

> Prioritize items on the agenda placing items, with more of a likelihood to be accepted, first on the agenda. This fosters staff interactions that are cooperative which is a prerequisite for discussing more controversial issues. Also, provide time slots for each item to keep the meeting on task.

> Stay confined to agenda items. Any issue raised that is not on the established agenda should be placed at the conclusion under "new business" or deferred until the next meeting.

> Assign responsibilities along with target dates for completion of designated tasks.

Treuille and Stautberg (1988, p. 69) offered the following suggestions for managing a meeting:

> If presenting results of a study or a report that has required the assistance of others, acknowledge their contributions. Publicly crediting others ensures their future participation and encourages others.

> Agree in advance on the ground rules for your meeting, and make sure the participants understand them. For example, may questions be asked during the presentation or should they be held to the end? Will there be a break? Do they need to take notes or is the material summarized in a handout?

Guard against one or two people monopolizing the discussion. Ask more retiring attendees for their opinion.

Summarize the results of the meeting before disbanding. If time permits and the group is small, let each attendee offer his/her final thoughts.

End on a positive note. Even if there are unresolved issues and you need to meet again, focus on what has been accomplished.

Put your meeting notes in a file, in case questions arise later, with a cover memorandum stating that a meeting was held on a certain date, attended by various staff.

Close the meeting on time. Overextending the meeting often leads to "diminishing returns." Anxious participants may feel the leader is insensitive to their other commitments or obligations.

Have a recorder for each meeting. Better yet, tape the meeting. Keep a written record to remind the faculty and staff about commitments, responsibilities, and obligations.

Edit and distribute the minutes on the following workday. This reinforces a sense of ownership on what transpired.

In Figure 9.7 is an evaluation of meeting form. You could use this example or modify for your use.

TYPES OF MEETINGS

The Committee Meeting: various chairpeople and committees report on their activities. Feedback from faculty may be solicited along with recommendations and alternatives. An example is a curriculum committee developed for the purpose of self-study or standards of quality.

(Continued on Page 197)

I. **Group Climate**

What was the general group atmosphere? Place an X at the appropriate place on each line.

Formal ●——●——●——●——●——●——● Informal

Competitive ●——●——●——●——●——●——● Cooperative

Hostile ●——●——●——●——●——●——● Supportive

Inhibited ●——●——●——●——●——●——● Permissive

Open ●——●——●——●——●——●——● Closed

II. **Participation**

1. How did you feel about your particpation during that session? Circle one numeral.

1	2	3	4	5	6
Very Satisfied	Quite Satisfied	Somewhat Satisfied	Somewhat Dissatisfied	Quite Dissatisfied	Very Dissatisfied

2. Check a place on each scale that shows how you think others participated:

All people talked ___ 1 ___ 2 ___ 3 ___ 4 ___ 5 Only a few talked

All members involved ___ 1 ___ 2 ___ 3 ___ 4 ___ 5 All members uninvolved

All resources used ___ 1 ___ 2 ___ 3 ___ 4 ___ 5 Group failed to use most resources

The following questions on patterns of communication are best suited for an observer:

1. Who talks? For how long? How often?

2. Whom do people look at when they talk?
   a. Single persons: possibly potential supporters
   b. The group as a whole (scanning)
   c. No one

3. Who talks after whom, or who interrupts whom?

4. What style of communication is used (assertions, questions, tone of voice, gestures, etc.)?

Source: Shipman, N.J., et al. (1983). *Effective time-management techniques for school administrators.* Englewood Cliffs, NJ: Prentice-Hall, Inc. Printed by permisison.

Figure 9.7. Evaluation of meeting.

Figure 9.7. Continued.

III. **Group Effectiveness**

The following questionnaire measures participant's reactions to a meeting. After each item mark an X in the box that best shows your reaction to this meeting.

	AGREEMENT		DISAGREEMENT	
	Strong	Mild	Mild	Strong
1. The results of this meeting were worth the time.	☐	☐	☐	☐
2. I was given adequate opportunity to state my beliefs about subjects dis-cussed by the group.	☐	☐	☐	☐
3. Our meeting was efficient.	☐	☐	☐	☐
4. I am satisfied with the attention and consideration that others gave to my ideas and opinions.	☐	☐	☐	☐
5. We wasted too much tim in this meeting.	☐	☐	☐	☐
6. The group effectively used my knowledge of the subjects dis-cussed.	☐	☐	☐	☐
7. The most important topics were never discussed.	☐	☐	☐	☐
8. I had adequate opportunity to influence our conclusions and de-cisions.	☐	☐	☐	☐

The Policy Meeting: focuses on issues which may influence school procedure, policy or administrative directives. An example is a decision on grading, examinations, or class rank.

The Planning and Problem Solving Meeting: focuses on a projective problem for prevention or early intervention. The goal is to pool and mobilize resources, perspectives and probable consequences of proposed solutions or alternatives. An example is how to decrease the school dropout rate.

The Debriefing Meeting: focuses on clarifying and understanding a major event which has directly or indirectly affected the faculty or staff. The emphasis is to provide accurate information and to correct distortions or conjecture. An example would be to assemble everyone following the sudden death of a colleague or student.

The Structured Task Force Meeting: focuses on participants gathering information and making recommendations. This is a long-term process where the group identifies causes of a problem, and generates specific action steps recommended to be implemented to resolve the problem. Recommendations are aired in public hearings for discussion and recommendation to the original plan. An example is changing accreditation standards.

EMOTIONAL BEHAVIOR IN GROUPS

In a group or in a meeting, individuals manifest different styles for reducing and expressing emotion. Kolb, Rubin, and McIntyre (1984) identified three "pure types":

The "friendly helper" orientation: acceptance of tender emotions, denial of tough emotions—"Let's not fight, let's help each other," can give and receive affection but cannot tolerate hostility and fight.

The "tough battler" orientation: acceptance of tough emotions and denial of tender emotions—"Let's fight it out"; can deal with hostility but not with love, support, and affiliation.

The "logical thinking" orientation: denial of all emotion—"Let's reason this thing out"; cannot deal with tender or tough emotions; hence, shuts eyes and ears to much that is going on.

Although this may be viewed as an oversimplification of group dynamics, it does provide some rationale to understanding the frustration a counselor feels when he or she (friendly helper) tries to facilitate a compromise among the principal (tough battler), the student, and his/her calculus teacher (logical thinking). In Figure 9.8 is summarized the emotional behavior in groups of the three groups.

An Inventory of Counselor Potential For Facilitating Staff Morale (Figure 9.9) concludes this chapter. The inventory can be viewed as generalized indication of how well you as a leader facilitate positive morale in your counseling department on the domains of leadership interpersonal relationships, rewards, student achievement, workload/caseload, facilities, responsibility, professional development, employee assistance, and conflict management. A comparison of how you rate yourself when compared to how your colleagues rate you could be an added dimension to this exercise.

(Continued on Page 204)

1. Friendly Helper	2. Tough Battler	3. Logical Thinker
A world of mutual love, affection, tenderness, sympathy	A world of conflict, fight, power, assertiveness	A world of understanding, logic, systems, knowledge
Task-Maintenance Behavior		
Harmonizing Compromising Gatekeeping by concern Encouraging Expressing warmth	Initiating Coordinating Pressing for results Pressing for consensus Exploring differences Gatekeeping by command	Gathering information Clarifying ideas/words Systematizing Procedures Evaluating the logic of proposals
Constructs Used In Evaluating Others		
Who is warm and who is hostile? Who helps and who hurts others	Who is strong and who is weak? Who is winning and who is losing?	Who is bright and who is stupid? Who is accurate and who is inaccurate? Who thinks clearly and who is fuzzy?
Methods of Influence		
Appeasing Appealing to pity	Giving Orders Offering challenges Threatening	Appealing to rules, regulations Appealing to logic Referring to "facts" and overwhelming knowledge
Personal Threats		
That he or she will not be loved That he/she will be overwhelmed by feelings of hostility	That he or she will lose his/her ability to fight (power) That he/she will become "soft" and "sentimental"	That his or her world is not ordered That he/she will be overwhelmed by love or hate

Source: Kolb, D.A., Rubin, I.M., & McIntyre, J.M. (1984). *Organizational psychology: An experimental approach to organizational behavior.* Englewood Cliffs, NJ: Prentice-Hall. Reprinted by permission.

Figure 9.8. Emotional behavior in groups.

Directions: Read each item below carefully and circle the response that indicates the extent to which you exhibit the behavior, use the skill, or hold the attitude expressed in the statement. Be honest in recording your response.

Response code: N = Never
                  S = Seldom
                  U = Usually
                  A = Always
                  NA = Not applicable

1.0. Leadership

1. I am concerned about how other counselors in my department feel about their work. N S U A NA

2. I let administrators and supervisors know how counselors in the school feel about their work. N S U A NA

3. I am sensitive to fluctuations in counselor morale in my department. N S U A NA

4. I note things that are associated with fluctuations in counselor morale. N S U A NA

5. I set standards and expectations that challenge counselors in my department. N S U A NA

6. I involve **all** counselors in setting or changing the mission, goals, or objectives of the department. N S U A NA

7. I work hard to provide the material and technical resources needed by counselors to do their work well and efficiently. N S U A NA

8. I willingly praise or offer positive feedback to counselors when a job is well done. N S U A NA

9. I keep the counselors in the department apprised of how well they are doing. N S U A NA

2.0 Interpersonal Relationships

10. I keep counselors apprised of condition that may affect the security of their jobs or assignments. N S U A NA

11. I help counselors who are RIFed to locate other positions. N S U A NA

Figure 9.9. Inventory of counselor potential for facilitating staff morale.

Figure 9.9. continued.

2.0 Interpersonal Relationships (continued)

12. I believe that counselors in our school do excellent work.   N   S   U   A   NA

13. I elicit feedback from colleagues on how I am doing with my job.   N   S   U   A   NA

14. My colleagues feel open enough with me to discuss professional or personal concerns.   N   S   U   A   NA

15. I feel open enough to discuss my professional and personal concerns with my counselor peers.   N   S   U   A   NA

16. I seek feedback and interaction from other staff members.   N   S   U   A   NA

17. I encourage counselors to seek interaction and involvement with other staff members.   N   S   U   A   NA

18. I avoid such personal amenities as a reserved parking space that is off-limits to my peers.   N   S   U   A   NA

19. I am honest in my interactions with others.   N   S   U   A   NA

3.0 Rewards

20. I give the counselors in my department free rein in carrying out their work.   N   S   U   A   NA

21. When I assign tasks to members in my department, I let them do their work without interference from me.   N   S   U   A   NA

22. I handle administrative problems promptly.   N   S   U   A   NA

23. I handle colleague requests promptly.   N   S   U   A   NA

24. I use a number of methods of rewarding fellow counselors for excellence.   N   S   U   A   NA

25. I recognize institutional departments with rewards occasionally.   N   S   U   A   NA

26. I recognize and reward other groups who support the department.   N   S   U   A   NA

27. I distribute tasks in the department to capitalize on individual strengths to provide maximum satisfaction for the counselor.   N   S   U   A   NA

28. I encourage others to let counselors know when they are doing a good job.   N   S   U   A   NA

Figure 9.9. Continued.

4.0 Student Achievement

29. I emphasize student achievement in the department. N S U A NA

30. I communicate to parents that student achievement is a department priority. N S U A NA

5.0 Workload/Caseload

31. I distribute the workload equitability among counselors in the department. N S U A NA

32. I make assignments based on training, experience, and expertise of counselors. N S U A NA

33. I provide opportunities for counselors to trade workload or responsibilities among themselves with little interference. N S U A NA

6.0 Facilities, Equipment, Supplies

34. I involve all counselors in selecting supplies and equipment needed to do their work. N S U A NA

35. I make sure office space is efficient and receptive. N S U A NA

36. I make sure that materials and equipment available to counselors are up-to-date. N S U A NA

37. I make sure that there are sufficient quantities of materials and equipment to share with the faculty and staff. N S U A NA

38. I enlist volunteers or others to take care of routine chores such as bulletin boards and to make the department atractive. N S U A NA

39. I systematically provide new materials and training in new technology for counselors. N S U A NA

7.0 Maintaining Responsiblity

40. I use a subtle form of peer pressure to establish acceptable norms for behavior in the department. N S U A NA

41. I appeal to counselors' feelings of fairness to regulate their behavior. N S U A NA

42. I take time to appreciate counselors for following rules and regulations. N S U A NA

Figure 9.9. Continued.

7.0 Maintaining Responsibility (continued)

43. I involve counselors in developing orientation or induction programs for new staff.   N   S   U   A   NA

44. I try to help each counselor become self-directing or self-starting.   N   S   U   A   NA

8.0 Professional Development

45. I provide or encourage staff development programs for counselors.   N   S   U   A   NA

46. I encourage counselors to develop specializations through professional development.   N   S   U   A   NA

47. I work closely with counselors in the department to plan in-service programs for the faculty and staff.   N   S   U   A   NA

48. Staff development programs are based on the latest research findings.   N   S   U   A   NA

49. Staff meetings in the department are cooperatively planned with all counselors.   N   S   U   A   NA

50. Follow-up programs or consultation is frequently used in in-service programs.   N   S   U   A   NA

9.0 Employee Assistance

51. I am concerned about counselors' personal problems.   N   S   U   A   NA

52. I would "carefront" a counselor in the department with respect to a personal problem.   N   S   U   A   NA

53. I am aware of any personal problems affecting a counselor in the department.   N   S   U   A   NA

54. I work with administrators, supervisors, or employee assistance programs to provide intervention or referral sources.   N   S   U   A   NA

55. I feel that helping others solve or manage their personal problems makes them better employees.   N   S   U   A   NA

10.0 Conflict Management

56. I accept conflict as a normal part of all orgnazations.   N   S   U   A   NA

Figure 9.9. Continued.

10.0 Conflict Management (continued)

57. I manage conflict in a manner that is beneficial to the department.   N   S   U   A   NA

58. I serve as a mediator for interpersonal conflict within the department.   N   S   U   A   NA

59. I request administrative intervention when I cannot handle interpersonal conflict in the department or among the staff.   N   S   U   A   NA

60. I assess the precipitating events, and the circumstances of each conflict before attempting to apply any conflict management techniques to the situation.   N   S   U   A   NA

Scoring the Inventory (Figure 9.9)

The inventory should be viewed as a diagnostic tool that provides a generalized indication of how well you as a leader facilitate morale in your department. By reviewing your scores in each section, you can isolate those areas where additional effort might improve morale and working relationships.

Scoring the inventory is simply done by completing the following table:

	Number		Weight		Weighted Scores
Count the number of As:	x		4	=	
Count the number of Us:	x		3	=	
Count the number of Ss:	x		2	=	
Count the number of Ns:	x		1	=	

Total weighted score
(Add number of As, Us, Ss, and Ns)

Divide total weighted score by total usable responses. This will give you your overall score.

Interpreting Your Score

Your overall score will be between 1 and 4. A score of 1 is the lowest possible score and a score of 4 is the highest possible score.

Lower scores mean the leader's behaviors, attitudes, and management skills tend to produce a very favorable climate for the morale of others in your department. Most people score between 1.51 to 3.50 with the lower scores reflecting a tendency for the respondent to have a negative effect on morale in that area, and the high scores indicating a positive effect on morale.

A Profile Illustration Could Be As Follows:

Overall	3.00
1.0 Leadership	3.10
2.0 Interpersonal Relationships	3.75
3.0 Rewards	2.00
4.0 Student Achievement	3.00
5.0 Workload/Caseload	3.40
6.0 Facilities, Equipment, & Supplies	1.00
7.0 Maintaining Responsibility	3.67
8.0 Professional Development	1.78
9.0 Employee Assistance	1.00
10.0 Conflict Management	3.76

Strong Areas: Interpersonal Relationships, Workload/Caseload, and Conflict Management.

Weak Areas: Facilities, Equipment, & Supplies; Professional Development; and Employee Assistance

To Resolve the Weak Areas:

- identify the problem,
- analyze potential reasons,
- establish a goal,
- generate alternatives,
- select the best fit, and
- evaluate results.

CHAPTER **10**

EDUCATIONAL AND OCCUPATIONAL GUIDANCE

Nothing is more tragic than failure to discover one's true business in life, or to find that one has drifted by circumstances into an uncongenial calling.

John Dewey

Nearly 80% of today's young people graduate from high school, and of these, well over half enter a college, university, or post-secondary institution of some kind. The school counselor assumes the responsibility at varying degrees for college counseling, scholarship and financial aid planning, career planning, interest and aptitude testing, as well as consulting with parents, teachers, and administrators. The counselor also advocates for students with college admissions officers, and often mediates resolutions of conflicts or misunderstandings with parents, faculty, and significant others over programs of study, future aspirations, and expectations.

Counselors also have been consistently charged with the responsibility of helping students discover their interests, aptitudes, abilities, achievements, and values. Inherently, all students must realize that their personal characteristics are unique, and that they can influence their decisions about future life goals. Career planning is an essential component that all students must undertake, and many factors should be taken into consideration in the career, academic preparation, and life planning process.

This arduous chore is compounded with the many training routes available for a variety of possible choices. Whether a student intends to go directly to work, to college, to the military, or a combination; all are dependent on time, involvement, cost, location, aptitude, interest, motivation, and aspirations. Empirically all these independent variables must be considered in relationship to future forecasts. This chapter provides perspectives, strategies, profiles, fact sheets, and integrated programs of studies to help the school counselor provide congruent, and timely educational and occupational information.

FUTURE FORECASTS

Curiosity about the future is as old as humankind. In the past, we have pleaded with the gods, asked the oracles, sought guidance from a soothsayer, followed our horoscope, or consulted with a futurist. A kaleidoscope of choices and changes are having more than a modest influence on our lifestyles and workstyles. Training has become a mammoth industry giving people new skills. The human services sector is also increasing with a demand for teachers, learning theorists, psychologists, video technicians, and writers. Everyone is rapidly becoming lifelong learners, where learning does not cease with the final chord of "Pomp and Circumstance." Counselors are continually being called on to assume the role of advocate, catalyst, and conduit for programs, services, and changing information. The following represents some of the critical changes which will influence educational and occupational choices (Naisbitt, 1984; Toffler, 1974).

Skills

In the next twenty years workers will have to change or upgrade their skills 4 to 5 times due to changes in the economy. New jobs created by technology require strong reading, writing, and computation skills. The more education and technical skills you have, the better your chances of employment.

Computer Literacy

Sixty percent of all jobs in the 1990s will require some degree of computer literacy. New technologies may reduce the importance of the printed word. The use of the computer in conjunction with information-handling technologies will make such phrases as "electronic mail, electronic offices, and electronic cottage" commonplace. Currently, graduating college seniors report that computers are the second most important thing they want to buy, following a car. Computers and robotics have boosted incomes because people can do more work in less time.

Women and Minorities

Women will spend up to 25 years in the labor market despite time out to raise families. Women also are going into business for themselves at a much higher rate than men. Government statistics show that by 1990, 65% of all new job applicants will be women. Almost 25% of the people in medical school, and a third of law students are women. As the millennium approaches, the labor force will be shaped more proportionately by women and minorities. Women will make up to 47% of the labor force by the year 2000, up from 44% in 1986. The percentage of minorities will climb to 26%, up from 21% (U.S. Department of Labor). In Table 10.1 are listed some traditionally male dominated fields in which women are expected to make some progress.

Information

We are in an information era—information rich where the growth of communications is dependent on information services as its primary industry. New communication technologies address the emerging electronic pathways of videotext, teletext, and outline databases. Education will be the driving force in our lives. Today 32% of high school graduates go to higher education compared to 8.5% in 1950.

TABLE 10.1
Some Traditionally Male Dominated Fields
In Which Women Are Expected to Make Some Progress

Occupation	Women in Field, 1980	Projected for 1990	Increase
Engineering	64,809	262,177	304%
Computer Programming	98,957	308,128	211%
Engineering Technicians	158,072	310,563	96%
Physicians	57,966	102,916	77%

Source: *USA Today: Tracking Tomorrow's Trends*, Copyright 1986, by Garret News Media Services and Anthony M. Casale. All rights reserved with gratis permission of Andrews and McMeel. Reprinted with permission.

Services

Industries providing services will offer more jobs than industries producing goods. Service workers will increase 35%; 8 out of 10 jobs will be in service areas, especially in technology such as genetic engineering, robotics, and telecommunications. Financial services, information processing, and factory automation will become key industries.

The insatiable demand for all services will generate 20 million new jobs by the year 2000, according to the Bureau of Labor Statistics. The hotel, restaurant, and other industries in the business of selling convenience to a consuming population are wanting "fast services for fastimes."

In Table 10.2 are listed those occupations that are fastest growing and those that are shrinking. The greatest overall growth within the next decade will be in clerical jobs in every category from file clerk to executive secretary.

Technical Skills

In the next decade, 80% of the new jobs will not require a four-year college degree, but will require training in technical

(Continued on Page 212)

TABLE 10.2
Best Jobs for the Future
Fact Sheet

JOBS ON THE RISE

Fastest Growing Occupations (1986-2000)

Biggest Percentage Increase

Paralegals 103.7%
Medical assistants 90.4%
Physical therapists 87.5%
Physical and corrective-therapy
  assistants and aides 81.6%
Data-processing-equipment
  repairers 80.4%
Home-health aides 80.1%
Podiatrists 77.2%
Computer-systems analysts 75.6%
Medical-records technicians 75.0%
Employment interviewers, private or
  public-employment services 71.2%
Computer programmers 69.9%
Radiological technologists,
  technicians 64.7%
Dental hygienists 62.6%
Dental assistants 57.0%
Physician assistants 56.7

Most Jobs Added

Retail salespeople .... 1.2 mil
Waiters, waitresses 752,000
Registered nurses 612,000
Janitors, cleaners, housekeepers 604,000
General managers, top executives 582,000
Cashiers 575,000
Truckdrivers 525,000
General office clerks 462,000
Food-counter and related workers 449,000
Nurses' aides, orderlies, attendants   433,000
Secretaries 424,000
Security guards 383,000
Accountants, auditors 376,000
Computer programmers 335,000
Food-preparation workers 324,000

JOBS IN DECLINE

Shrinking Occupations (1986-2000)

Biggest Percentage Decreases

PBX installers, repairers .... -23.1%
Textile-machine operators, tenders .... -25.2%
Statistical clerks .... -26.4%
Farmers .... -28.1%
Stenographers .... -28.2%
Chemical-plant and system
  operators .... -29.7%
Telephone-station installers,
  repairers .... -31.85%
Shoe-sewing-machine operators,
  tenders .... -32.1%
Industrial truck, tractor operators .... -33.6%
Gas, petroleum-plant and
  system jobs .... -33.3%
Railroad brake, signal,
  switch operators .... -39.9%
Railroad conductors, yardmasters .... -40.9%
Electronic-semiconductor
  processors .... -51.1%
Electrical-electronic assemblers .... -53.7%

Most Jobs Lost

Machine workers .... -19,000
Retail-delivery drivers .... -20,000
Stock clerks .... -23,000
Payroll, timekeeping clerks .... -25,000
College, university faculty .... -32,000
Child-care workers,
  private household .... -38,000
Stenographers .... -50,000
Textile draw-out and winding machine
  operators, tenders .... -55,000
Data-entry keyers,
  except composing .... -66,000
Sewing-machine operators,
  clothing .... -92,000
Typists, word processors .... -140,000
Industrial truck, tractor operators .... -143,000
Farm workers .... -190,000
Farmers .... -332,000

Source: U.S. Department of Labor, Bureau of Labor Statistics, April 1, 1986.

skills. New technology in manufacturing already displaces one and one-half million workers each year. An evolution of a pool of highly skilled service workers is also gaining momentum.

Sunbelt

One out of every six jobs in the next decade will be in the six states in the south and southwest; a new brand of economic regionalism.

Flexibility

The future is not going to be a comfortable time for people who cannot adapt and be flexible, or for people who don't have imagination and a willingness to take some risks. Important personal assets in the future will be to have the ability to be flexible, inventive, reliable, and have the capacity to deal with change and with other people. The development of decision-making and problem-solving skills will enhance a person's capability to respond to change.

Self-Reliance

We are actively becoming a society that seeks medical self-care and adjusts well to our self-serve and self-fix life-styles.

Choices and Decision Making

The new worker will not be happiest with strict work guidelines and clear tasks, but also will expect to find meaning in work. To recruit such workers, employers will begin to offer individualized rewards, i.e., not a fixed set of fringe benefits but a smorgasbord of options such as holidays, medical benefits, pensions, company stocks, insurance, and flextime.

Employers

Skills employers valued the most in recent high school graduates were typing and secretarial skills. The reason students are not chosen for jobs include

- poor academic/attendance records,
- lack of enthusiasm or interest in business,
- inability to express oneself, and
- inadequate preparation for the type of work.

Some companies also are looking for more of a personality type than a degree. Proctor and Gamble, for example, wants "impact players"—highly motivated students who are leaders on campus and who also inspire and influence others.

Change

The average person will make at least three career changes in their life time. The traditional one-company career is becoming increasingly obsolete. Pursuing a career revolves around the principles of "seek and find," what careers to initially seek and when to find another career as economic conditions change.

Flextime

One of the fastest-spreading time structured innovation in industry is flextime, which has reduced absenteeism and increased productivity. There will be an increase in flextime, night work, 24 hour services, and a part-time job market.

Marketing

Mass marketing will decline. Specific targeted marketing will increase. Marketers will aim for specific, targeted groups of customers through demographic targeting of interests, tastes, and needs.

Work Style/Life-style

Individualism, noncomformity, and personalization will become accepted at home and on the job. A career will become an on-going task of building a satisfying life that includes relationships, interests, and leisure activities. In Table 10.3 are listed what young people indicated as to how they want their lives to be different from their parents.

TABLE 10.3
How Do You Want Your Life to Be Different From Your Parents' Life

Better off financially 20%

Have a good marriage 12%

Be more open-minded 6%

No way 5%

Be more successful in work 4%

Get a better education 4%

Be happier 3%

Work fewer hours 3%

See more of the world 3%

Source: *USA Today: Tracking Tomorrow's Trends,* Copyright 1986 by Gannet News Media Services and Anthony M. Casale. All rights reserved with gratis permission of Andrew and McMeel. Reprinted with permission.

Self-Employed

The number of self-employed people in the U.S. increased 24% between 1974 and 1984; a growth rate much higher than the growth in the total work force. In the 1980s the number of people who worked for themselves grew at a rate four times faster than the number of people who work for a daily wage. Entrepreneurship adds another dimension of opportunity. Most jobs created in the next few years will be in the realm of small businesses.

Aging Workforce

Over the next decade, sweeping changes will occur in the work force. Between now and the year 2000, the population of people age 16 to 24 will actually drop at a rate of six-tenths per year, according to Howard Fullerton, a demographic statistician for the U.S. Bureau of Labor Statistics. While people in that age group made up nearly a quarter of the labor force in 1972, their contribution will fall to 16% by the year 2000. As the pool of younger workers shrinks and the need for reliable skilled workers increases, employers inevitably are going to have to do more to retain their older workers than they currently are dong. Programs such as using senior employees as consultants on special projects or as mentors to young people, slowing phasing-in retirement, and flexible or reduced work schedules are some options that corporations are beginning to implement.

Diversity in Living

No longer does one standard way to live exist. According to the National Center for Health Statistics, some futurists have described the decade of the nineties and beyond as the "single society." The unmarried will play a more integral part in the society. Blended families, single-parent families, friends who regard one another as families will all make up the diversity of living in contemporary society. DINKS (double-income-no-kids) is a particular family style that will become an accepted alternative just as much as "YUPPIES with Puppies" were in the eighties.

Careers

Within the next decade, one-half of the U.S. workers will be immigrants, according to Nestor E. Terlecky, president of NPA Data Services in Washington, D.C. With no training or education youth can expect to compete with a growing population of immigrants, who are willing to work long hours with few amenities.

Anyone with a developed skill will have many job opportunities. Technologists will be very scarce and anyone with computer skills will be in demand. Any variation of health-care profession will be in demand. For example, an often overlooked and up-coming profession is medical-record technician.

Other promising occupations will be social work with an increasing need for child-protective agencies, delinquency diversion programs and work with the aging (a growing population in the life span). Teachers, too, will be much in demand, not only in the schools, but increasing in demand in corporations which will spend millions of money on training employees to perform their jobs more effectively and efficiently.

By the twenty-first century, approximately 25% of all working Americans will work at home. Many will own their own business. Those who work in a traditional office will encounter opportunities for flex-time. Job insecurity will be a greater concern. With corporate mergers and aggressive takeovers, companies will be more inclined to fire workers. This will foster less loyalty among employees who will be more willing to leave their present job for a better opportunity.

Old-fashioned Values

Faith Popcorn, founder of New York's Brain Revenue, a future forecasting group, predicts that the decade to the twenty-first century will be embracing a return to old-fashioned values. Life in the fast lane—heavy drinking, drugging, and conspicuous consumption—will be passe. Quiet living, self-control, self-discipline, and proactive community concern will be the hallmarks of the coming century. In Table 10.4 are listed life values high school seniors consider important and how these values changed with time.

A COMPREHENSIVE SYSTEM

Educational or occupational guidance referred to as a comprehensive system of services and programs in the school setting (reflecting the needs of students and the community) is designed to assist the student in attaining academic adjustment, educational competence, and career exploration. Empirically, traditional outcomes can be measured by such things as increased grade point average, increased test scores, or follow-up studies of graduates.

In the arena of career decision and development, counselor intervention has had some empirical validation. For example,

(Continued on Page 218)

TABLE 10.4
Life Values Seniors Consider Important

Percent of high school seniors in 1972 and 1982, and four years later, who felt that certain life values were "very important," by sex: 1972-1976 and 1982-1986

| | Percent of 1972 Seniors | | | | Percent of 1982 Seniors | | | |
| | 1972 | | 1976 | | 1982 | | 1986 | |
	Male	Female	Male	Female	Male	Female	Male	Female
Being success-ful in work	86.5	83.0	80.3	69.7	88.2	85.5	84.0	77.2
Having steady work	82.3	73.7	79.3	62.1	88.0	84.4	84.2	76.3
Having lots of money	26.0	9.8	17.7	9.4	41.3	24.1	27.8	16.9
Being a com-munity leader	14.9	8.0	9.2	4.2	11.3	5.9	9.5	4.5
Correcting inequalities	22.5	31.1	16.2	17.1	11.8	11.7	10.7	10.9
Having children	--	--	--	--	37.0	47.0	41.4	56.2
Having a hap-py family life	78.6	85.7	84.2	86.4	81.6	86.3	86.8	87.8
Providing bet-ter opportun-ities for chil-dren	66.6	66.2	59.8	58.8	71.0	68.7	68.4	67.4
Living closer to parents or rel-atives	6.8	8.2	7.7	11.9	15.0	15.7	12.9	19.8
Moving from area	14.3	14.6	6.7	6.4	14.4	12.8	9.0	7.4
Having strong friendships	81.2	78.7	76.1	72.1	80.4	79.1	76.5	75.0
Having leisure time	--	--	65.4	60.1	70.2	68.8	70.1	68.9

--Data not available.

Source: U.S. Department of Education. (1987). National Center for Education Statistics, National Longitudinal Study and High School and Beyond Surveys.

through group problem-solving methods, students can be helped to understand the relationship between educational and vocational development, to clarify goals, and to acquire skills in identifying and using relevant information for their decision making (Babcock & Kauffman, 1976; Martin & Stone, 1977). Students utilizing computer-based career guidance systems make larger gains than nonusers in such characteristics as degree of planning and decision making, knowledge of use of resources for career exploration and awareness of career options (Meyer, Strowig, & Hartford, 1970). Further, minority students who are assisted in deciding upon vocational objectives are typically found to have a more positive self-concept and higher ideal than those who do not have such objectives (Higgins, 1976).

This represents a selected sampling of positive interventions with occupational and educational planning. Prospectively such concepts as skilled workers, information handling technologies, flexibility, and inventiveness, creates a new mosaic of variables which will influence educational and occupational decisions in a changing economy punctuated by increasing technology and shifting demographics. National and local trends also seem to direct the focus and the thrust of programs and services to students and their families. Moreover, three distinct subpopulations within a school setting require different kinds of information. They are the college-bound, the noncollege-bound, and the marginal or the minority student. These specific needs must also be evaluated from the perspective of educational opportunities, occupational projections, and changing value systems.

CAREER EDUCATION VERSUS CAREER DEVELOPMENT EDUCATION

A distinction needs to be made between "career education" and "career development education." Career education is teaching occupational information with an existential hope that the student will arrive at an informed choice. Career development education, in contrast, encourages the processing of occupational information conditionally as a means to shape hypotheses about one's self and to eventually arrive at a considered choice.

Education for career development contributes to the personal growth of students in ways that complement academic as well as vocational curricula.

The National Career Development Association (formerly National Vocational Guidance Association) maintains that the application of life stages to career development education provides a means for describing the development of career competence. The goal of career development is "to stimulate" the student's progress step-by-step through four stages. A step-by-step description, combining the notions of life stages and career management tasks (Figure 10.1) appropriate to each stage provides a way of ordering curriculum by enabling the counselor or teacher to anticipate the kinds of learning experiences students will most likely respond to and profit from (Herr & Cramer, 1984).

EDUCATIONAL AND OCCUPATIONAL ASSESSMENT

Guidance career planning and educational decisions, i.e., educational/occupational assessment is probably the oldest and one of the most fundamental activities in the schools. The inherent purpose is to provide students with the necessary vocational and educational data to make informed decisions. They are not separate entities performed by designated specialists (e.g., the career counselor). Rather, they are an integral part of the instructional program and the responsibility of everyone who's vested interest in the growth and development of youth. Fundamentally, every opportunity should be utilized to integrate academic and career planning, with the selection of courses that relate to appropriate career clusters.

Srebalus, Marinelli, and Messing (1982) stated that educational/occupational guidance is an organized, systematic program to help the individual develop self-understanding of societal roles and knowledge about the world of work. Career education, on the other hand, is the lifelong totality of experiences through which one prepares to engage in work. Career guidance is one aspect of the preparation; it entails

(Continued on Page 221)

A formal curriculum with a progression of skills and self-awareness exercises which proceed through the grades to bring students to a point of self-awareness and maturity to deal with the transition to work or college or both.

Grade	7th	8th	9th	10th	11th	12th
	• Learn about guidance resources, vocational, biographies, guidelines and publications, computer programs and video or multimedia systems, and suggest post-secondary alternatives.	• Develop 5 year plan of program of studies	• Attend seminars on study skills, how to read for understanding, build vocabulary, use mnemonic devices	• Actively connecting college or other post-secondary training to careers	• Take the PSAT, an important experience in the college grooming process	• Take a full course load; take electives that provide a marketable skill
	• Explore careers and develop aspirations	• Differentiate among programs and courses based on testing and academic preparation	• Take challenging core courses and electives to balance interests	• Concentrate on writing and speaking well in all classes	• Take interest inventories such as the CAT if you plan to go to work after high school	• Implement the mechanics of the admissions process; armed services registration
	• Facilitate decision making	• Review testing history: integrate achievement, aptitude and interest	• Integrate critical thinking skills across the curriculum in all subjects	• Attend test-taking workshops and develop proscriptive plans for skill development such as quantitative comparisons, vocabulary, and analogies	• Attend the Junior Post-secondary Fair: learn about college admissions, other post-secondary options, job seeking and job keeping seminars	• Read all literature for colleges or other post-secondary opportunities
	• Meet with students in small groups to promote effective study skills: time management, memorizing, managing a notebook, test-taking, note-taking	• Assess interests, values, and abilities	• Become involved in career related clubs such as Future Teachers, Medical Club, Junior Achievement	• Investigate colleges according to interests, programs of study, and location	• Participate in the AP program	• Develop and refine your academic and personal profile
	• Reinforce the basic skills of reading, writing, listening, speaking, studying and thinking	• Develop realistic plans	• Attend family meetings on college options, financial aid opportunities, college admission requirements, summer school alternatives		• Meet with college representatives and representatives from apprenticeships	
	• Be active in academic, extracurricular and community activities	• Seek summer enrichment courses in academic weaknesses				
	• Participate in family meetings re: student school/parent concerns	• Develop parent support groups as in informal network of parents who advise and assist school counselors in career, college information, and financial aid				

The Counselor as Disseminator of Information
• Send out montly newsletters on college admissions, careers and curriculum
• Prepare a planning guide for the college bound student and one for the job-seeking student
• Prepare exit packages for the marginal student who drops out of school

Figure 10.1. Program of studies: Academic and career planning guide.

active assistance with the development of decision-making skills and the framing of occupational and educational plans. While some overlap occurs between career education and career guidance, career education stresses direct experience and activities related to occupational skills and attitudes. Educational and occupational guidance emphasizes the process of planning, decision making, and the implementation of well articulated plans.

This inseparable marriage between occupational and educational guidance must be repeatedly interwoven into the backdrop of course offerings, academic preparation and decision making. Students, parents, and teachers, however, often need more accurate information to make their decisions.

For assessment purposes, interest inventories have generally been accepted as one fairly accountable means of matching characteristics of individual clients with various careers or occupations. A high level of sophistication has occurred in the use of interest tests in career counseling and educational programs. According to Tittle and Zytowski (1978) approximately 3,500,000 interest types proposed by Holland (1973) are also widely used in vocational guidance and research. Trait factor assessment instruments based on Holland's six types include his own *Vocational Preference Inventory (VPI)* and *Self-Directed Search (SDS)*; the *Unisex Edition of the Act Interest Inventory (UNIACT)* used in the *Act Assessment Program (the "Act")* and *Strong-Campbell Interest Inventory (SCII)*; the *Career Assessment Inventory (CAI)*, a "blue-collar" version of the SCII; the *Harrington-O'Shea System for Career Decision-Making;* the *Ohio Vocational Interest Survey;* and the *Kuder General Interest Survey* have served as a graphic aid for vocational guidance and research vis-a-vis Holland's types.

In a study entitled "Are secondary schools still using standardized tests?" Engen, Lamb, and Prediger (1982) surveyed tests used nationally at the secondary school level. The study yielded the following list of career guidance tests/inventories ranked according to their use at any grade level for at least one percent of the schools in the sample (highest first):

- *Armed Services Vocational Aptitude Battery* (ASVAB)
- *Differential Aptitude Test* (DAT)

- *General Aptitude Test Battery* (GATB)
- *Kuder Occupational Interest Survey* (Form DD)
- *Strong Vocational Interest Blank* (SVIB)
- *Strong-Campbell Interest Survey* (SCII)
- *Kuder Vocational or General Interest Inventory* (Form C or E)
- *Ohio Vocational Interest Survey* (OVIS)
- *Self-Directed Search* (SDS)
- *California Occupational Preference Survey* (COPS)
- *Judgment of Occupational Behavioral-orientation* (JOB-O)
- *Vocational Interests Experience and Skills Assessment* (VIESA)

Combined Instruments

Congruency of information between educational preparation and occupational decisions will occur as instruments are combined. Compatible combinations can occur along two significant areas:

- aptitude and achievement domains will be linked to interests, experiences, and work values; and

- all types of test data also can be interlinked to occupational information.

Currently, the major college admission test which combine aptitude, interest, and experience is the *ACT*, while the SAT includes measures of aptitude and experience. The *Differential Aptitude Test* includes an optional "career planning program." The *ACT Career Planning Program (American Institute for Research, 1976)* assess ability, interests, values, and information. The *SRA Placement and Counseling Program* (Science Research Associated, 1978) combines the *SRA Achievement and Ability Series* with the *Kuder-Form E* (Kuder, 1976).

Test publishers have also been combining educational and occupational information with test data. For example, the *Ohio Vocational Interest Survey* (Psychological Corporation, 1981) has been cross referenced with the *Dictionary of Occupational Titles* (DOT). The *California Occupational Preference System* (COPS) interfaces with a *Career Briefs Kit, Career Cluster Booklist,* the *DOT,* and the *Occupational Outlook Handbook.*

INTERPRETING TEST DATA

One of the counselor's responsibilities is to assist the client in gathering and interpreting relevant test data. Test scores, however, only serve as starting points for discussion to help individuals consider and clarify for themselves what their attitudes and preferences are regarding the direction they wish to go. The practice of basing important decisions on tests alone is unsound. Test data cannot provide infallible predictions of human behavior (such as success in college). The whole course of an individual's potential development at any particular time evolves from a complex interweaving of heredity, experience, learning, and responsiveness to environmental cues. Moreover, one cannot conclude on the basis of test data that any racial, cultural, or socioeconomic group is superior or inferior to any other group. One merely can estimate how well an individual may function in the culture for which the test is appropriate. Fundamentally, the best indicator of one's future success is past performance. The following caveats should be incorporated in articulating to others about what tests mean:

A score serves to show where a person stands in a distribution of scores of his/her peers.

Aptitude tests (intelligence tests, I.Q. tests) cannot measure innate potential or characteristics.

An aptitude score merely projects how successful individuals will be with academic learning, particularly more difficult accelerated parts of the curriculum. At any grade level, all students are capable of learning some of the course content, but not all students are capable of understanding the more difficult and the more abstract.

Aptitude tests do not measure strength, persistence, or motivation. Essentially, we can all recognize motivation but we cannot measure it.

Interest inventories do not measure how much interest a person has in any collective domain, but only reflects what direction his/her interests have taken.

Worker traits on interest inventories have been isolated from the vast complexity of occupational interactions as a convenience for interpretation.

Interest inventories cannot measure unique characteristics, they measure only traits common to many people in the general population.

A score on an interest inventory indicates the number of ways in which one's likes and dislikes match people in a particular occupational group. These similarities often have to do with what one dislikes or rejects rather than with what one likes or chooses.

A focus on the test rather than the individual is inappropriate. Human potential and behavior is too complex to be reduced to one isolated score.

Interpretation of any test score in isolation is detrimental. As many variables as possible should be considered when evaluating an individual's potential.

The extent to which test scores can contribute to sound educational decisions depends on proper interpretation and use of test scores. Frequently, updating norms and better communication of test results to parents and the public are critical strategies to assessment and placement.

Finally, the onus of responsibility for the use of test information and decision making belongs to the individual. If an individual does not perceive the relevance of the test data, the explanation of the meaning of the scores is not likely to affect the individual's decision.

In Figure 10.2 is a checklist that a counselor can use regarding the organization and administration of testing program. The checklist includes seven areas.

This checklist is divided into seven parts each labeled with a capital letter. The numbering of the question is continuous throughout the entire checklist.

A. Coordination, Leadership, and Philosophy

	Yes	No
1. Is there an active testing committee representative of some or all of the staff of the school/district?	____	____
2. Is there a written statement of the duties of this committee?	____	____
3. Do members of this committee have course work in the area of tests and measurements?	____	____
4. Is there a system-wide testing director?	____	____
5. Is there a written statement of the purposes of the school/ district's testing program?	____	____
6. Are these testing program purposes in harmony with the stated philosophy and objectives of the whole school program and with school and district policies on assessment?	____	____
7. Are school board members, parents, and other citizens well-informed as to the testing program?	____	____

B. Inservice Training Programs Related to Testing

8. Are inservice training opportunities provided for those who administer, score, and interpret standardized tests?	____	____
9. Are inservice opportunities provided to teachers for improvement of teacher-made classroom tests?	____	____
10. Does the school staff professional library reference areas covering teacher-made classroom tests, uses, and interpretation of standardized tests?	____	____
11. Are specialists in the area of tests and measurements available for assistance with problems as they arise?	____	____

Source: ERIC/CAPS: Resources for Guidance Program Improvement. The University of Michigan. Reprinted by permission.

Figure 10.2. Checklist on the organization and administration of the testing program (1986). Reproduced by permission from ERIC Counseling and Personnel Services Clearinghouse, Ann Arbor, MI: The University of Michigan, School of Education.

Figure 10.2. Continued.

C. Selection of Tests

	Yes	No
12. Are all tests selected by recognized professional and technical standards?	____	____
13. Do those selecting tests have specimen sets available for study and such reviews of tests as appear in Buros' Mental Measurement Yearbooks?	____	____
14. Whenever practical, are tests field-tested on small samples of students before broad application?	____	____
15. Are all tests based on objectives that are appropriate for the ability level and instructional program of the students involved?	____	____
16. Is there a periodic evaluation of each test in the program to determine whether it should continue to be used?	____	____

D. Testing Facilities

17. Are rooms where testing takes place satisfactory in terms of

	Yes	No
a. freedom from outside distractions?	____	____
b. adequate lighting?	____	____
c. adequate ventilation?	____	____
d. work space for each student?	____	____
18. Are there adequate, carefully supervised facilities for storage and control of testing materials?	____	____
19. Are all testing supplies subject to continuing inventory and checked as to usefulness?	____	____

E. Administration and Scoring of Tests

	Yes	No
20. Are teachers and counselors involved in determining when tests will be administered and for what purpose?	____	____
21. Is the person administering the test always prepared for the task?	____	____
22. Are the purposes and importance of each test made clear to students before the test is given?	____	____

Figure 10.2. Continued.

23. Are persons present to assist with the administration of tests to groups when desirable?   ____ ____

24. Is the timing of the testing disruptive of the other activities of the school?   ____ ____

25. Do teachers and counselors spend an inordinate amount of time scoring, tallying, graphing, and filing test results?   ____ ____

26. Are test scorers always carefully instructed for their tasks?   ____ ____

27. Are all student answer sheets carefully checked for possible errors in scoring?   ____ ____

28. Are services of a trained psychologist or psychometrist available for testing individual students?   ____ ____

F. Facilities and Means for Use of Test Results

29. Are tests filed in places easily available to the persons who should use them?   ____ ____

30. Are definite means employed to encourage wider and more thorough use of test results?   ____ ____

31. Are there rooms, private and quiet, in which counselors and others can confer with pupils?   ____ ____

32. Are cumulative test records carefully reviewed periodically, so as to be sure that test data and other material are properly organized and as easily useable as possible?   ____ ____

33. Is a test handbook describing the testing program and covering such areas as uses and interpretation of test information readily available for teacher and parent reference?   ____ ____

34. Are counselors and teachers encouraged to make use of the item analysis technique for studying difficulties of individuals and their classes as a whole?   ____ ____

G. General

35. What are the strong points in the testing program?

_____

_____

_____

Figure 10.2. Continued.

36. What are the weak points in the testing program?

    _____

    _____

    _____

37. What improvements can be made in the testing program during the coming year?

    _____

    _____

    _____

CHAPTER 11

COUNSELOR AS CATALYST FOR COLLEGE DECISION MAKING

> There are techniques of being intelligent. It is not easy to acquire the proper use of the mental tools which we have thoughtlessly inherited or which are implicit in the construction of our brains. Severe effort and long practice are required.
>
> Perry W. Bridgment

> The fusion of knowledge is the most creative act of the human mind.
>
> Elwood Murray

Projections from the last three decades reflect a changing profile of the perspective college graduate. For example, in the last three decades:

The proportion of high school graduates going on to college increased from 25% to 60%.

The proportion of college students older than twenty-five years of age increased from 20% to 40%.

The proportion of freshmen who enrolled in at least one college credit course while still in high school went from near 0 to 13%.

The proportion of freshmen who delayed entry into college from high school grew from a small percentage to 33%.

Entering college right after high school graduation and continuing through four years of full-time coursework only applies to a small minority of students in the nation.

An analysis by the National Center for Education Statistics entitled "A Descriptive Summary of 1980 High School Sophomores: Six Years Later," found that two-thirds of those who graduated in 1982 had received some postsecondary education by 1986.

Of those who had enrolled in college, however, only 22% remained on the traditional path by 1986.

The percentage of freshmen who expect to work at least part-time while in college grew from a small percentage to 40%.

The percentage of bachelor degrees in arts and sciences (compared to professional degrees) fell from a substantial majority to about one-third.

The proportion of all college students who would be characterized as full-time, living on campus, and age 18 to 22 fell from a majority position to 17%.

The proportion of all college students who are members of a racial minority group rose from less than 5% to 19%. However, during the years 1975 to 1982, 29% more Blacks graduated from high school, but Black enrollment in college dropped 11%. For Hispanic college enrollment declined 16% (Frontiers of Possibility, 1986).

COLLEGE AND UNIVERSITY
EXPECTATIONS

Nearly all colleges and universities will offer remedial programs in writing, reading, mathematics, and study skills for underprepared students. While many of these students will be from racial minority groups, the majority will be White and will come from families with lower incomes. These students also may be low in motivation and self-esteem in relation to academic work.

Nearly all colleges and universities will incorporate systematic testing and placement into remedial, regular, and honors courses to insure matriculation.

A four-year College Board and Educational Testing Service study revealed that academic ratings class standing and SAT scores are three times as important as personal attributes at these selective schools:

- University of Richmond,
- Bucknell,
- Colgate,
- Harwick,
- Kalamazoo,
- Kenyon,
- Occidental and Williams Colleges, or
- Ohio Wesleyan Universities.

At some highly competitive schools, such factors as the interview recommendations, and extracurricular activities also play a significant role.

James Crouse and Dale Trusheim with their book *The Case Against the SAT* using data on nearly 3,000 students compared the selection decisions that would have been made using high school grade-point averages alone with those that would have been made from grade-point averages and SAT scores combined. From their thorough critique they concluded:

> Colleges make identical admissions decisions, either to
> admit or reject, on a great majority of their applicants

whether they use the SAT along with the high school record, or the high school record alone. The SAT therefore, has very little impact on who is in colleges' freshman classes and who is not. It is, in effect, statistically redundant. (Crouse & Trusheim, 1988, p. 257)

The American Association of College Registrars and Admissions Officers (AACRAO) and the College Board designed a survey to all institutions of higher education. Responses were obtained from 1,463 institutions. When asked what single characteristics or credentials they considered "most important" in making their admissions decisions, 40% of all four-year institutions indicated academic performances, as measured by grade point average and class rank (Conner, 1983, p. 36).

The survey also revealed other factors institutions considered most important or very important. In Table 11.1 are summarized those factors that institutions have considered for admissions decisions. These findings reinforce the rhetoric that a student's academic record has more influence than any other factor on a college or university admissions decision. Admission tests are important, but ultimately it is a student's course history that seems to matter most.

Without additional exceptions, probably one is safe to say that measures of an applicant's academic success in high school (grades, rank-in-class, and courses taken) and measures of how well the applicant compares with other students across the state and nation (with SAT or ACT scores) are clearly the factors given the most emphasis by college admissions personnel.

The Scholastic Aptitude Test (SAT) is currently being revised. This is a means for the College Board to maintain one step ahead of the critics. Some of the changes under revision are

- including an essay,
- increasing the amount of reading comprehension to as much as 80% of the verbal section,
- using open-format questions in the math section, and
- including an algebra achievement test in the math section.

TABLE 11.1
Applicant Credentials Considered Most Important or Very Important by Four Year Institutions in Making Admissions Decisions

Credential	Percent of Institutions Public	Private
Academic performance in high school (GPA or RIC)	77	84
Aptitude tests (SAT, ACT, etc.)	63	55
Pattern of secondary school subjects	25	38
Recommendation from high school	4	24
Interview with faculty member, alumnus, etc.	6	23
Personal essay or autobiographical statement	3	13
Recommendation from employer, etc.	1	13
Declaration of major	9	7
Portfolio, etc., to demonstrate prior work	6	7
Health statement	5	7
Achievement test scores	4	7
Ability or inability to pay college costs	1	4

Source: Connor, J.D. (1983). Admissions policies and practices: Selected finding of the AACRAO/CEEB survey. *NASSP Bulletin, 67,* 460. Reprinted by permission.

A COLLEGE EDUCATION
IN THE WORKPLACE

Workers with four years of college earn about 60% more than workers with only a high school education.

Ninety percent of those who majored in accounting, chemistry, computer science, engineering, mathematics, and nursing who were in the labor force entered college-level jobs.

Seventy percent of those who majored in agriculture and natural resources, arts, communications, English, and the social sciences entered a college-level job within a year of graduation.

In the 1960s, 36% of the new jobs were in professional and managerial areas, 53% were in service and clerical areas. In the 1990s, 28% of the new jobs will be in professional and managerial areas, 40% in clerical and service areas, and 32% in other areas.

Seventy-five percent of the new jobs generated between 1982 and 1995 will be in service-producing industries:

• transportation,
• telecommunications,
• public utilities,
• trade,
• finance,
• insurance,
• real estate,
• medical care,
• hotels,
• nonprofit organizations and business, and
• personal and professional services.

For college-educated workers, the greatest employment expansion will occur in such fields as

• health care,
• engineering,

- computer science (including sales and management), and
- elementary education.

The least expansion is forecasted for secondary education, agriculture and natural resources, accounting clerks, and drafters.

According to Audrey Forrest, Director of Instructional Design and Assessment for the American College Testing Program,

> in the next fifteen years, our country will experience a critical need for citizens with highly developed reasoning and communication skills. People who do not attend college are less likely to develop these skills than those who do attend. It is imperative that the flow of students into, through, and out of the higher education system be managed to ensure that a maximum number of students seeking access to the system do indeed succeed. (Forrest, 1987)

KEEPING OPTIONS OPEN

In the report of the College Board's Twelve-Member Commission on Precollege Guidance and Counseling entitled *Keeping Options Open* (1986), it was recommended that precollege guidance and counseling be extensively revised and made equal with instruction to stem the considerable waste of human talent occurring in the nation's schools. A second report by the National College Counseling Project entitled *Frontiers of Possibility* (1986) found similar results and concluded that many of the nation's 25,000 high schools are not serving their students.

One-half of the prospective students interviewed in a recent Carnage Foundation study indicated they did not have enough facts to make an informed decision about where to apply for admission, and parents echoed an even stronger need to be informed (Boyer, 1987). Matriculation is critically linked to making an initially satisfactory choice.

A critical study of the college process revealed the following perceptions regarding decision making for college selection (Matthay, 1989):

Visits to college campuses were significantly more helpful to students attending the private, 4-year liberal arts college (highly competitive) than to students attending all the other types of institutions (p=.0001).

Use of computer information systems was significantly more helpful to students attending all other types of institutions (p=.01).

College fairs were significantly more helpful to students who attend the 4-year private secular college (competitive) than to those attending all others (p=.01).

Satisfaction with overall assistance received in college decision making was significantly higher for students attending the 4-year, private liberal arts college (highly competitive) and the 4-year private secular institution (competitive) than for students attending the 4-year private liberal arts college (highly competitive) and the public, 2-year community college (p=.007).

Satisfaction with choice of college was significantly higher for students attending the 4-year, private liberal arts college (highly competitive) than for students attending all other types of colleges. The least satisfied students were those attending the 4-year, public nonresearch university.

Matthay (1989) concluded that the four most helpful resources in the college selection process are college visits, college catalogs, parent involvement, and the school counselor. These data suggest that

- college planning should begin in the middle school years,

- counselors should emphasize the importance of visiting colleges and should prepare students and their families to critically evaluate college selections,

- regional education centers should be used to provide libraries of catalogs and videos, and

- high schools should ensure access of their students to visiting college representatives.

Even with brochures, letters, college fairs, college catalogs, and campus visits, high school students and their families still feel inadequately informed or lacking in enough facts to make an informed decision.

In Table 11.2 are the indicated rank of perceptions of helpfulness of seventeen resources in assisting students with college selection with the top four most helpful resources being visits to colleges, college catalogs, parents and family, and the school counselor. The least helpful were computer software packages and college coaches.

When univariate analysis was used to determine statistically significant differences in perceptions of helpfulness based on type of college attended, the following findings emerges from the study:

The college catalog was more helpful to students who attend a 4-year, private secular college (competitive) than those who attend the public community college (noncompetitive) (p=.01).

Parents and family were more helpful to students attending the 4-year, private liberal arts (highly competitive) and the state 2-year technical college than to students attending the 4-year, public nonresearch university (competitive) (p=.0002).

The school counselor emerged as a more helpful resource to students attending the 4-year, private secular college than to students attending the 4-year, private liberal arts college (highly competitive) and the public community college (noncompetitive) (p=.01).

Interviews with admission representatives on college campuses were significantly more helpful to students at the 4-year private secular college (competitive) than to students at all the other types of colleges (p=.001).

(Continued on Page 241)

TABLE 11.2
Perceived Helpfulness of Resources
For All types of Colleges Combined

Rank	Mean	SD	Resources
1	3.4	1.29	Visits to colleges
2	2.9	1.07	College catalog
3	2.8	1.30	Parents or family
4	2.7	1.22	School counselor
5	2.7	1.21	Friends who attended the college
6	2.7	1.20	College admissions representatives
7	2.7	1.29	Interviews with college admissions representatives
8	2.5	1.11	College guides and directories
9	2.4	1.15	College fairs
10	2.3	1.13	High school teachers
11	2.2	1.11	General group sessions during college day
12	2.2	1.13	College information nights
13	2.0	1.04	Films or tapes on specific colleges
14	2.0	1.03	Films or tapes—general information on colleges
15	1.9	1.15	Private college counseling services
16	1.8	1.08	College coaches
17	1.7	1.01	Computer information programs

Source: Matthay, E.R. (1989). A critical study of the college selection process. *The School Counselor, 36*, 5, p. 9. Reprinted by permission.

Fundamentally, students who need the most guidance for making decisions about attending college are those whose parents may not have had the college experience. Parents with a college education tend to have children who attend college. This is a stronger correlation than SAT scores. Parents without a college education, however, often don't know how to play the college admissions "game." Chapman, O'Brien, and DeMasi (1987) found low-income students indifferent to the counselor's role in assisting with post-secondary decision making.

The school counselor's college advising responsibility is especially important in low-income and minority families where parents are unable to share the experience of college with their child. Lee and Elkstrom (1987) found that counselors often devote more time to college-bound, middle and upper-income White students than to others. They concluded that family income is the major determinant of the education a student receives. Many researchers have warned that current trends might eventually lead to a dual school system in the United States, one for the rich and one for the poor.

The National College Counseling survey confirmed what many have suspected about the variation across the country in school settings, in college attendance rates, and in college counseling practices. They found the following:

> School size greatly influences the availability of resources devoted to college counseling, especially the number of counselors with college counseling duties.

> The patterns of college attendance are affected dramatically by the family income profile of the school. Fewer students from lower income schools attend a four-year institution than do students from upper income schools.

> High schools drawing students from more well-to-do families offer more exposure to colleges through programs such as fairs, visits from college representatives, parent meetings, and the new information technologies. Counselors at upper income schools spend a large portion of their time on college counseling duties.

The most frequently mentioned problem (by 16% of the respondents) was the lack of sufficient time to get to know students and carry out effective college counseling. Other identified problems included

- the need to help expand student horizons, i.e., to consider more college options, to think more independently, to strive for higher goals;

- insufficient financial resources, resulting in small staffs, student/counselor rations that are too high, and small operating budgets;

- student apathy and indifference toward taking responsibility, meeting deadlines;

- the counselor's difficulty in keeping up to date with financial aid developments, college admissions requirements, and career information; and

- too many peripheral responsibilities for counselors, including many non-college duties such as managing student discipline and doing clerical work (Frontiers of Possibility, 1986).

The study found that effective college counseling programs share a number of common characteristics. First, they start working early with students and their families. Second, they help families find ways to finance higher education. What becomes increasingly important is for counselors to assist in dismantling the financial aid barrier for all income levels. To do so will necessitate coordinating community human resources. Third, successful programs also require the full support and commitment from the principal. Finally, effective college counseling involves the larger community in the success of the students. Community goals, school mission, and college counseling or other post-secondary training alternatives should be fully integrated into the total school program.

Concurrently, many students come into counseling offices often pressured from family and friends to declare a major course of study for a career field that they might know little about, choose a school from glossy brochures or enticing videos, sort through an abyss of acronyms, and fill out form after form to be eligible to qualify for scholarships in everything from the Daughters of the American Revolution to the local recreational athletic association.

Studies on attrition continue to reveal that most students leave college or universities for one or more of the following reasons:

- inadequate academic preparation,
- lack of finances, and/or
- poor college choice.

What becomes paramount is for students and their families to be counseled so that when they leave high school all of their post-secondary options are commensurate with their ability, aptitude, achievement, and aspirations.

Many proponents support the development of a college guidance curriculum as an explicit sequence of activities designed to carry students through their school academic experiences and career possibilities. The goals of the curriculum would include challenging student potential and enhancement of self-esteem, broadening experiences and aspirations, and preparing students to make comprehensive and flexible decisions. The college guidance curriculum should be intricately woven into the academic curriculum.

Finally, the Commissions on Precollege Guidance and Counseling (College Board Publications, 1986) and the National College Counseling Project (Frontiers of Possibility, 1986) recommended

- a focus on student needs with college counseling acting as part of a long-term guidance curriculum;

- attention to appropriate counselor qualities (student advocate, effective manager/leader, and political savvy);

- counselor/principal cooperation and faculty involvement;

- parent/family or significant other involvement; and

- emphasis on intervention on elementary or middle school level especially underserved students, who may feel that Harvard and Radcliffe are not within their reach. If they do, and if the same thing were to happen at other private colleges, we would end up with substantial economic and racial segregation in our system of higher education (Harvard-Radcliffe Colleges, 1986).

Concurrently, most graduates not going to college are attending proprietary trade and business schools with minorities making up to 32% of enrollment in these schools. The number of minority students enrolled in proprietary schools has climbed sharply in the past five years.

BOLD INTERVENTION PROGRAMS

Bold intervention programs such as Upward Bound can help reverse the decline in enrollment of minorities in higher education. Several other innovative programs also are available.

Upward Bound

The purpose of the program is to provide disadvantaged secondary school youth with the skills and motivation needed to successfully pursue post-secondary education. Upward Bound programs for needy and talented minority students expose them to skill-building and enrichment courses, as well as provide consistent support and attention. Participants receive instruction in reading, math, English, and study skills, academic and career counseling, college entrance examination preparation, cultural activities, and career exploration.

Options for Excellence

This program was established by the College Board in 1981. It has two goals; increase the number of college-bound minority students and improve the college preparatory curriculum for all students in the public and private secondary schools.

Talent Search Programs

Talent search programs such as the Johns Hopkins University's Talented Youth Program focus on advance study in all the major disciplines including the performing arts.

Project Stay

Collateral programs for parents and non-college bound, such as Project Stay can bring special educators to the school to tutor the most needy students.

In addition, schools and communities with a high proportion of lower income families who aspire for higher education can develop creative links to develop resources and programs.

Business Communications Resources Utilized

Programs which draw directly on the resources of the business community include:

Project Involve. Local businesses offer apprenticeship opportunities to students interested in furthering their understanding of a particular business or profession.

Cooperative Work Program. Students who have developed a particular career interest may leave school early in the afternoon to work part-time at a local business.

School/Business Partnerships. Programs which involve teachers in local business (during the summer) for a brief period of time can promote the transition from school to work. School-business collaborations augment the educational system's ability to serve at-risk students by providing greater access to work experience, increased personal attention, and more relevant preparation for finding and keeping a job. Collaborative programs that also promise college-scholarship support for precollegiate students who earn their diplomas are the most popular recent trend in school-business partnerships.

Cooperating Hampton Roads Organizations for Minorities in Engineering (Crome)

CROME'S mission is to increase the number of minorities who enter engineering, science, mathematics, and related technical fields. CROME'S goals are to

- identify, nurture, and assist minority students to succeed in engineer, science, mathematics, and related technical fields;

- provide training activities and programs designed for teachers to encourage minorities to pursue careers in technical fields; and

- form partnerships among businesses and corporations, higher education institutions, school systems, professional organizations and governmental agencies to assist in fulfilling CROME's mission; and obtain resources from various sectors of the commuity to conduct program activities.

P-ACT+

The American College Testing Program offers a new testing and guidance program for high school sophomores to help students get a head start on planning for college and careers. Dubbed P-ACT+, the program consists of four parts:

- academic tests in reading, writing, mathematics, and science reasoning;
- an interest inventory;
- a study skills assessment; and
- a student information section.

The program represents a dramatic step in providing assistance to students earlier in the educational process to maximize the impact of high school as preparation for post-secondary education and careers. The interest inventory results are reported as regions on ACT's "World-of-Work Map," a graphic representation of career choices. The study skills assessment analyzes student responses to determine the student's knowledge of effective study habits in six areas:

- managing time and environment,
- reading textbooks,
- taking class notes,
- using resources,
- preparing for tests, and
- taking tests.

SCHOOL BASED PROGRAMS

In addition to bold intervention programs, several special consumer/community focused programs are available that energetic counselors can design or implement to meet local needs.

Encourage more minority students to take college entrance examinations. Scholastic Aptitude Test preparation programs are a natural extension of the counseling office in cooperation with academic disciplines such as English and mathematics. Minority students made up only 7% of the million high school students who have taken the Scholastic Aptitude Test annually. Taking the Preliminary Scholastic Aptitude Test (PSAT) as early as the tenth grade can provide the counselor and counselee with a diagnostic tool to assess areas (such as vocabulary or reading comprehension) that may need remediation. Having the school division pay for the registration fee would be an added incentive to encourage participation.

Develop programs to help students discover alternatives for financing their education and ways they can support themselves while in college.

Provide inservice for mathematics and English teachers on PSAT/SAT content. For example, mathematics scores increase with credits earned in algebra and geometry.

Increase options for post-secondary education and occupations through repeated counseling and planning sessions five-year courses of study.

Mail PSAT information to parents of all 10th and 11th grade students who are in geometry or algebra.

Promote summer enrichment programs at local universities for rising ninth grade students to learn critical thinking skills, problem solving, test-taking strategies, vocabulary, computer technology, and high school program planning to prepare students to become National Merit Semifinalist. National Merit Semifinalist are only identifed one time as part of the PSAT (PSAT/NMSQT-National Merit Scholarship Qualifying Test).

Develop a system-wide item analysis of the PSAT and give the results to home schools to develop Individual Academic Improvement Plans (IAIP).

Provide greater recognition of student academic achievement through honors banquet in each secondary school, and receptions for Presidential Academic Fitness Award nominees, National Merit Scholarship merit winners, the National Achievement Scholarship for Outstanding Negro Students, the National Hispanic Scholarship Awards Program, etc.

Have a school bulletin board showing median SAT achievement and advanced placement scores of the previous freshman class at various colleges and universities.

Inherently, counselors must ensure that all levels of students are not academically stereotyped or tracked in such a way that will endanger future college admission or college success. In addition, counselors could do the following:

develop programs with alumni to educate potential college-bound students about college life, coping skills, and survival strategies;

offer tutorial assistance, career planning, and an active career counseling program;

link choice of classes tightly with career and college preparation;

network with local colleges and universities that offer precollege programs or enrichment summer institutes for minority students;

implement an "Academic or Homework Hotline" (A local cable television or radio station could provide help to students having trouble with homework. Students could call and receive help from honor students and teachers. Such a program is not only good public relations, it also demonstrates to students and their families a community interest in their academic success and well-being); and

encourage English composition teachers to focus on critical thinking skills, analogies, vocabulary, and reading comprehension as early as the seventh grade..

THE GROWING COMPLEXITY OF FINANCING A COLLEGE EDUCATION

Federal Programs	Student Loans
State Programs	Armed Services
College and School Programs	Career Incentive Programs
Scholarships	Work-Study Programs
Grants	Subsidized Loans

More than 3,100 colleges, universities, technical institutes, junior colleges, and other institutions of higher learning are in the United States from which to choose. From 1973 to the present, the overall cost of attending a public, four-year college or university rose 143%. Even more overwhelming, the increase for private colleges or universities rose 199%.

Nearly Half of All Post-Secondary Students
Receive Financial Aid

Almost 50% of the nation's post-secondary students received some form of financial aid in 1986, according to the first comprehensive survey of how much students pay for their education. In summary, the following were reported:

> Only 6% of undergraduates relied exclusively on financial aid to pay for post-secondary education.

> Of all students enrolled in 1986, 38% received grants, 24% received loans, and 6% participated in work-study programs.

> The average amount of all aid received by full-time undergraduates was $3,813; the average of federal support was $2,973—almost twice the amount of state aid.

> The federal government was the largest single source of aid for students assisting 35% of undergraduates.

> The annual college costs reported by those surveyed averaged $6,000.

> Students at private, for-profit institutions were more likely to receive financial aid than those at public institutions or private nonprofit schools (*Education Week*, May 11, 1987).

In a recent annual survey of 3,087 of the nation's colleges and universities, the average total cost of a year at college climbed 6% in 1986-87, the sixth consecutive year that such costs had outpaced the overall inflation rate. The average cost per year for on-campus students attending four-year public colleges or universities is $5,600 or more annually.

In addition, the average annual total cost of attending a private university is over $10,000.

Based on a public opinion poll conducted by the College Board, 80% believed that college costs are rising so quickly that college will soon be unaffordable for persons from average or below average income families. Tuition at America's colleges and universities has been rising at roughly twice the rate of inflation. This means that the student's family must invest on the average from $20,800 to $42,000 in a four-year undergraduate degree. For students attending the most prestigious private institutions, the price can run to $60,000 or more.

Such increases may inadvertently create an elitist system of education in the United States; a system which eventually would be accessible only to those primarily in the upper-income levels. With the Reagan administration, student financial aid shifted from outright grants to subsidized loans. The "bottom-line" is that federal aid has significantly diminished. Many costly colleges in the early 1980s strapped with increased operating funds critically reviewed their own financial aid disbursements. Several colleges announced that in a number of admissions cases, an applicants financial aid status might affect the possibility of acceptance (Hassan & Reynolds, 1987). Some ominous projections: parents of freshmen in 2003 could expect to pay at least $64,212 for a four-year education at a public university. The average cost of obtaining a four-year degree at a private university will top $90,000.

According to Ernest L. Boyer, President of the Carnegie Foundation (1986), rising college costs take on special significance when compared with family income. In a survey of college students, they found that more than 40% of all undergraduates reported that they came from families with an annual budget (before tax income) of less than $30,000; 16% were from families with an annual (before tax) income of less than $15,000. On the average, four-year colleges or public universities cost almost 11% of the median family income. Private colleges and universities claim 29%, and elite private universities 42% of the median family income.

The cost of a college education is increasingly becoming a genuine financial burden for everyone, and a deepening chasm for low and middle income families. The average family with college aged children will find itself facing a tuition payment that will be second only to the cost of purchasing a house in a typical family's financial history.

FINANCIAL AID SOURCES
AND MISCONCEPTIONS

Financial aid officers are finding that financial aid dollars on a state and federal level are not keeping pace with the cost of attendance. Family financial planning and creative alternatives in payment plans are rapidly becoming a part of college's admissions services. College financial aid office could soon be called "family financial planning offices."

In Figure 11.1 are listed misconceptions about financial aid.

Mistaken beliefs about the costs of going to college—and the means available to help pay for it—may be a major factor in preventing many students from pursuing higher education, a 1988 survey conducted for the Council for Advancement and Support of Education (CASE) suggested.

The survey of 1,001 middle and secondary school students and other young people found, for example, that most see college as considerably more expensive than it really is. Respondents estimated that the average annual tuition and fees at a four-year state college totaled $6,841, compared with the actual average of $1,566 as measured by the College Board. For four-year private schools, students estimated annual costs at $10,843, compared with the actual $7,693.

Moreover, many young people apparently do not realize how much financial aid is available. A substantial number of those polled agreed with or were unsure about a series of statements (below), each of which, CASE said, is incorrect.

More information on the survey, conducted by the Gallop Organization, is available from CASE, Suite 400, 11 Dupont Circle, Washington, D.C. 20036-1207.

Percentage of Students Who Believe That:

College financial aid is available only from the Federal government.

Financial aid is given only to students whose parents cannot afford to pay for schooling.

Students cannot receive aid for an expensive private school if their parents can afford a state school.

Almost all financial aid is set aside for minority students.

Students with average grades do not qualify for aid even if they are accepted for admission.

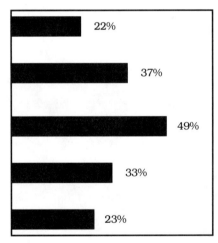

Source: *Education Week*, October, 26, 1988, Vol. VIII, No. 8

Figure 11.1. Financial aid misconceptions.

CHAPTER 12

COUNSELOR AS OCCUPATIONAL CONDUIT FOR THE NONCOLLEGE BOUND

"The talents needed are no clever hands or a strong back."
Anonymous

The noncollege bound constitute a population who may have not absorbed the prevailing middle-class belief that a college degree is an essential prerequisite for economic, personal, and social fulfillment. Approximately 20 million Americans between the ages of 16 to 24 are not likely to seek a college education (The William T. Grant Foundation Commission on Work, Family, and Citizenship, 1988). Yet, a college degree is not the only way to develop the talent of tomorrow's workers. Many opportunities exist outside the college classroom to develop marketable skills and talents which can lead to worker productivity. The successful transition from school-to-work, however, requires a strong school community commitment to close the widening gap between educational institution opportunities and career ladder employment.

SHIFTING VOCATIONAL PLANS

Astin (1967), studying the shifts in vocational plans that occur during high school, observed that the shifts tend to move students away from science and technology, and toward courses in business education. Subtle differences existed between the noncollege bound and the noncollege vocational/technical student. The two groups differ considerably from each other in their inventoried interests as measured by the Career Assessment Inventory, a blue collar version of the Strong-Campbell Interest Inventory (Thompson, 1985).

The educational orientation between noncollege bound and vocational/technical students reflects an indifference or dislike for school and course work. Vocational/technical students are substantially lower on the educational orientation than their noncollege bound counterparts. They also demonstrated a strong preference for mechanical activities and for skilled trades and technical occupations. The noncollege bound/ nontechnical student exhibited an indifference to these activities. Vocational/technical students as a whole preferred to work with things more than people, while the noncollege bound/ nonvocational technical student showed more variability as a group.

Counseling implications are present because of differences between these two groups. Vocational/technical students seem to be more career specific in occupational aspirations; to have made an occupational choice; to have assumed a vocational identity when compared to their noncollege bound counterpart. The noncollege bound seemed to be less advanced in vocational maturity or self-development reflecting a stage of vocational experimentation, with many interests.

Unrealistic vocational choices during adolescence are likely to lead to occupational instability in adulthood. Unrealistic, weak, or unstable choices are those which are inconsistent with the individual's interests, abilities, personality, attributes, work values, or available opportunities. A poor choice does not permit an individual to enhance self-concept (Super, 1957), cope with important developmental tasks (Havighurst, 1953), or achieve self-actualization (Maslow, 1954).

The period following high school for noncollege bound uncertain students could more likely be characterized as floundering or making haphazard occupational choices before beginning a stable career. In addition, the growing pattern of being disenfranchised from gainful employment results primarily from the action of prospective employers, from adult attitudes toward inexperienced youth, and from the economic health of the labor market. Often this is the period when graduates look back at their high school experience and counseling services with disdain and disappointment, as they continue to meet with rejection and frustration in the workforce because they lack job-entry skills.

Essentially, the school's task has been to find viable means to create linkages from one institutional setting to another. Parenthetically, schools are in an advantageous position to develop creative and innovative approaches for the transitional challenges confronting indecisive students. In addition to providing multiple opportunities for on-the-job training, internships, apprenticeships, and job shadowing, students are in need of realistic experiences that will take them out of the confines of the classroom and into settings where they can learn the skills, attributes, and approaches necessary for a successful transition. For example, to further innovative ways of linking education to work, the school and counselor as facilitator could become lucrative centers for part-time work and part-time education through job-sharing with other youth interested in the same arrangements. The school could develop a variety of educational leave programs or support student entrepreneur projects in which young people generate employment for themselves. A work/experience curriculum could increase a student's sense of efficacy and worth. Such orientations could reciprocate an expectation of economic independence which could increase work effort and employment following a program.

ECONOMIC BARRIERS

Recent economic data reveals that between 1979 and 1985, the United States suffered a net loss of 1.7 million manufacturing jobs. A fast-changing economy has produced millions of new jobs in the service and retail sectors, but with wages at only half the level of a typical manufacturing job. These patterns are damaging to both youth and society. The William T. Grant Foundation on Work, Family and Citizenship (1988) provides a unique perspective to explore the strengths of America's young men and women, their families, and the programs and community institutions that serve them. The commission provides the following correlations of significant barriers for youth in their transition from school-to-work.

Twenty million of America's 16-to-24 year olds will not go to college. Many of these young people will not be able to support themselves financially or provide for a family, thus they probably will become part of a pattern of declining economic status and diminished opportunities. Noncollege youth are losing ground financially. Changes in America's economy have resulted in drastically fewer well-paying jobs in fields that were previously open to them, particularly, manufacturing.

Many of the new jobs available to high school graduates are in the service sector, often low-paying with few benefits. Other staggering statistics reveal the following:

> Employed young men ages 20 to 24 with only a high school diploma earned 28% less in 1986 than their counterparts in 1973. Income deceased 24% for Whites and 44% for Blacks.

> In 1984, 12% of all young men ages 20 to 24 reported having no income at all, as compared with 7.3% in 1973.

> In 1985, only 43.7% of young men 20 to 24 years old with a high school diploma had incomes high enough to support a three-person family above the poverty level, as compared to 60% of similar youth in 1973.

> Of the 3.1 million family households headed by youth under 25 in 1985, 30% had incomes below the poverty level, almost double the rate of the early 1970s (Thiers, 1988).

Far fewer youth, even with high school diplomas, are now able to obtain full-time, year-round employment. In March 1986, nearly 75% of all male high school graduates (under 20 and not attending college) were working. However, only 65% of these young male workers held a full-time job. Overall, less than 49% of America's noncollege bound high school graduates were working full-time one or two years after receiving their diplomas. By contrast, in March 1974, 73% of the male graduates held full-time jobs.

Similarly, in March 1986, only 42% of female high school graduates (under age 20 and not attending college) were employed full-time, a rate one-fourth lower than in March 1968.

In 1986, young males 20 to 24 who had high school diplomas and who had jobs earned 28% less in constant dollars than the comparable group of youth in 1973. The income drop was 24% for Whites and 44% lower for Blacks.

While earning power among working youth had declined, more of these young people also report no earnings. In 1984, 12% of all 20 to 24 year old males said they had no earnings, up from 7.3% in 1973.

Of the 3.1 million family households headed by youth under age 25 in 1985, 30% had incomes below the poverty level, nearly double the rate of the early 1970s.

Among families headed by a person under 25, the poverty rate almost doubled from 1973 to 1985, from 15.9 to 30.2%. The poverty rate of young White families doubled from 11.7 to 24.7%, while the rate for young Black families also rose markedly, from 42.9% in 1973 to 62.1% in 1985.

Among Black high school graduates under age 20, and not enrolled in college, only 49% were working, and of those, only 45% were employed full-time. Thus, only one of every five Black graduates was able to find full-time employment.

Analyses of data by Professor Andrew Sum of Northeastern University from the "National Longitudinal Survey of Young Americans" (The W.T. Grant Foundation Commission on Work, Family, and Citizenship, 1988) also reveals significant correlations between levels of academic skills and youths' prospects for participation in society. Research is confirming the high cost of failure in school. For examples:

Girls, who by age 14 or 15 have basic skills scores in the bottom fifth, are five times as likely to become mothers before age 16 as those scoring in the top one-half.

Young women, who by age 17 or 18 have very weak basic skills, are two and one-half times as likely to be mothers before age 20 as those in the top one-half of the basic skills distribution.

Young men who by age 17 or 18 have very weak basic skills are three times as likely to become fathers before age 20 as those scoring in the top one-half.

Young adults ages 18 to 23 with basic academic skills in the bottom fifth of the distribution relative to their peers in the top half are

- 8.8 time more likely to have left school without a diploma,

- 8.6 times more likely to have a child out of wedlock,

- 5.4 times more likely to be receiving some form of public assistance,

- 5.0 times more likely to be poverty-level in income and not in schooling of any type,

- 3.6 times more likely to be not working, not in school, and not taking care of a child, and

- 2.2 times more likely to have been arrested in the previous year.

When youth who graduated in 1980 in the bottom quarter of their class are compared with graduates in the top one-half of their class:

- those in the bottom quarter were only one-fifth as likely to be in college (either graduate or undergraduate school), five years after graduation; and

- those in the top one-half of academic skills distribution were 70 times more likely to be enrolled in college and majoring in engineering, math, or physical science programs than those in the bottom quarter.

Young people who do not attend college need help in their transition from high school to a viable career. These young people need more systematic follow-up and assistance. Educators are beginning to recognize that they should form alliances with employers and community leaders to give them a viable incentive and appropriate counseling. Other suggestions include the following:

Redirecting vocational education. Vocational education alone does not prepare young people well for specific jobs. The hands-on approach, however, does offer students a valuable and effective way to acquire the basic skills and general ability they will need to be successful in a wide range of endeavors.

Provide incentives. Low motivation and low expectations for success in the workplace limit students' educational achievement. Recent experiments guaranteeing post-secondary and continuing education, guaranteed employment, or guaranteed training to students who do well seem to motivate young people to work hard in school.

Align career information and counseling. Such services offered in the schools or through community agencies, can make young people aware of job opportunities, career options, by exposing them to adult role models.

***Community mentor and community-based organiza-
tions.*** Such programs as Project Success in Roanoke,
Virginia, and the Dropout Prevention Program in New
York City, rely extensively on community groups to
provide many essential counseling and supportive
services.

Some strategies that employers, schools, and youth-serving
organizations can collectively undertake to facilitate the
transition from school to work could be to

- expand the hiring of recent high school graduates
  directly into career ladder positions rather than
  low-wage, dead end jobs;

- reevaluate hiring criteria, making certain that ability
  to do the job is considered more important than
  age, credentials, dress, or diction;

- make apprenticeship training available to 16 to
  20 year olds;

- have potential employers work with schools to provide
  better cooperative education placements for students;

- establish a career information center to provide
  job-hunting skills, educational and training
  opportunities, and financial aid possibilities;

- create incentives such as guaranteed employment,
  training opportunities, and financial aid incentives;

- create incentives such as guaranteed employment
  and training to students in local schools conditional
  on successful completion of basic skills or other
  academic criteria;

- emphasize primary prevention and early intervention
  of students in academic trouble and improve the
  school-to-work transition processes;

- make improved guidance and counseling services more readily available to "all" students, not merely the problem student or the college bound student;

- work with public and private authorities to develop creative incentives and substantial long-term rewards (e.g., college tuition, apprenticeships, guaranteed jobs) for excellence in academic, service, or work-related activities; and

- develop contractual relationships with neighborhood merchants for young participants to provide needed supervised services in return for financial support of special community organization programs.

MARGINAL STUDENTS

Most public schools have a percentage of students who feel that they will not experience success in school; those students who are at the lower one-half of achievement and in the bottom 25% of the class as measured by grade point average. They also are the subpopulation within the school who dislike academic work and also have attendance problems. Many of these marginal students have a unique peer group which maintains its own social system and serves to alienate them from adults and peers.

Traditional intervention programs have focused on the preconceived notion of "what is wrong" with these students. Assumptions often focus on tracking students into unstimulating courses that stigmatize the students as remedial and less likely to enhance intellectual development. The perpetual circle of failure, truancy, and remediation accumulate to increase the probability that these students will not engage in the kinds of intellectual activities required to participate in contemporary society.

According to Wehlage (1983) a number of effective programs do exist, such as Reuther Education at Large (REAL), Reuther Alternative High School (Kenosha, Wisconsin).

The program has one full-time counselor/coordinator
and three half-time teachers certified in math, science,
English, and social studies.

The program is self-contained and students stay together
as a group, taking all their courses from the four staff
members.

REAL's important features include flexibility afforded
both staff and students, and group identity that is
established by keeping the small group of students
together all day.

REAL's experimental component in the second semester
includes gutting and renovating an old house or building
in the community. In conjunction with contractors and
labor unions, students are taught about wiring, plumbing,
heating, dry walling, and a variety of construction
skills.

Another REAL experimental component is one where
students start a small business based on the Junior
Achievement Model. Involvement in service projects
is a central component.

Another collaborate project is the Lincoln Educational
Alternative Program (LEAP), Lincoln High School, Wisconsin
Rapids, Wisconsin.

LEAP serves 25 students selected by the program's
two full-time teachers.

The program is two semesters long and prepares students
to reenter the schools traditional curriculum.

LEAP courses are individualized to remediate students
and build their self-confidence in their ability to perform
academically.

LEAP is self-contained.

A unique component is enrollment in a psychology class with an emphasis on group counseling and coping skills dealing with personal, social, and family problems and human behavior. The course sets the tone and builds a spirit of cohesiveness and community.

Wehlage (1983) offered the following suggestions for local program planning for intervention with the marginal student:

Develop a formal written plan or proposal that spells out a rationale, describes the target population, states program goals, outlines administrative operations, and describes courses to be offered.

Take an inventory of assets and strengths of personnel, as well as roadblocks which may be encountered with administration.

Develop criteria for admission and termination into and out of the program.

Survey the community to identify sources of support and sites for the experimental and work components such as: Optimists, Rotary, Chamber of Commerce, daycare facilities, shopping centers, community colleges, as well as a host of service organizations are all potential resources.

Have on-going community and team building activities routinely such as parties, competitions, ceremonies, and recognition.

Planning academic components so that some work will be

- individualized;
- drill and practice;
- cooperative and group centered;
- explicit, short-term, and clearly achievable; and
- designed to challenge students and encourage personal growth.

Recognize that planning the experimental component involves

- recruiting work sites,
- monitoring sites to ensure students are punctual and reliable, and
- monitoring to ensure that adults understand the purpose and goals as a written contract.

Evaluate the program according to written objectives such as changes in attendance, achievement, credits, and testimony from students, parents, teachers and employers. Information should be shared with the school and the community.

Inherently, for most young people who have dropped out of school both physically and emotionally, more hours of traditional schooling in traditional settings will not be the answer.

The William T. Grant Foundation Commission on Work, Family, and Citizenship (1988) recommended the following alternatives:

Intensive training in academic skills. This component should be added to all employment training programs that do not currently incorporate it. Concentrated remediation using Individualized Academic Improvement Plans (IAIP) and competency based curricula should be developed.

Job Corps. Evaluations of the nation's largest training program for dropouts has shown that Job Corps graduates have higher earnings, remain employed longer, and more often go to full-time study. The Job Corps provides society a net return of $1.46 for every dollar invested. Those who took part in the Job Corps earned an average of 15% more per year than a similar group of nonparticipants. A higher share of participants also completed high school, entered the military, and stayed off social service roles. Although studies reveal that the cost per participant in the Job Corps has been high (currently about 9,500) the benefits of the program exceed the cost.

The Job Training Partnership Act (JTPA). The potential programs under the JTPA for serving at-risk youth has not been adequately realized; only 5% of eligible youth are currently being served. Moreover, these programs tend to direct their efforts to the young people who are easiest to reach, teach, and place in jobs.

Alternative School Program. Hundreds of alternative secondary schools throughout the nation offer dropouts or potential dropouts a last opportunity to resume their education. Success programs challenge students academically and provide individual counseling by caring adults.

The Armed Forces. Although only 9% of all recruits lack high school diplomas, demographic changes may increase this proportion dramatically. Armed Forces' programs designed to upgrade the academic and work skills of members should be expanded, in order to guarantee that no member will return to civilian life without both a general equivalency diploma and a marketable job skills.

In conclusion, the school counselor must continue to develop skills and methods that are unprecedented in order to deal with the specific needs of the subgroups within each school population. Unless this challenge is met, youth unemployment and discontentment with schooling will persist as critical issues facing educators.

Fact sheets on topics for career decisions, job seeking, and job seeking skills can be used to provide career entry information in a concise and factual manner.

CHAPTER **13**

PROGRAM DEVELOPMENT

"Alice: Would you please tell me which way I ought to go from here?"

"Chesire cat: That depends on where you want to get to."

Alice in Wonderland

Unlike research, program development and evaluation are processes designed to collect relevant information for use in making decisions about counselee needs and current counseling programs and services. Essentially, "what gets measured gets done." The inherent benefits to counselors, students, and constituents of the school community (although not all inclusive) are

- to provide evidence of the positive impact of counseling programs and services to students, faculty, parents, and community organizations;

- to identify the needs not met with the present program;

- to determine the relative effectiveness of programs, services, methods, and materials, to date;

- to obtain information for designing a staff development and parent consultation program;

- to provide information for support of the present program or for enhancing specific areas such as clerical help, parent volunteers, and or more staff; and

- to clarify and communicate the role of the school counselor and exemplary services as an integral part of the school program.

Historically, school counselors have resisted the potential of systematically planning, implementing, and evaluating their school counseling program. When counselors fail to evaluate their services, others tend to do it for them and frequently with inappropriate or inadequate data. School counseling programs and services are invariably assessed every time an administrator, school board, or school division makes a decision about fiscal commitments, facilities, personnel, or resources. Numerous authors (Peer, 1985; Aubrey, 1983; Hayden & Pohlmann, 1981; Shaw, 1977) have openly criticized counselors' aversion to program development and accountability. All critics stress the potential for change. Demands for accountability, however, generates a variety of anxious responses from educators:

- some react with anger and frustration,

- some withdraw and become cynical, and

- others tend to focus program goals and services to only that which can be measured.

With the growing tendency for counselors to become more involved in the "services" curriculum, many seem beleaguered by occupational stress from task overload. Task overload occurs when too many activities are required without enough time, energy, material, resources, or staff to adequately complete the task. Task overload becomes a more serious dilemma when some tasks are not essential counseling activities. Counselor roles which assume all residual and ancillary administrative and secretarial tasks (such as clerical work, discipline, attendance, schedule changes, and athletic eligibilities) remain incongruent when compared to counselor preparation programs.

School counselors are often thrust into a compromising condition between ideology of specific role and function; incompatible institutional pressures; conflicting organizational goals; and increasing performance expectations from colleagues, consumers, and constituents. A serious need exists to clearly articulate role and function and to operationalize counselor efforts in a more consumer/community centered program model (Ibrahim, Helms, Wilson, & Thompson, 1984). Inherently, school counselors work in an accountability-based system and they are consciously forced to examine their effectiveness within the unique social system of school-as-institution, or school-as-community.

ROLE CONFLICT AND
ROLE AMBIGUITY

The range of tasks and functions normally assigned to school guidance and counseling programs serve to further dilute the resources available for counseling, and at best is wasteful of professional counselor skills. In addition, a disproportionate distribution of core programs and services exist across localities, as well as inconsistent student-to-counselor ratios which may vary from 170:1 to 510:1 in the same school division. This generates much public skepticism regarding accountability and continuity of programs and services, within and between school divisions across the nation.

As early as 1964, Kahn, Wolfe, Quinn, Snoek, and Rosenthal suggested chronic role conflict and ambiguity often resulted in a "rather marked sense of futility" (1964, p. 120). **Role conflict** results when incompatible demands are placed on the worker (Harrison, 1980). Role conflict is the simultaneous occurrence of two or more sets of inconsistent, expected role behaviors for an individual task or function. This invariably occurs, for example, when school counselors are asked to make out schedule changes or confirm athletic elegibilities when a great many students need personal or group counseling.

Role ambiguity is a lack of clarity regarding the appropriate behavior for a particular occupation (Abdek-Halim, 1982;

Beehr & Newman, 1978; McGrath, 1976). Role ambiguity can occur when the counselor has no clear knowledge of his or her role and function, is considered quasi-administrative, or lacks the personnel to adequately complete the task. Role conflict and role ambiguity invariably create stress on the occupation of school counseling. The challenge for contemporary school counselors, according to Hargens and Gysberg (1984) is to make the transition from the ancillary services concept to that of a comprehensive, developmental program; a program that is an equal partner with other education processes such as instruction or extracurricular activities.

Other contemporary researchers, such as Day and Sparacio (1980) and Wells and Ritter (1979), found a number of disturbing role mutations that have seriously damaged the professional image of school counselors. Peer (1985) in a national survey further revealed the lack of statewide commitments to the content and quality of school counseling services which seem to undermine the overall quality of programs. He further outlined a strong trend toward counselor role abuse, weak program design, and the underdelivery of services in such areas as career and academic advising, group guidance, and group counseling. Only when counselors can collectively describe their role and function will they be able to respond to these criticisms, and develop comprehensive models of accountability. Fundamentally, counselors need to routinely examine the rationale and goals for counseling programs and services and examine whether program goals are compatible with annual school plans and consumer needs.

Concurrently, the broad range of benefits entitled "student services" continues to exist with no consistent definition or standard pattern for providing these services (Carey, 1977). Confusion punctuates the responsibilities and the functions of school counseling and other support services. Trends in recent studies point to the blatant discrepancies which exist between services students report needing and the services they actually receive. For example, in 1971, Van Riper surveyed 735 ninth grade students and found that "the counselor was rather easily identified as a person who helped with school problems; and not clearly identified as a person who helped with personal problems" (p. 54). Levitson (1977) administered a Guidance Self-Evaluation Survey to 550 high school students grades ten, eleven, and twelve and found that students would rather consult a parent (29%) or a friend (54%) than a counselor (only 4%) if they had a personal problem. Wells and Ritter (1979) with a sample of 550 high school students found similar results.

Students would go to a counselor for help to change a class (81%) or to determine graduation requirements (80%). The same group of students, however, were not likely to seek out a counselor for help with a problem with a friend (6%), with a question about sex (4%), or with a personal problem (4%).

Most recently, Hutchinson and Bottorff (1986) sought to compare students' assessments of their expressed needs for counseling services with what they actually received from their high school counselor. Participants in the study consisted of 250 college freshmen from 21 states representing 152 high school guidance and counseling programs in a wide variety of small, medium, and large schools. These authors found the largest discrepancy between the services students reported needing and the services they actually received in the area of career counseling. A majority of students (89%) believed they needed career counseling in high school; only 40% of those students surveyed, however, reported that they received career counseling (Hutchinson & Bottorff, 1986). In addition, three of every five students (60%) placed counseling for personal problems in a category of high need. Yet, only one of every five students (21%) received such counseling in school. Finally, students in this study thought they had little need for four services offered by their counselors: checking attendance and truancy (1%); disciplining (3%); record keeping (3%); and testing (10%). Student self-reports seem to substantiate a frequent criticism of school counseling programs that appear to function quite differently from counselor preparation programs, their defined roles, or from the expressed needs of students served. Student self-reports of counseling services are perhaps the most disheartening.

Even though the most important resource a student has is the school counselor, students report that: "they don't point you in the right direction; that they are there only to help students with very serious emotional problems; and that the price for a conversation with a caring adult was to risk being considered a problem case" by one's peers (Powell, Farrar, & Cohen, 1985, p. 46). The more sophisticated the counseling program, the greater the pride it took in its successful extrication from traditional tasks such as scheduling, disciplining, college admissions, and routine advising, the activities which serve to distort the whole counseling relationship (Powell et al., 1985, p. 49).

Moreover, what are often defined as counseling functions do not require training and preparation, do not require special skill, and can be handled by most of the paraprofessional or volunteer personnel currently utilized in the schools. One recourse for the school counselor, practitioner, or counselor educator is to develop and implement a comprehensive, consumer-specific delivery of programs and services.

PREDICTORS OF QUALITY SERVICES

From the perspective of program development, Wagenaar (1982) found two categories of variables which are predictors of quality services. The first, is counseling resources as seen by students which include

- educational counseling,
- employment counseling,
- self-awareness counseling,
- frequency of discussion of future plans with counselors,
- counselor visibility, and
- availability of desired information.

The second, is counseling activities as defined by counselors and include the amount of time spent with students, and how this time is divided among specific areas such as career guidance, the variety of employment placement strategies implemented, the number of college funding sources recommended, the ratio of students to counselors, and the use of interest inventories.

Unfortunately, school counseling has waxed and waned around a set of loosely related programs and services whose focus shifted with changing demographics, and cultural trends, or administrative expectations. Schools have sought to provide "comprehensive" services by the capricious addition of new strategies and activities in response to the identification of new student needs. As a consequence, a number of selected institutional problems have evolved:

- duplication of efforts by several school personnel;
- confusion about counselors' roles and increasing ambiguity;
- lack of continuity in services and coordination of activities;
- unresearched assumption about the relationship between counselor activities and program goals to student needs and outcomes;
- focus of attention and energy on a few student subgroups (e.g., the college bound, special education students, and behavior problems);
- unrealistic expectations for the accountability of school counseling problems and services; and
- discrepancies in identifying, monitoring, and evaluating the outcomes of programs, activities, and services.

A Comprehensive Consumer/ Community Centered Model

Instead of a set of loosely related services, school counselors need to operationalize their efforts into a comprehensive consumer/community center program model which would

- consist of interrelated and interdependent services organized around an accountable consumer-based model;
- become an integral part of the entire education process, involving parents, students, faculty, and administration in the students' course of study and experiences;

- address the social, emotional, educational, and developmental needs of all students K to 12;
- be student-outcome oriented rather than counselor activity centered; and
- contain a self-monitoring system to provide for systematic program improvement which reflects the needs of the school/community.

COUNSELOR OBJECTIVES VERSUS PROGRAM OBJECTIVES

Finally, Lombana (1985) maintained that it is important to acknowledge two important objectives of equal value which should orchestrate the counselor's work: counselee (student) objectives and program (institutional) objectives. The difference between the two types were illustrated by Lombana (1985) and are shown in Figure 13.1.

The outcome of a counselee objective is demonstrated in terms of specific student behavior or accomplishment. When the counselor assume responsibility for student behavior, program objectives may reflect outcomes such as the following:

- students will decrease their dropout rate by 5%,
- college bound seniors will identify three colleges to which they plan to apply by October 31, and
- peer counselors will be able to model attending behaviors and active listening by the end of six training sessions.

The outcome of program objectives is demonstrated in terms of counselor behavior or accomplishment. The counselor explicitly assumes responsibility for performing a function for the benefit of others, but he/she is not accountable for the ultimate behavior changes in other individuals. Program objectives provide credibility for many counseling tasks, demonstrate the value of job descriptions, and illustrate the necessity for counselors to negotiate their roles to meet institutional norms. Counselee objectives reflect a commitment to identified consumer needs of students, parents, and staff.

(Continued on Page 278)

Differences

Program Objectives		Student Objectives
* derived from job descriptions	* derived from need assessments	
* target = counselor(s)	* targets student(s)	
* outcome stated as counselor accomplishments	* outcome stated as student behavior(s)	
* stable over time	* changes often	
* related to program goals	* related to program goals	
* outcome is observable and measureable	* outcome is observable and measureable	
* provides specific direction for counselor(s)	* provides specific direction for counselor(s)	

Similarities

Source: Lombana, J.H. (1985). Guidance accountability: A new look at an old problem. *The School Counselor, 32,* 5, 340-346. Reprinted by permission.

Figure 13.1. Counselor objectives versus program development.

A comprehensive school counseling program, however, should be based on both program and student objectives. An illustration is as follows:

The counselor will coordinate the school testing program.

The counselor will coordinate parent-teacher conferences.

The counselor will facilitate small group counseling.

All seniors will develop tentative post-secondary plans by November of their senior year.

At least 80% of the students who participate in the "young mothers group" will graduate.

At least 95% of the teachers who participated in the teacher/parent conferencing program will show significant improvement in their conferencing skills with parents.

The first three items are program objectives characterized by a focus on counselor implementation based on formal job descriptions, role statements, and district-wide performance objectives which remain relatively stable over the course of time. The last three items focus on counselee or other parent/teacher/consumer/community needs. These evolve from needs assessment data and will fluctuate as consumer-based needs change. Student and program objectives establish the context in which the counselor performs routine and long-term programs and services. This is enhanced with a student-focused model for the development of counseling service (Harmon & Baron, 1982). From this perspective, activities, and strategies are observable, measurable, and lend credence to performance based evaluation procedures. Potential intervention is also outlined from crisis intervention to developmental counseling. In Figure 13.2 is presented a student-focused model for the development of counseling services.

In Figure 13.3 (see pages 281-286) is represented selected outcomes on seven constructs for student outcome which operationalizes both program objectives and student outcomes to foster a consumer/community centered program model and

(Continued on Page 280)

Purpose of Intervention	Levels of Intervention	Goals	Strategies
Crisis	I Students and those in the immediate environment	To intervene in the crisis situation to (1) stabilize the individual(s) in crisis; (2) facilitate on-going assistance and/or referral; and (3) provide support, reassurance, and/or counseling for those in the immediate environment affected by the student in crisis.	Walk-in Counseling Crisis Team Telephone Counseling Case-centered Consultation Support Groups
	II. Staff, faculty, student leaders, peer counselors and others who work with students.	(1) To communicate information concerning the recognition of students in crisis; (2) to provide training in crisis intervention; and to provide consultation for those working with the student(s) in crisis.	Case-centerd Consultation Workshops Case Conferences Media Presentations Cooperative Planning
	III Social System	To identify and remedy environmental factors which exacerbate student crisis.	Environmental Design
Remediation	I Students and those in their immediate environment.	To assist in overcoming skill deficits and to resolve intrapsychic and environmental conflicts.	Individual Counseling Group Counseling Skill Development/Focus Groups Telephone Counseling
	II Staff, faculty, student leaders, peer counselors, and others who work with students	To communicate information related to remedial resources, the detection of students in need of such services and referral procedures.	Case Conference Case-centered Consultation Media Presentations
	III Social System	To advocate systematic changes for enabling students with emotional problems to function within the university community.	Committe Work Consultation Media Environmental Design
Development	I Students and those in the immediate environment	To assist students in exploring, understanding, and acting upon the social, emotional, and cognitive dimensions of various developmental tasks (e.g., establishing personal identity, developing autonomy, learning to make decisions and to manage emotions).	Developmental Structured Groups Workshops Media Presentations Academic Coursework Seminars Informal Classes
	II Staff, faculty, student leaders, peer counselors, and others who work with students.	To provide training and consultation in methods and skills for facilitating student growth and development.	Program Development Consultation Case-centered Consultation Workshops Presentations Media
	III Social System	(1) To identify and advocate the alleviation of barriers within the system which hinder student development; and (2) assist in the creation of environments which provide a proper balance of challenge and support for students in their growth process.	Research Consultation Committee Work Environmental Design

Source: Harmon, F.M., & Baron, A. (1982). The student-focused model for the development of counseling services. *The Personnel & Guidance Journal,* *60,* 5, p. 49. Reprinted by permission.

Figure 13.2. A student-focused model for the development of counseling services.

delivery of targeted services. A similar outline needs to be made for each major aspect of the counseling and guidance program, e.g., educational/occupational information, parent-teacher consultation, individual and group counseling, and pupil appraisal and assessment.

SUMMARY

In summary, educators as counselors should be encouraged to help plan evaluation studies to appraise the quality of counseling programs and services. Specific suggestions for improving programs and services should be obtained from a cross-section of the constituents served. Dialogues about accountability should be heeded as an opportunity to provide clear, concise definitions of counselor role and functions; to improve cooperation among school professionals in implementing objectives; and to develop clearly stated goals. With systematic evaluation and routine accountability, educators can securely defend services and obtain adequate fiscal resources to support them.

Construct: Program Development and Research

Outcomes: To maintain on-going monitoring of programs, student outcomes, and progress.
To provide feedback for continuing program development, implementation, and improvement.
To indicate strengths and weaknesses of the counseling program.

Target Population: Teachers, administrators, students, community organizations, and advisory boards.

Developmental Program Objectives	Guidance & Counseling Strategies	Outcomes	Resources
Program objectives and counselor functions are determined by the needs of students, legislative mandates, and school/community expectations	Assist with follow-up studies of former student's post-high school experiences. Implement opinion surveys to solicit evaluations of the guidance program by students, teachers, administrators, and parents.	Assess and respond to student and community needs. Analyze and respond to existing program needs. Assess available and potential resources.	Bulk mailings of follow-up postcards or questionnaires. Counseling Program Evaluation Forms Time Logs Counseling Program Manual

Construct: Educational/Occupational Information

Outcomes: To develop an awareness of the opportunities in the educational setting.
To develop an awareness of the world of work and an accurate occupational self-concept.

Target Populations: All Students

Developmental Program Objectives	Guidance & Counseling Strategies	Outcomes	Resources
The student will decide on a curriculum and electives that are consistent with his/her abilities, interests, and future career objectives. The student will become aware of the training requirements and needed skills at different occupational levels.	Course registration Selected Group Activities on employment counseling, job placement, job seeking and keeping strategies Meetings with representatives from post-secondary opportunities	Students will have selected a curriculum consistent with his/her ability and interests. Course selection will be in agreement with tentative career selection	Interest and Aptitude Batteries Faculty and Staff Community Speakers Occupational Outlook Handbook Career Center and Materials

Figure 13.3. Student Outcome Program Development Model.

Figure 13.3. Continued.

Construct: Educational/Occupational Information (continued)

Developmental Program Objectives	Guidance & Counseling Strategies	Outcomes	Resources
The student will participate in activities to develop an awareness of his/her potential occupational abilities, interests, and strengths.	Use of the Career Center and Information Systems S.A.T. preparation programs Local tours of business and industry Individual and group guidance Shadowing experiences	Students will verbalize and demonstrate understanding of training requirements, skill development and economic and social rewards	GED Procedures Armed Services Resources

Construct: Coordination, Information Management, and Dissemination, Time Management

Outcomes: To select, organize, and utilize educational, occupational, and personal development information.
To provide students and parents with information to make decisions.
To employ time management strategies to prevent task overload.

Target Population: Students, Parents, Faculty

Developmental Program Objectives	Guidance & Counseling Strategies	Outcomes	Resources
The counselor serves as the liaison between the school, the student, and the parent; follow up services and conferences. The counselor establishes and maintains communication networks with human service personnel at all levels within the school division.	Placement-registration, special education coordination Student Records—enrollments, withdrawal, record maintenance, reporting to parents, credit check, grade point average Scheduling, adjustments, registration, returning from alternative education	Provide systematic organization of vital information Orient or monitor student new to school, students returning from alternative education, students with academic or behavioral difficulties; students who drop out	Cumulative Record Release of Information Form Computerized Information Services Verification of Birth Application Grade Transmittal Form

Figure 13.3. Continued.

Construct: Parent Consultation/Teacher Consultation

Outcomes: To encourage the development of an accurate and realistic concept of the student in the educational setting.

Target Population: Parents, Students, and Teachers

Developmental Program Objectives	Guidance & Counseling Strategies	Outcomes	Resources
The parents will be given an opportunity to become aware of their child's abilities, interests, and achievements.	Group conferences with parents to process testing information, interests, and abilities	Parents will have a knowledge of their child's abilities, interests, and achievements.	Easy to understand resource material
	Clarify tests' relationships to vocational directions	Parents will be able to recognize their child's strengths and weaknesses.	Permanent records as appropriate
The parents will be aided in becoming aware of the vocational abilities, interests and aptitudes, potentialities, and limitations of their children.	Publications/Visitations	Parents will be able to link their child's aptitudes and interests to perceived occupational directions.	Slide presentations
	Parent Conference Days		Newsletters
Parents will be given the opportunity to formulate educational expectations for their child which are consistent with the child's interests, abilities, and tentative career choice.	Junior Parent Night		Staff, Parents, Outside Resources Speakers
	Back to School Night		
	Newsletters		
	Parent Career Planning and Development Groups		

Construct: Individual and Group Counseling

Outcomes: To assist students to increase knowledge of self and others, and to eliminate self-defeating behaviors.
To assist students to learn appropriate modes of interpersonal interaction and communication with the school, home, and community environments.

Target Population: Students, Parents, Teachers, and Administrators

Developmental Program Objectives	Guidance & Counseling Strategies	Outcomes	Resources
The counselor shall know and apply theories and techniques which facilitate effective individual and group counseling relationships and provide assistance with interpersonal concerns.	Survey students to determine topics for individual or group counseling; provide the needed opportunities during the year when the topics may be discussed in a secure environment.	Students will demonstrate their needs on survey data, anonymously.	Counseling Units:
		Students will be able to describe their strengths and list areas they wish to improve.	Loss
			Leadership
			Conflict Resolution
			Communication

Figure 13.3. Continued.

Construct: Individual and Group Counseling (Continued)

Developmental Program Objectives	Guidance & Counseling Strategies	Outcomes	Resources
The counselor shall understand that counseling is developmental emphasizing the acquisition of knowledge and skills needed for self-direction and independence.	Collaborate with teachers, administrators, and parents to identify and refer students in need of special services, such as mental health, special education, rehabilitation, welfare, and health.	Students will demonstrate appropriate developmental social skills when interacting with others.	Divorce Assertiveness Dealing with Anger Weight Groups Eating Disorders
The counselor shall provide intervention strategies for students who experience some unique developmental concerns as the handicapped, gifted, students with chemical abuse problems, children of single parent families, and minority students.	Develop procedures by which teachers may identify and refer students with learning problems, students who are disruptive, and those who may be potential dropouts.	Students will be able to list the steps in the decision-making process and apply them to a specific situation. Teachers and administratorss will utilize counselor skills and services to promote a school climate that is conductive to students' social and emotional growth.	Decision-Making Teen Mothers/Fathers New School Orientation Dating
In individual or group counseling, the counselor provides confidential setting to assist students to examine and understand their feelings, attitudes, concerns, or behavior.	Arrange conferences for the purpose of studying the individual needs of students; participants in case conferences would be counselors, teachers, administrators, parents, visiting teachers, nurses, doctors, school psychologists, and others who may contribute to a better understanding of the student.	Teachers, parents, and administrators will seek the input from counselors for child study teams and parent-teacher conferences. Teachers, parents, and administrators will support the counseling process.	Step-Parents Step-Teen COA's Alateen Brochures
The counselor functions in such a way that he/she is perceived as being accessible, concerned and an understanding helper.	Distribute to students, parents, teachers, and administrators information explaining the services of the guidance and counseling department, including the availability of individual and group counseling and the procedures for securing these services.	Teachers and administrators will provide opportunities for counselors to meet students in groups. Students will become more self-sufficient.	Flyers Newspaper Articles Conflict Management Peer Counseling Handbook Resources
The counselor will demonstrate an understanding of growth and change in human behavior, and apply techniques and processes which are appropriate to individual or group needs.		Students will demonstrate their needs on survey data and questionnaire anonymously.	Ways to Increase Self-Esteem

Figure 13.3. Continued.

Construct: Individual and Group Counseling (Continued)

Developmental Program Objectives	Guidance & Counseling Strategies	Outcomes	Resources
The counselor will use counseling procedures that enhance self awareness and implement positive behavior and facilitate students' participation in both groups and individual counseling.	Provide information in the counseling office and at meetings that the counselor serves as facilitator in conferences; consultant in interpreting individual and group needs, and counsels for individuals and groups.	Students will be able to describe their strengths and list areas they wish to improve.	Group Counseling Resources Workshop in Skill Development
The counselor is able to establish with the student(s) a close relationship characterized by respect, understanding, openness, acceptance, and trust.	Provide group counseling for students in crisis such as separation and divorce, underachievers, teenage mothers, or other school adjustment problems.	Students will demonstrate appropriate developmental social skills when interacting with others.	Assertiveness Skills Problem-solving Skills Stress-management Skills
The counselor recognizes group dynamics; i.e., typical stages of group development; various leadership styles; and conditions under which groups enhance personal growth.	Conduct counseling groups for enhancing personal growth of students who do not have serious problems; asset to understand themselves better in areas of communication, decision-making.	Students will be able to list the steps in such life skills as decision making and conflict management and integrate it into their beheavioral repertoire.	Conflict-resolution Skills Interpersonal-relations Skills Intrapersonal Skills
The student will become aware of self-defeating behaviors as well as behaviors that foster greater interpersonal relationships.	Group counseling for target groups and self-referred students.		
The student will become aware of his/her needs in relation to a variety of social groups of which he/she is a part.	Classroom guidance and/or individual or group counseling for such probelms or areas of interest as: dating, sex education, drug and alcohol abuse, running away, family conflicts, interpersonal relations, underachievement, absenteeism, study skills, personal/educational/career goal setting, student adjustment, self-concept, and peer pressure.		
The student will become aware of his/her interpersonal strengths and blind spots in his/her fucntioning in various social systems of which he/she is a part.	Peer facilitation or peer counseling groups		

Figure 13.3. Continued.

Construct: Pupil Appraisal Assessment

Outcomes: To assist students and faculty to develop realistic expectations based on the assessment of interests, aptitude, and abilities.

Target Population: Students, Faculty, and Parents

Developmental Program Objectives	Guidance & Counseling Strategies	Outcomes	Resources
The counselor shall assess the characteristics of students; analyze and interpret data; communicate student needs and potentials; apply results in program planning.	Explanation of standardized testing program; modifications of testing program. Relate academic grades to standardized test results	Students, faculty, and parents will indicate understanding of test results through identification of abilities, interests, and achievements in the educational setting.	Test Profiles and Manuals Videos and Films Portions of Student Records
The counselor shall demonstrate knowledge of major functions, strengths, and limitations of those tests and instruments that are widely used to assess aptitude, achievements, interests, and personality traits.	Synthesize data in order to answer questions about individuals and groups. Provide group and individual test interpretation: DAT, SRA, SAT, PSAT/MERIT, ACT, ASVAB, KUDAR INTEREST INVENTORY, MINIMUM COMPETENCY TEST, CAREER ASSESSMENT SURVEY, LITERACY PASSPORT TEST, IOWA TEST OF BASIC SKILLS	Students, faculty, and parents will have knowledge of how their grades relate to standardized testing and will be able to answer questions asked about this relationship.	Registration Guides Student Handbook Faculty Handbook

Construct: Professionalism and Ethical Standards

Outcomes: To demonstrate to the school and community that counselors are professional educators who are dedicated to the enhancement of the worth and dignity, potential and uniqueness of each individual.

Target Population: Parents, Teachers, Administrators, and Students

Developmental Program Objectives	Guidance & Counseling Strategies	Outcomes	Resources
The counselor shall articulate ways to make the school goals explicit and public; make the counselors' contributions to institutional goals specific; and foster mutual accountability for goal achievement.	School, community and consumer needs assement Annual school goals In-service programs for teachers Workshops for parents News articles in school or local paper	Annual school goals and counseling program goals are compatible. Performance and outcome are accountable to consumers. Roles of support personnel are clearly understood.	Faculty Handbook Counselors Support Personnel Other Helping Professionals in the community

CHAPTER 14

PROGRAM EVALUATION

"Crafty men condemn studies; simple men admire them; and wise men use them"

Francis Bacon

An important differentiation should be made between research and program evaluation. **Research** is conducted to discover new knowledge, to advance current knowledge, and to substantiate theory. It is service oriented. For example, "Would coaching students on the Scholastic Aptitude Test improve test scores over those students who were not coached?" By contrast, **program evaluation** seeks to provide meaningful information for immediate use in decision making. It is program oriented. For example, "Do counselors need to spend more time counseling students and less time doing administrative tasks such as scheduling?"

School counselors invariably neglect to take advantage of empirical research to support their counseling goals and objectives. This area of focus is easy to relinquish when one's role and subsequent responsibilities are already seriously overextended. Past research and potential benefits of counseling, however, should be included in the rationale and justification of potential counseling interventions and services.

Although not all inclusive, a compendium of empirical studies over the last decade reveals the benefits of counseling, especially in the arena of longitudinal studies, career decision making, enhancing the self-sufficiency of at-risk students, and improving students' self-esteem. (Additional research implications are provided in Chapter 3, School Counseling Definition and Benefits.)

RESEARCH SUPPORT

Fundamentally, the guidance process helps students to become competent decision makers, to select high school courses responsibly, and to make school plans more congruent with their abilities than is true of students not exposed to such processes (Griggs, 1983; Sloan, Staples, Cristol, Yorkston, & Whipple, 1975). Students exposed to the counseling process tend to organize their concept about themselves in a more congruent way; and to reconcile their differences between ideal and real self-concepts more effectively than persons without such experiences (Morrison & Thomas, 1975; Schunk, 1981; Tyler, 1969; Washington, 1977).

In the arena of career decisions and development, counselor intervention also has had some empirical validation. For example, through group problem-solving methods, students can be helped to understand the relationship between educational and vocational development, to clarify goals, and to acquire skill in identifying and using relevant information for their decision making (Babcock & Kauffman, 1976; Martin & Stone, 1977; Stewart & Thoresen, 1968). High school students exposed to model reinforcement and reinforcement counseling participate more intensely in external information-seeking behavior than students not so exposed (Krumboltz & Thoresen, 1976). Further, young adult career adjustment was found to be related to awareness of choices; information and planning based on choices; and processing occupational, psychological, educational, and economic information while in high school (Super, 1969).

With minority, disadvantaged, or at-risk students, the literature provides a number of positive counselor interventions. During periods of transition, counselors who are specifically trained can provide personal counseling, resolve interpersonal conflicts, and coordinate groups designed to improve students' human relations skills and their understanding of different racial/ethnic groups to reduce racial prejudice and conflict (Gordon, Brownell, & Brittell, 1972; Higgins, 1976; Katz & Zalk, 1978; Lewis & Lewis, 1970). Individual counseling in combination with counselor connected training programs designed to develop interpersonal, physical, emotional, and intellectual skills which are transferable to home, school, and community can reduce the recidivism rate for youthful offenders (Lewis & Boyle, 1976). Disadvantaged youth who participate in counseling are more likely to achieve salary increases and job satisfaction than those who do not (Herr, 1978).

In the arena of self-esteem, interpersonal growth and adjustment, the counseling process and the potential benefits are well documented. The higher the degree of therapeutic conditions provided by the counselor, the more likely it is that the counselee will achieve constructive change (Berenson & Carkhuff, 1967; Egan, 1980; Egan & Cowan, 1979; Herr, 1976; Lewis & Schafner, 1970). In addition, secondary students who have been assisted through counseling have overcome debilitating behaviors such as anorexia, depression, and substance abuse (Beck, Rush, Shaw, & Emery, 1979; Burns, 1981; Lazarus, 1981). Teams of counselors, teachers, principals, and parents who work closely together in dealing with emotional or social problems that interfere with the use of children's intellectual potential help to increase general levels of student achievement (Bertoldi, 1975; Thompson, 1987). Finally, either group or individual counseling extended over a reasonable period of time helps students whose ability is average or above to improve their scholastic performance. Better results are likely if guidance processes focus on the causes of underachievement and ways to remediate them than if a more general approach is taken (Carrol, 1979; Corey & Corey, 1983; Herr, 1976; Larrabee & Terres, 1984; Schmidt, 1976). Students who have been helped by counselors to evaluate their problems, to divide them into components, and to master these components one at a time gain self-confidence (Bennett, 1975; Herr, 1976; Zimmerman & Ringle, 1981). Moreover, a rise in the self-esteem of students exposed to guidance and other counseling processes is related to reduction in dropout rates, absences, and improvement in conduct and social adjustment (Bennett,

1975; Jones, 1980; Tyler, 1969; Wiggins, 1977). School counselors also have provided direct and indirect counseling intervention and a variety of roles with exceptional students (Cochrane & Mareni, 1977; Hohenshil & Humes, 1979; McDowell, Coren, & Eash, 1979; Morse, 1977).

PROGRAM EVALUATION

Counselors must actively take the initiative to define their role, develop comprehensive programs, and educate teachers, administrators, parents, students, and other significant persons about counseling programs and services.

A recent national survey indicates that 72% of counselors (K-12) involve themselves in evaluation and accountability activities as a means of enhancing their program and their own professional growth (American School Counselor Association, 1989, p. 15). However, as many as 41% of the counselors surveyed indicated that they collect accountability data because it is required by their supervisors. The liability of having "significant others" require accountability activities is that they generally determine the methods to be used (e.g., time-consuming logs) as well as what they want to observe.

In Figure 14.1 is presented an example of The Counselor's Time Study Analysis Form. To code so as to do computer analysis of several weekly analysis sheets Figure 14.2 is provided with codes for different counselor activities. Figure 14.2 demonstrates the complexity of counselor role and the diversity of services. Random time analysis (i.e., taking random days in the month, or weeks in a quarter) could periodically be collected to analyze encumbrances on counselor time. Adhering to such a log on a daily basis, however, could easily undermine a counselor's professional integrity. Thus, the log perhaps is more germane to practicum students rather than practitioners.

Unlike research, program evaluation is a process designed to collect relevant information for use in making decisions about counselee needs and current counseling programs and

(Continued on Page 294)

Counselor: _____   School: _____

Directions: Indicate all the areas in which you spend your time on the weekly schedule. Indicate times to the nearest half or quarter hour. Also indicate the task code from the Figure 14.2.

	Assessment	Occupational Guidance	Educational Guidance	Group Counseling	Individual Counseling	Research	Support Personnel Consultation	Teacher Consultation	Parent Consultation	Referral	Placement	Public Relations	Professional Meetings	Administrative Duties	Miscellaneous (specify)	TOTAL HOURS
MONDAY — Hours / Code																
TUESDAY — Hours / Code																
WEDNESDAY — Hours / Code																
THURSDAY — Hours / Code																
FRIDAY — Hours / Code																
AFTER HOURS — Hours / Code																

(Example: Crisis Counseling 2.00 hrs, Code 20)

Figure 14.1. The Counselor's Time Study Analysis

**(EO) = EDUCATIONAL/
        OCCUPATIONAL GUIDANCE**

01 planning and preparation time
02 orientation for new students
03 orientation to curriculum changes
   and graduation requirements
04 group guidance for careers
05 group guidance to show relationship of school to work
06 group guidance for scheduling
07 group guidance for job seeking
   and job keeping skills
08 group guidance on test-taking
   skill development
09 orientation for scholarship and
   award competitions
10 class assemblies
11 S.A.T. preparation workshops
12 orientation for college
13 orientation for post-secondary
   educational experiences

**(CO) = INDIVIDUAL AND GROUP
        COUNSELING**

14 individual counseling re: academic progress
15 personal counseling
16 interpersonal counseling
17 counseling for targeted groups
18 counseling for self-defeating behaviors
19 peer counseling groups
20 crisis counseling
21 personal growth counseling

(RE) = RESEARCH

22 follow-up surveys of former students
23 needs assessments-teachers and
   administrators
24 needs assessments-parents and
   teachers
25 program evaluation
26 self audits

(SC) = STAFF CONSULATION

27 teacher consultation
28 teacher conference groups
29 teacher-student conferences
30 teacher-parent conferences
31 with support personnel
32 with personnel in special education
33 introduce private agency liaison
34 staff meetings in and out of the
   building
35 in-service to faculty

(PC) = PARENT CONSULTATION

36 parent conferences
37 group conferences
38 grade level parent nights
39 conferences on testing
40 back-to-school night
41 parent career planning and development groups
42 parent volunteers
43 financial aid information

**(PL)(REF) = PLACEMENT AND
            REFERRAL**

44 parent orientation
45 college or post-secondary
   representatives
46 student referrals
47 parent referrals
48 test interpretation
49 special education facilitation
50 community agency referrals
51 placement academic
52 placement vocational training
53 placement alternative education
54 placement gifted and talented;
   magnet schools

Figure 14.2. Suggested code numbering for different counselor
activities.

Figure 14.2. Continued.

(ADMIN) = ADMINISTRATIVE DUTIES

55 test scheduling and administrative
56 registration
57 schedule changes
58 transcripts
59 reports
60 recommendations
61 credit checks
62 dissemination of information
63 collating information
64 hall duty
65 preparing mailings
66 distributing report cards
67 calling absentees
68 collecting homework assignments
69 filling out reports
70 miscellaneous

(PR) = PUBLIC RELATIONS

71 community relations
72 newsletters
73 public service announcements
74 calendar of events
75 counselor's report card accountability log
76 cooperative efforts with advisory boards
77 newspaper articles

(PRO) = PROFESSIONALISM

78 in-service training
79 evaluation and program development
80 professional meetings
81 graduate work

services. Essentially, "what gets measured gets done." The inherent benefits to counselors, students, and constituents of the school community (although not all inclusive) are

- to provide evidence of the positive impact of guidance programs and counseling services to students, faculty, parents, and community organizations;

- to identify the needs not met with the present program;

- to determine the relative effectiveness of programs, services, methods, and materials, to date;

- to obtain information for designing a staff development and parent consultation program;

- to provide information for support of the present program or for enhancing specific areas such as clerical help, parent volunteers, or more staff; and/ or

- to clarify and communicate the role of the school counselor and exemplary services as an integral part of the school program.

EVALUATION OF PROGRAMS

Needs assessment tend to be performed on a periodic program-oriented, "crisis management" basis with few efforts to coordinate the administrative assessment with other programs and services within the school. The dichotomy of administrative "felt needs" versus consumer articulated "real needs" are perhaps an oversimplification of a more pervasive problem.

While numerous models of needs assessment are available (MacDevitt & MacDevitt, 1987; Orthner, Smith, & Wright, 1986), needs assessment is generally bound by four distinct parameters. First, the target population (parents, students, teachers, administrators, etc.) must be determined; second, a method (survey, interview, etc.) must be specified; third, some measurement scheme (Likert scale, forced choice, semantic differential, etc.) must be developed; and fourth, data must be interpreted to decision makers. Experts in the field (Attkisson, Hargreaves, Horowitz, & Sorenson, 1978; Rossi & Freeman, 1982) agreed that need assessments are conducted to develop an understanding of the service-related needs of program recipients.

Rossi and Freeman (1982) listed three contact methods suitable to soliciting need assessment information. These are key informant, community forum, and survey sampling. The **key informant approach** uses contacts with leaders and others, especially knowledgeable about problems concerning the target population. The main disadvantage of this approach is the possibility of bias when the key informant is part of the program. The **community forum approach** involves attracting program recipients to meetings where discussion-generated issues and needs are noted and recorded. Limitations of the community forum approach include problems in attracting a true cross section of program constituents and the possibility of obtaining mostly negative information. The third approach, **survey sampling,** using a structured questionnaire, is the most popular approach and has the potential of obtaining precise need-related information.

Figure 14.3 is an example of a Postcard Follow-up that could be sent to those who have not returned the form within a reasonable time period.

Figure 14.3. Postcard follow-up.

PROGRAM AUDIT

The role of the school counselor through specific guidance programs and counseling services is to help in the creation of an effective learning climate for each student within the school arena. This process involves educational/occupational information, counseling, consulting, student appraisal, placement, and referral.

Both guidance programs and counseling services are concerned with developmental issues of individuals in cognitive, effective, social, and interpersonal domains. Counselors working with students, parents, teachers, administrators, and other support personnel operationalize their collective efforts with comprehensive objectives based on specific needs identified in a consumer/community-center program model.

The eleven constructs to consider in a program audit include the following:

1. Educational or occupational guidance—a comprehensive system of functions, services, and programs to assist students in personal adjustment and educational competence.

2. Counseling—a method or technique applied to individuals or groups to enhance their personal development and psychosocial competencies involving a dynamic relationship between counselor and counselee.

3. Research—activities that validate the counselor's perception of the need for change or demonstrate that a new technique, strategy, or intervention accomplished a goal.

4. Staff consultation—the mutual sharing and analysis of information with the instructional staff for making decisions about strategies for helping students.

5. Parent consultation—the mutual sharing and analysis of information with parents and family for making decisions about strategies for helping students.

6. Placement—to assist student to move to the next level of their educational program or to continue a program of advanced education or employment upon leaving the secondary program.

7. Referral—utilizing agencies, organizations, or individuals to assist individuals in reaching their full potential.

8. Pupil appraisal—administrating, interpreting, and evaluating test results, and placemats in alternative educational programs.

9. Program development—planning, assessing needs, and providing a systematic program for the delivery of services.

10. Public relations—communicating guidance and counseling roles and functions; programs and services; inherent benefits to those inside and outside the school system.

11. Professionalism—activities to assure counselors maintain professional growth and contribute to the profession.

EVALUATION OF SERVICES

Within the private business sector, such sophisticated accountability models as *Management by Objectives (MBO)*, and *Program Planning and Budgeting Systems (PPBS)* have been used with considerable satisfaction. Yet, such concepts as "the profit motive" are inappropriate in the school's service curriculum." Structure, organization, and systematic evaluation are accountable components of the evaluation process in the school arena. The fundamental steps in program evaluation of the counselor as practitioner are outlined in five simple steps.

First, **organize and chair an evaluation or advisory committee** consisting of counselor(s), administrator(s), parent(s), teacher(s), student(s), and significant community members to study current guidance program and counseling services. This assure collective input and a comprehensive commitment to the evaluation process. An example of some questions advisory committee members should consider answering include the following:

Do teachers understand the basic academic needs of their students and the program of studies for different groups of students, (i.e., vocational, academic, handicapped, etc.)?

Do any school policies (such as an attendance or suspension policy) jeopardize students' matriculation or academic performance?

Do teachers help students develop academic strategies, study skills, test taking techniques, or time-management strategies which enhance their performance?

Do teachers and the administration routinely review test results from standardized or criterion-referenced tests and then design instructional delivery and program objectives to respond to student needs?

What are teachers and staff doing to further students' occupational and career development?

What special provisions or services are utilized for the identification and education of the exceptional and the at-risk student (e.g., students who are learning disabled, gifted, talented, potential drop-outs, pregnant teens, and underachievers)?

What counseling services are in place to meet the emotional, developmental, interpersonal, and social needs of all students?

Second, *survey all consumers of the guidance program and counseling services.* Develop and conduct a needs assessment of program goals and student outcomes for student, teachers, parents, and counselors. Program evaluation seeks to provide meaningful information for immediate and long-term decision making, as well as planning. To obtain the most from surveys the following guidelines should be considered:

Have a clear sense of purpose and rationale of "why" you want to do your needs assessment. Develop a conceptual basis for your survey work to provide future growth and change in meeting students', parents', and teachers' needs.

Think about the contributions of the survey to the decisions to be made. Anticipate how the information coming out of the survey will contribute to administrative decision making, and how it may generate new services. Design the instrument on a Likert Scale which may be analyzed by SCANTRON or other computerized scoring means. When composing questions for your survey, evaluate each question according to the following criteria:

- Is the question necessary?

- Why are you asking it?

- Will the question obtain important information accurately and without ambiguity?

- Is the ordering of questions in the survey systematic to elicit the necessary information in a cost-effective manner?

- Does the format of the questionnaire lend itself to efficient and consistent analysis of data?

- Is the survey easy to read and easy to understand?

- As a final check, read the survey for redundant questions, confusing questions, jargon, lack of clarity, or "educanese."

- Field-test the survey for clarity, brevity, and understanding.

Sample evaluation surveys of guidance programs and counseling services for teachers, administrators, students, and their families are provided in Figures 14.4, 14.5, and

(Continued on Page 301)

The purpose of this survey is to collect your honest opinion of the guidance program and counseling services in your school. Please indicate the extent to which you are satisfied with the quality and scope of these services.

Read each statement and rate the extent to which you agree with the statement. If you do not have enough information to rate an item, leave it blank. Please complete as many items as you can.

1 = Strongly Agree   2 = Agree   3 = Disagree   4 = Strongly Disagree

Teacher or Administrator: Circle one   School: _____

1. The administration supports the guidance and counseling services as an integral part of the educational curriculum.   1   2   3   4

2. There is a written policy concerning the confidentiality of student records.   1   2   3   4

3. There is adequate secretarial assistance for the guidance and counseling department.   1   2   3   4

4. The counselor(s) periodically provide(s) an in-service session to teachers and administrators on the programs and services of the guidance and counseling department.   1   2   3   4

Figure 14.4. Teacher and administration evaluation of guidance program and counseling services.

❊   ❊   ❊

School: _____   Grade: _____

The purpose of this survey is to collect your honest opinion of the guidance program and counseling services in your school. We want to find out if there are some things we could do to serve you better.

Read each statement and rate the extent to which you agree with the statement. If you do not have enough information to rate an item, leave it blank. Please complete as many items as you can.

1 = Strongly Agree   2 = Agree   3 = Disagree   4 = Strongly Disagree

1. I can trust my counselor.   1   2   3   4

2. I see my counselor soon after my request for an appointment.   1   2   3   4

3. My counselor understands me.   1   2   3   4

4. If I had a personal problem, I would feel comfortable discussing it with my counselor.   1   2   3   4

Figure 14.5. Student questionnaire of guidance and counseling services.

Dear Parent(s) or Guardian: School: _____

The purpose of this survey is to collect your honest opinion of the guidance program and counseling services in your school. We want to find out if there are some things we could do to serve you better.

Read each statement and rate the extent to which you agree with the statement. If you do not have enough information to rate an item, leave it blank. Please complete as many items as you can.

1 = Strongly Agree   2 = Agree   3 = Disagree   4 = Strongly Disagree

1. I have had a conference with my child's counselor.   1   2   3   4

2. I know about the counseling services which are available   1   2   3   4
   for my child at school.

3. I have discussed my child's educational program with   1   2   3   4
   a counselor.

4. I am familiar with my child's course of study and   1   2   3   4
   graduation requirements.

5. The counselor has met with my child(ren) this year to   1   2   3   4
   discuss academic planning.

Figure 14.6. Parent evaluation of guidance and counseling services.

14.6. Only a few items are provided in each figure to illustrate the type of information elicited..

Third, **plan carefully and organize a realistic time schedule** to conduct your needs assessment. This must be done from the initial survey refinement to the formal presentation to significant decision makers in the school community. Pay careful attention to time constraints and survey constraints of the typical school year, e.g., state mandated testing schedules, division mandated holidays and/or vacations, and the opening or closing of school would not be the best time to conduct a survey.

Fourth, **analyze data** for results that provide a guide to short-term and long-term action-goals. Analysis should be action oriented and focus on proactive decisions. For example, "the survey said," 60% of minority students and 75% of all parents said they need assistance in college planning and meeting financial costs.

Fifth, *communicate the results concisely.* Separate relevant from irrelevant information; important from unimportant data; and glean the most salient points from the data for articulation. Report the findings to significant others at their level of understanding. Address PTAs, PTOs, student groups, business and community leaders, school board, supervisors, faculty, and administration. Program development and evaluation is a collective effort. Program development consists of identifying new program components, establishing performance objectives, allocating resources, and identifying relationships between observed improvements and program changes or related observed improvements to original documented needs.

In Figure 14.7 are five critical steps in need analysis that must be considered and then followed. The first step is a function of the Evaluation Committee. They should assist with all five steps.

In Figure 14.8 are presented six steps in evaluating a program. Time schedule for each step is also provided.

By enhancing and evaluating areas identified as needing improvement, counselors choose to demonstrate a genuine interest in improving guidance programs and counseling services. The fundamental purpose is to relate program goals to student outcome and to modify the delivery of services to a more consumer/community centered program model. Furthermore, practitioners or supervisory staff also may want to differentiate between questions that focus on "effort" versus "effectiveness" versus "efficiency." The relationship among these three variables are presented in Figure 14.9.

One kind of question you may have is about program services: "What services did we actually provide and to whom?" Such questions are about program effort. An example of an effort questions is "How many ninth grade students at Central High School were trained as peer counselors this year?" An effort question about a parent program could be:

(Continued on Page 306)

- Identify who will receive the need assessment and how the need assessment will be used. The former could be counselors, administrators, supervisors, PTA/PTO, advisory boards, etc.

- Describe target populations which may be underserved. For example, they may include gifted and talented, the handicapped, underachievers, at-risk students, or important services for often neglected average youth. Discrepancies between existing services, as well as assets and deficits, could be identified.

- Identify consumer/community centered needs. Describe problems and identify solution.

- Assess the importance of the identified needs and prioritize intervention strategies.

- Communicate results to signficant others both internally and externally. Be objective and use language that others can understand.

Figure 14.7. Critical steps in need analysis.

STEP 1: **Choosing an Evaluation Question**   Date Completed: _____
(Meeting 1: Week 1 of Evaluation Year)
Questions to be answered

____ Part 1: Review the model of your program.

____ Part 2: Raise questions about your program. What do you want to know?

____ Part 3: Discuss effort, effectiveness and efficiency in relation to your questions.

____ Part 4: Identify a purpose and audience for the evaluation.

____ Part 5: Choose the question your evaluation will answer.

STEP 2: **Designing an Evaluation**   Date Completed: _____
(Meeting 2: Week 2 of Evaluation Year)
Evaluating Design

____ Part 1: Consider possible evaluation designs.

____ Part 2: Choose the design that fits your question and situation.

____ Part 3: Define your sample.

STEP 3: **Designing Measurement Instruments**   Date Completed: _____
(Meeting 3: Week 3 of Evaluation Year)
Outcome Measure

____ Part 1: Measuring the results of your program.

____ Part 2: Deciding on background data.

(Meeting 4: Week 4 of Evaluation Year)
Implementation Measurement

____ Part 3: Consider instruments for measuring implementation.

STEP 4: **Building a Data Collection Plan**   Date Completed: _____
(Meeting 5: Week 5 of Evaluating Year)
Organizing and Collecting Data

____ Part 1: Plan how to collect the data. How often will you collect it? Who will do it?

Source: U.S. Department of Health & Human Services, Public Health Service (1981), Alcohol, Drug, Abuse, and Mental Health Association.

Office for Substance Abuse Prevention, Division of Demonstrations and Evaluation, 5600 Fishers Lane, Rockville, MD 20857.

Figure 14.8. Six-step checklist to evaluating your program.

Figure 14.8. Continued.

_____ Part 2: Pilot test instruments and collection plan.

(Meeting 6: Week 6 of Evaluation Year)
Troubleshooting Measures and Collection Procedures

_____ Part 3: Monitor field reports on measures and procedures. Adjust as needed.

STEP 5: Analyzing the Data   Date Completed: _____
(Meeting 7: Week 7 of Evaluation Year)
Planning for Data Analysis

_____ Part 1: Choose analysis procedures.

_____ Part 2: Design tables and graphs for reporting results.

_____ Part 3: Begin collection of data.

_____ Part 4: Monitor data collection regularly.

(Meeting 8: Week 45 of Evaluation Year)
Analysis of Data

_____ Part 5: Analyze data.

STEP 6: Reporting the Findings   Date Completed: _____
(Meeting 9: Week 47 of Evaluation Year)
Evaluation: Articulation

_____ Part 1: Complete "dummy" graphs and tables for reporting findings and plan presentation of data.

_____ Part 2: Role play presentation to target audience, adding data needed to respond to audience questions.

_____ Report your findings to identified audiences.

(Meeting 10: Week 50 of Evaluation Year)
Making Use of What You've Learned

_____ Part 4: Adjust your program based on what you've learned.

Celebrate Your Accomplishments!

Note: Meetings 1, 5, and 9 should involve your whole staff.

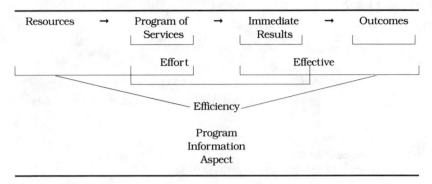

Source: Hawkins, J.D., & Nederhood, B. (1987). *Handbook for evaluating drug and alcohol prevention programs.* Rockville, Maryland: Office of Substane Abuse Prevention, U.S. Department of Health and Human Services.

Figure 14.9. Relationship of effort, effectiveness, and efficiency to a program model.

"On the average, how many of the three sessions on Planning for College did parents attend?"

Another question you may ask is whether you achieved the immediate results you wanted. Follow through on the previous question, you might focus on: "How may parents in the Planning For College session actually talked with their child and began the college planning process?" This is a question of program effectiveness in achieving immediate results. In this example, the outcome that the program sought was to increase family communication and assertiveness on college planning.

A third type of question is about the efficiency of service delivery. This includes cost-per-unit of service and cost related to benefits achieved. For example, you may ask: "How much did it cost per student to provide training for peer counseling in the school?" This is a question of the relationship between resources and program services (cost-per-unit of service). What was the cost in resources to produce the services that resulted? Alternatively, you also may want to know how much it cost to reduce the rate of failure among freshman by 50%. This is a question of the relationship between resources, program services, and outcomes (i.e., a cost-benefit analysis). Sometimes, before you can answer efficiency questions, you must have the answer to effort and effectiveness questions.

In Figure 14.10 is an exercise in identifying effort, effectiveness, and efficiency. Try responding to each item and then check your response with answers provided.

EVALUATION DESIGN

The designs which follow reflect the aspect of evaluation called product or outcome evaluation. The focus is to identity counselor needs and program goals which are carefully executed to meet student needs. Some designs are time-consuming and anchored in social science theory. Other designs are appealing because of immediacy and simplicity. Local needs, talents, and institutional constraints will tend to promote one design over the other within respective school divisions. Eight approaches are available.

Experimental Research Approach

The Experimental Research Approach includes the pretest— posttest control group design; the posttest only control group design, and the before-and-after control group design. The experimental approach depends on random assignment of subjects to treatment controls and requires that treatment and control conditions be kept constant for the length of the study. This is most appealing to the counselor educator at local colleges or universities. Experimental research designs in a contemporary school setting, however, can be difficult with such barriers as obtaining parental consent from students to participate and, obtaining release time from the student's academic classes. In addition, the ethical considerations regarding students who do or do not receive an experimental service is a philosophical issue of "equity versus equality" in schools.

(Continued on Page 309)

Directions: Place an A by a sentence if it is asking an effort question. Place a B by a sentence if it is asking an effectiveness question. Place a C by a sentence if it is asking an efficiency question.

_____ 1. Are parents satisfied with our counseling program?

_____ 2. Which recruitment approach yields the most parent volunteers at the least cost?

_____ 3. Does student participation in our peer counseling program reduce the reported use of alcohol?

_____ 4. How many parent workshops did we provide in the 1989-90 school year?

_____ 5. Which was the most cost-effective recruitment strategy for parent participation in parent workshops raffles or free child care?

_____ 6. Do SAT preparation workshops signficantly increase verbal and math scores?

_____ 7. Did radio advertising or community flyers do the best job of advertising our "Parent Information Night?"

_____ 8. How much influence did seminars co-facilitated by college alumni have on senior attitudes about attending college?

Answers: B, C, B, A, C, B, C, B

Source: Adapted from Hawkins, J.D., & Nederhood, B. (1987). _Handbook for evaluating drug and alcohol prevention programs._ Rockville, MD: Office for Substance Abuse Prevention, U.S. Department of Health and Human Services.

Figure 14.10. An exercise in identifying effort, effectiveness, and efficiency.

Quasi-experimental Approach

The Quasi-experimental Approach such as the static-group comparison design and the nonequivalent control group design could be utilized. An educational resource such as by Borg and Gall (1983) provides limitations for making generalizations by such an approach. Once again, the limitations previously addressed in the previous approach applies here also.

Tabulation Approach

The Tabulation Approach represents the simplest approach to program evaluation where the counselor maintains a log of the number of counseling sessions, students seen, parents contacted, and other relevant counseling activities. Some possible criteria evaluating performance or effectiveness following counselor intervention are academic achievement, improvement in standardized test scores, increase in personal adjustment, better school attendance, greater self-understanding, improved teacher/parent/student relationships, or the reduction of self-defeating behavior. These represent tangible, observable or measurable changes in student behavior.

Follow-up Approach

The Follow-up Approach uses surveys to collect information and consumer satisfaction with programs and activities from students after they leave school. **Satisfaction Surveys** can be randomly given to students, parents, teachers, and employers to determine the degree of satisfaction various target groups have with the school guidance program and counseling services. This approach can be enhanced with the use of open-ended questions. Patton (1980) provided explicit procedures to elicit the most useful answers from respondents.

Questions should not suggest the dimension of response. Instead of "Did you find . . . helpful" try "What was your feeling about . . .?" Instead of "Do you find that . . . causes you problems?" try "What do you think about . . .?"

Questions should presuppose that the respondent can give answers but should avoid using "why?" Instead of "Are there reasons why people do not use . . .?" or "Why do people not use . . .?" try "What kinds of barriers keep people from using . . .?" instead of "Can we make this service easier to use?" try "How can we make . . .?"

Ask one question at a time, but do not ask questions that can be answered dichotomously. After reasons, likes, or barriers have been elicited, explore them individually with probes: "Say more about . . .?" or "What do you mean by . . .?"

Let respondents use their terms. They may use a different name or conceptualize a service at a different organizational level than does the questioner. Instead of "When did you first think about applying to Grant University?" try "What program of study are you in?" "When did you first think about starting your program?" Larsen, Attkisson, Hargreaves, & Nguyen (1979) also provided the following recommendations to increase the usefulness of consumer surveys:

- focus on dissatisfaction, through use of open-ended questions and by examination of relative satisfaction;

- examine satisfaction trends over time, and

- include specific questions about barriers to service.

Case Study Approach

The Case Study Approach is a longitudinal study of the counselee as he or she progresses through a program or curriculum. It can be used to illustrate methods of counseling or program aspects which enhanced self-sufficiency skills. Once again, this is time consuming.

Expert Opinion Approach

The Expert Opinion Profile involves submitting a profile of counseling staff qualifications and program components to consulting experts such as counselor educators for their evaluation or comparison to other existing programs. A parallel is self audits, where counselors rate themselves according to established criteria of successful counseling or program development. The *Counselor Role Repertoire Needs Assessment Survey* (Thompson, 1986) assess the expressed importance and expressed attainment of counselor role and function on eleven counselor constructs. This survey evaluates the counseling program and essentially is a school division audit of program needs.

Time/Cost Approach

Time/Cost Analysis is an accountability model which relates the estimated cost of the counselor's activities to the accomplishment of guidance goals and outcome. Krumboltz (1974) however acknowledge that the actual implementation of his model poses a number of limitations such as determining the amount of uniformity required in descriptions of counseling outcomes and activities.

Discrepancy Evaluation Approach

The Discrepancy Evaluation Model is another comprehensive evaluation method for program evaluation. It has been lauded as the most useful model to improve guidance programs and counseling services. It describes the discrepancy between a standard of performance and the performance itself. The model focuses on the gaps that exist between *what is* and *what ought to be*. The model emphasizes normative expectations and involves three phases (Kaufman & English, 1979):

- goal setting, identifying what ought to be;

- performance measurement, determining what is; and

- discrepancy identification, ordering differences between what ought to be and what is.

Summary for Evaluation Design

Specific need is indicated where measured performance is lower than desired levels. Needs also may be ordered by the size of the gap between performance or service goals; larger gaps indicating greater needs. Target programming of services begins in the area of the largest performance gap.

All these approaches are conducted to "assist some audience to judge and improve the worth of some educational objective" (Shufflebeam & Webster, 1980, p. 85) but none is all comprehensive or program conclusive by itself. Inherently, program evaluation involves obtaining the kinds of information which will be useful in developing, implementing, and improving the school guidance program and counseling services.

EVALUATION OF PROFESSIONALS

To observe counselors is often difficult; therefore, to evaluate what they do is hard to achieve. Guidance, consultation, or small group counseling often do not lend themselves to participation from an outside observer. Brechenridge (1987) offered a systematic performance improvement program that enables administrators to evaluate counselor job performance. By sharing performance criteria, both counselors and administrators can focus on significant counseling behaviors for evaluation.

In Figure 14.11 is an example of a performance evaluation criteria from the administrator's perspective. In Figure 14.12 is an example of a school counselor performance evaluation.

Procedure

District administrators, supervisors, and counselors should select criteria for evaluation from a review of counseling philosophy, job description, job objectives, state and national organizational publications, codes of ethics, role statements, standards, and other school district evaluation systems.

(Continued on Page 319)

Performance Area I—Counseling Skills

A. Demonstrates appropriate communication skills; e.g.,
   1. Allows time for student reflection and reaction
   2. Provides opportunity for balanced dialog with students
   3. Demonstrates a flexibility of approaches in meeting the needs of students
   4. Exhibits sensitivity, empathy, congruence, and acceptance necessary for establishing rapport
   5. Demonstrates listening skills
   6. Demonstrates confrontation skills
   7. Provides opportunity for students to recognize, identify, and express feelings
B. Promotes student growth and development; e.g.,
   1. Promotes self-responsibility in the students being served
   2. Promotes opportunity for student decision making, problem solving, and goal setting
   3. Promotes development of the students' full potential
   4. Promotes the development of the students' self-esteem
   5. Promotes the opportunity for students to deal with their emotions
C. Provides a flexibility of approaches in meeting the needs of students
D. Demonstrates sensitivity and awareness of clues from the student.

Performance Area II—Guidance Skills (Instructional)

A. Prepares students for learning; e.g.,
   1. Focuses attention of the learners
   2. Reviews previous learning
   3. Develops a mental readiness for new learning
B. Communicates objectives and purposes effectively to students; e.g.,
   1. Explains what is to be learned and why
   2. Communicates in language understood by the learner
C. Employs appropriate methods of presentation; e.g.,
   1. Determines how much to teach
   2. Uses appropriate sequences
   3. Selects effective methods to convey content

Performance Area III—Organizational and Planning Skills

A. Provides opportunities for varied counseling and guidance approaches; e.g.,
   1. One-to-one counseling
   2. Group counseling
   3. Developmental guidance and counseling
B. Articulates goals of program to students, staff, and parents; e.g.,
   1. Parent meetings
   2. Student meetings
   3. Newsletters
   4. Public relations
C. Plans and organizes the counseling complex so that it is an aesthetically pleasing and a functional area; e.g.,
   1. Area presents an inviting atmosphere
   2. Area is functionally neat, tidy, and presents a friendly orderliness
   3. Materials are accessible and pleasantly displayed
   4. Furniture is appropriate to the function
D. Organizes student information for effective use; e.g.,
   1. Maintains accurate, current files
   2. Provides functional access to student files while protecting student confidentiality

Source: Hayden, C., & Pohlmann, N. (1981). Accountability and evaluation: Necessary for the survival of guidance programs. *NASSP Bulletin, 64,* 477, p. 61.

Figure 14.11. Performance evaluation criteria: Adminstrator perspective.

Figure 14.11. Continued.

E. Demonstrates effective personal planning and organization, e.g.,
   1. Uses time effectively and responsibly (is on time)
   2. Is available to students, parents, and staff
   3. Works well as a part of team

Performance Area IV—Positive Interpersonal Relationship
A. Develops a positive working relationship with students; e.g.,
   1. Reacts with sensitivity to the needs and feelings of students
   2. Makes an effort to know the students as individuals
   3. Shows trust in students and respect for their rights
B. Develops a positive working relationship with staff members; e.g.,
   1. Works cooperatively with other staff members
   2. Reacts with sensitivity to the feelings and needs of other staff members
   3. Makes use of other support services as needed
C. Develops a positive working relationship with parents/guardians; e.g.,
   1. Responds appropriately to parental concerns
   2. Provides a climate that encourages communication between parent/guardian and counselor
   3. Cooperates with parents in the best interest of the students
   4. Supports and participates in the parent/guardian—counselor relationships
   5. Facilitates parent teacher conferences
D. Demonstrates concern for all students; e.g.,
   1. Displays nonsexist, multicultural attitudes in counseling styles
   2. Demonstrates understanding and acceptance of different racial, ethnic, cultural and religous groups
   3. Exhibits acceptance of all students regardless of the lifestyle practiced in the home
   4. Avoids stereotyping
E. Creates an environment conducive to effective communication and the development of good rapport; e.g.,
   1. Demonstrates a sense of humor
   2. Demonstrates predictable behavior and positive emotional stability
   3. Demonstrates a positive enthusiastic attitude

Performance Area V—Professional Responsibilities
A. Exhibits an awareness/knowledge of the total secondary counseling and developmental program; e.g.,
   1. Demonstrates awareness of the 6-12 counseling program
   2. Possesses the body of knowledge essential to counseling; e.g., career guidance, youth risk prevention, group counseling, post-high school options, financial aid, special education, etc.
B. Makes appropriate referrals; e.g.,
   1. Refers to professional support staff
   2. Refers to community resources
C. Demonstrates a sense of responsibility; e.g.,
   1. Completes duties promptly and accurately
   2. Assumes professional duties expected of a counselor
   3. Maintains regular attendance
   4. Pursues personal wellness as a lifestyle
   5. Participates in building and district-wide committees
D. Participates in professional activities and organizations; e.g.,
   1. Contributes to the profession
   2. Participates in activities contributing toward professional growth and development
E. Demonstrates awareness of, and practices professional ethics; e.g.,
   1. Maintains confidentiality
   2. Treats colleagues with respect, courtesy, fairness, and good faith

Name: _____	Position: _____	Date: _____
School: _____	Evaluator: _____	

Evaluation Guidelines

The evaluation of the guidance program and counseling services is a cooperative process. It involves those who plan, administer, and implement programs and services, as well as those who receive them. The appraisal of guidance and counseling activities should be based on the objectives of the particular program. These objectives should grow out of the needs and interest of the students and the philosophy of the individual school.

Information can be obtained by any combination of counselor evaluation conference, review of annual plan, or observation.

Performance Rating Code

1 = Commendable (C)
Performance is regularly in the range of professional excellence.

2 = Acceptable (A)
Performance meets expectations. Evaluatee is encouraged to continue professional growth.

3 = Ineffective (I)
Immediate improvement is required. Identified problems must be dealt with as indicated.

4 = Not applicable or not observable (NA)

Evaluator(s) is (are) to evaluate each major performance area. Indicate by circling level of performance. Major categories marked "ineffective" shall have additional comments.

PRORAM ADMINISTRATION AND INFORMATION MANAGEMENT

	C	A	I	NA
A. Effectively plans, coordinates and administers counseling services	1	2	3	4
B. Identifies and uses available resources which provide services to students	1	2	3	4
C. Disseminates current and correct information on curriculum offerings, occupational information, school regulations, and referral requirements	1	2	3	4
D. Interprets counseling services to students, staff, parents, and community	1	2	3	4
E. Demonstrates effective knowledge of and compliance with policies, regulations, and guidelines in meeting assigned duties	1	2	3	4

Figure 14.12. School counselor performance evaluation.

Figure 14.12. Continued

Program Administration and Information Management (continued)

	C	A	I	NA
F. Develops program plans based on appropriate needs of assessment information	1	2	3	4
G. Provides for the annual evaluation of the counseling program in the school	1	2	3	4
H. Gathers, interprets, and appropriately uses data, including standardized testing information, on students and programs	1	2	3	4

ASSESSMENT AND PLACEMENT

	C	A	I	NA
A. Administers and interprets the results of the testing program to students, parents, teachers, and administrators	1	2	3	4
B. Gathers, interprets, and appropriately uses data, including standardized testing information, on students and programs	1	2	3	4
C. Interprets data from the cumulative records for students, their parents, and others who are professionally concerned	1	2	3	4
D. Works with teachers and administrators to assist with the placement of students in appropriate courses, programs, and grade levels	1	2	3	4
E. Works with employers, vocational coordinators, and community and state to assist in the appropriate placement of students in part-time and full-time employment	1	2	3	4
F. Works with special services and teachers in identification, placement, and follow-up of students with special needs	1	2	3	4

EDUCATIONAL AND OCCUPATIONAL GUIDANCE

	C	A	I	NA
A. Assists students in making wise choices on gaining admission to post-secondary programs, including information on work, apprenticeships, loans and scholarships	1	2	3	4
B. Helps students discover, evaluate and understand their interests, abilities, and aptitudes and relates this information to educational and occupational planning	1	2	3	4
C. Facilitates the implementation of College Night or Career Day	1	2	3	4
D. Meets with assigned students for program planning and graduation requirements	1	2	3	4
E. Works with administration and staff in developing school policies and curriculum to meet student needs	1	2	3	4
F. Ensures implementation of a balanced program of guidance services to include: orientation, counseling, placement, and follow-up	1	2	3	4

PARENT AND STAFF CONSULTATION

	C	A	I	NA
A. Serves as a resource person to parents and staff on the growth and development of children	1	2	3	4
B. Communicates with parents through phone calls, letters, home visits, group meetings, etc.	1	2	3	4

Figure 14.12. Continued

Parent and Staff Consultation(Continued)

	C	A	I	NA
C. Assists teachers in correlating guidance with classroom instruction	1	2	3	4
D. Consults with teachers, parents, or administrators to understand student behavior and developmental needs	1	2	3	4
E. Accepts the concept of a parent-teacher partnership in a child's education and career planning	1	2	3	4
F. Cooperates with other members of the staff in planning guidance program goals, counseling services, and objectives	1	2	3	4
G. Works to establish and maintain open lines of communication with students, parents, and staff concerning academic and behavioral progress of all students	1	2	3	4

COUNSELING

A. Provides counseling services for all students in individual and/or group settings	1	2	3	4
B. Provides the goals and rationale for counseling groups to staff and administration	1	2	3	4
C. Schedules counseling sessions with each student according to needs and provide opportunities for self-initiated counseling sessions	1	2	3	4
D. Plans counseling in groups with at-risk students based on local need	1	2	3	4
E. Plans counseling in groups for life adjustment concerns and developmental needs	1	2	3	4
F. Employs students as natural helpers as part of a peer counseling program	1	2	3	4

PUBLIC RELATIONS

A. Promotes positive parent-school-community relations	1	2	3	4
B. Establishes monthly/annual calendar of counseling activities	1	2	3	4
C. Uses all available communication media to publicize and acquaint the community with the guidance program and counseling services of the school	1	2	3	4
D. Plans and articulates an on-going program of orientation and program placement to feeder schools and parents	1	2	3	4
E. Implements and facilitates a Guidance Advisory Committee	1	2	3	4
F. Demonstrates self-control in interations with the school community	1	2	3	4

PROFESSIONALISM AND ETHICAL STANDARDS

A. Respects the dignity and worth of every individual	1	2	3	4
B. Demonstrates good human relations skills	1	2	3	4

Figure 14.12. Continued

Professionalism and Ethical Standards (continued)

		C	A	I	NA
C.	Continues professional growth through conferences and mettings, advanced study, and division-wide interaction	1	2	3	4
D.	Interprets the program of counseling services to school and personnel	1	2	3	4
E.	Respects the confidentiality of students, parents, and school personnel	1	2	3	4
F.	Keeps counseling staff informed of current mandates and changing needs	1	2	3	4
G.	Complies with administrative directives and school policy	1	2	3	4
H.	Ensures that oral and written communications are clear, accurate, and grammatically correct	1	2	3	4
I.	Demonstrates effective knowledge of and compliance with policies, regulations, and guidelines in meeting assigned duties	1	2	3	4
J.	Demonstrates punctuality	1	2	3	4

COMMENTS OR CONDITIONS

_____

_____

_____

_____

_____

_____

Attachements: Yes _____   No _____   Date: _____

Recommended for Re-employment

Yes _____   No   _____   Conditionally _____

*Counselor's Signature _____ Date _____

Evaluator's Signature _____ Date _____

* Counselor's signature only represents receipt of this document and in no way implies acceptance of the evaluation. If the counselor feels that this evaluation is improper, the counselor may file a written rebuttal with this document.

Training sessions should be provided for administrators to familiarize them with the philosophy of observation, procedures, and techniques of the evaluation process.

Observations should occur on three separate occasions with both a pre-observation and post-observation conference.

The counselor should prepare a form for discussion at the pre-observation conference. The counselor selects two of the 22 criteria items on the form for observation and feedback.

The form also asks clarification on the following questions:

- What are the objectives for this activity?

- What activities will take place?

- Are there any aspects of the activity you would like the observer to note?

- Are there special circumstance of which the observer should be aware?

- How will you know if the objectives were met?

All three observations should focus on different counselor functions: small group, individual counseling, classroom guidance, conferences, etc.

In summary, educators as counselors should be encouraged to help plan evaluation studies to appraise the quality of guidance programs and counseling services. Specific suggestions for improving programs and services should be obtained from a cross-section of the constituents served. Dialogues about accountability should be heeded as an opportunity to provide clear, concise definitions of counselor role and function; to improve cooperation among school professionals in implementing objectives; and to develop clearly stated goals. With systematic evaluation and routine accountability, educators can securely defend services and obtain adequate fiscal resources to support them. It represents an approach that serves to operationalize both the outcome of program objectives and the outcome of student objectives to foster a consumer/community centered model of guidance program goals and counseling services.

CHAPTER 15

DEVELOPING EFFECTIVE PUBLIC RELATIONS

As educators, we believe that knowledge is information without meaning until it is shared with others, or put into practice

Anonymous

Many of us have a tendency to assume that what we know well is common knowledge to others. Consequently, guidance and counseling services provided by the school counselor in and outside of the school setting often go unnoticed by parents, colleagues, and constituents. The knowledge explosion is contributing to this void in program articulation.

More and more, we have become the convenient receptor of paper forms and continually changing information processing technologies. The knowledge explosion is punctuated by paper. Paper within institutional bureaucracies has become necessary to document, record, report, and justify, as well as to teach new information to students, parents, educators, and helping professionals. We have evolved to the level where a practicing counselor's work is almost useless, (perpetuating more cost than benefit within the time investment ratio) if it is not adequately documented for reference and dissemination to confused or inquiring consumers. Many school counselors, naturally feel beleaguered by the pace of rapid change.

Declining school enrollments, tightly extended budgets, reforms within the curriculum, demands for accountability, and a growing number of at-risk student subpopulations are dismal facts of life for many counseling programs. Concerns for accountability also have received national attention. For example, Gallop polls of public attitudes toward schools revealed some alarming evidence that guidance and counseling is viewed less positively today than a decade ago. In the 1971 Gallop poll (Gallop, 1971), reducing the number of counselors on the staff was ranked fourth of 16 proposals for cutting school costs, with 32% of those surveyed favoring such a recommendation. Eleven years later, another Gallop poll (Gallop, 1982) found that reducing the number of counselors was ranked second of nine methods of cutting school costs, with 49% of the respondents endorsing such a measure.

MARKETING

In the last decade, corporations, universities, hospitals, social agencies, as well as political groups have engaged in aggressive public relations campaigns which continue to demonstrate the value of effective public relations programs. Public relations and marketing strategies have gained a permanent and respected place within the management structure of these groups or organizations.

Public relations defined could be considered "the planned effort to influence opinion through socially responsible and acceptable performance based on mutually satisfactory two way communication" (Cutlip & Center, 1971), or "Public relations is the management function which evaluates public attitudes, identifies the policies and procedures of an organization with the public interest and plans and executes a program of action to earn public understanding and acceptance" (Griswold, 1947).

Marketing is a critical component of school counseling public relations programs. During the past decade, school public relations has evolved as a true profession, anchored in research and knowledge about how attitudes are formed. Public relations also has evolved as an important component of counseling programs throughout the nation in both public and private schools. It is more than publicity, which merely announces or provides a statement of fact. Public relations is communicating counseling roles and functions, programs and services, costs and benefits to those inside and outside of the school division. To be effective, it must be positive, consistent, and consciously integrated into the total counseling program.

Yet, many counselors, acutely aware of the needs of school and community, find the thought of having to "sell" their programs disconcerting. Images of being a "hard-selling, fast-talker" often come to mind. Marketing, however, is different from selling. **Selling** focuses on the needs of the seller, converting a product into cash. **Marketing** focuses upon identifying the needs of the counselee or consumer, then researching, planning, creating, and delivering a service to satisfy those needs. Kotler (1975) in his book *Marketing for Nonprofit Organizations,* stated:

> Marketing is the analysis, planning, implementation, and control of carefully formulated programs designed to bring about voluntary exchanges of values with target populations for the purpose of achieving organizational objectives. It relies heavily on designing the organization's offerings in terms of the needs and desires, and on using effective communication, and a system of delivery to inform, motivate, and educate. (p. 23)

From this perspective, counselors can position their programs and services as essential offerings in the school, their community, and their districts. Most plans call for an investment in up-to-date creative programming, and greater community involvement. The dividends are the enhancement of the image and perceived value of counseling. Counseling is highly marketable, addressing the needs of all people of all ages, from the elementary school child to the senior citizen.

Within this context, marketing has developed three major concepts: segmentation, perceptual mapping, and positioning. **Segmentation** seeks to break down the market into discreet blocks of counselees or potential counselees. **Perceptual Mapping** attempts to find out what students, parents, alumni, teachers, business leaders, community leaders, and other groups perceive to be the nature of school counseling programs and services, along with its strengths and weaknesses. **Positioning** (which relies heavily on segment analysis and perceptual mapping) tries to build on widely held perceptions with the right audiences such as P.T.A./P.T.O., support agencies, parents, and other helping professionals. An essential component is to know precisely what are your program's strengths and weaknesses.

Parenthetically, marketing should not be confused with selling or advertising. In marketing, the effort is a more scholarly endeavor of systematically understanding who your counseling program is serving, why they come, why they don't come, and how you might better serve students, parents, teachers, and others. Marketing is an invaluable tool in helping to improve your program's communications with others and to establish your comparative advantage over other programs and services within the school-as-community. Positioning yourself more visibly to gain support for programs and services is critical to survival.

Most marketing plans call for up-to-date, creative programming, quality dissemination, increased student recruitment, greater community involvement, and the enhancement of the image and perceived value of counseling. Designing a workable marketing plan for your program and its services requires the basic steps of any planning activity:

- assessment of needs,
- setting goals and objectives based upon needs,
- formation on strategies to reach the goals and objectives,
- implementation of strategies, and
- assessment and evaluation of progress.

Selecting marketing strategies and implementing them is vital for a successful marketing plan. In choosing strategies and plans of action, use a form to list each strategy and the need it is meeting, required resources, the person responsible for following through the strategy, a timeline for completion. Putting it in writing provides a time frame for accountability and responsibility. In Figure 15.1 is a worksheet for implementing strategies related to public relations.

(Continued on Page 326)

GOAL: To plan and implement strategies for successful marketing of my program.

WHY: The main reason I need to do this is

_____

_____

WHO: This stragegy is primarily deisgned to reach:

          ❏ Community

          ❏ Parents

          ❏ Legislators

          ❏ Students

          ❏ Administration

          ❏ Other Faculty

          ❏ Board Members

          The first strategy I want to implement is: _____

          _____

WHICH: Critical limitations which might prevent me from doing this are

          1. _____

          2. _____

          3. _____

          4. _____

HOW: Can I overcome these limitations?

          lim. 1, actions _____

          lim. 2, actions _____

          lim. 3, actions _____

          lim. 4, actions _____

WHAT: Steps required to implement this strategy are

              Step   By When   Who else is involved

          _____   _____   _____

          _____   _____   _____

          _____   _____   _____

SUPPORT: The support network person with whom I will remain in communication while
          I implement this strategy is

          _____

WHERE: I will communicate at least once per month on the _____
AND   to share my success and to identify my needs for assistance, additional resources,
WHEN   and the like.

Figure 15.1. Worksheet for implementing strategies.

Know Your Audience

When planning strategies, know your internal and external audiences. Your internal audience will involve students, advisory committees, faculty and staff, administration, and support personnel. The external audience will include school board members, feeder schools and parents, out-of-school adults, the general public, senior citizens, media representatives, local human service agencies, and professional groups with interests similar to those of counselors. Develop internal and external strategies which are germane to your own particular setting, and which are within your realm of available resources. An illustration of a communication model for internal and external audiences is included as Figure 15.2.

INTERNAL MARKETING STRATEGIES

Educate

Develop yearly school counseling calendars for dissemination to students and their families. Be creative and include pictures of the school, a personal profile of the staff, or special events. Provide standardized test dates, interim report, report card dates, college nights, financial aid workshops, career days, class orientations, and/or other pertinent dates.

Provide monthly calendars for faculty and staff to promote support and commitment to educational, occupational, and interpersonal counseling programs and services.

Use flyers, pamphlets, posters, and photos to promote courses, programs, and services with students, parents, and instructional staff.

Create a slide-tape or video presentation covering curricula, and program offerings for multiple promotional use (i.e., with staff feeder schools, students, and parents).

(Continued on Page 328)

INTERNAL	EXTERNAL
Students, especially those who are involved in school newspapers, annuals, and other extracurricular activities	**Advertising agencies** who may provide consulting help or even specific campaign assistance
School board members who have many business and civic contracts	**Sales promotion directors** in advertising and publicity from large retail stores who may assist in implementing a school-community relations program
Secretaries who can create favorable impressions in phone contacts and influence persons visiting the school on business	
	Chamber of commerce executives who should be able to present schools to newcomers in the community
Teachers of business, advertising, English, marketing, and vocations who have skills in communicating school information	
Staff members who arrange work experince for students and contact potential employers in the community and interpret the school to them	**Civic officials,** e.g., mayor, city manager, county commissioners, recreation directors, who are positive toward the schools and project favorable attitudes to others in the community
Coaches who influence student and community interest in the sports program of the school	**Alumni** of all ages who can identify with the school, know about its development, and support its programs
Teachers who are sponsors of other extacurricular activities, i.e., dramatics, bands, chorus, and who cultivate community support for their groups	**Classes in advertising** in local colleges and who may be involved in universities helping develop specific public relations project
	Media personnel in the community who can help get news and feature coverage for schools into newspapers, radio, and local television

Source: Pfeiffer, I.L., & Dunlap, J.B. (1988). Advertising practices to improve school-community relations. *NASSP Bulletin,* Vol 72, No. 506.

Figure 15.2. Internal and external advertising practices.

Train students as peer counselors to serve as articulation agents of the guidance and counseling program. (See Chapter 4 on Developmental Guidance Counseling for details).

Invite the principal or other administrators to sit in on a guidance and information session.

Advise other staff or support personnel of activities for which counseling are related to the improvement of instruction and/or curriculum.

Conduct periodic school assembly programs aimed at specific student interests, adjustment needs, or developmental concerns (e.g., drug and alcohol abuse, time management, decision making, interpersonal relationships, or communication skills).

Provide a list of services and specific functions counselors provide, post it for teachers and staff, highlighting special areas of expertise such as scholarships, college advisement, and group counseling.

Develop and conduct workshops and seminars to assist the instructional staff in such areas as motivation, testing, stress and time management, communication skills, or parent conferencing.

Conduct workshops for student government or leadership groups within the school on topics such as team-building, communication, consensus reaching, problem solving, and leadership.

Involve

Have teacher support groups for students to promote wellness or provide an arena where students can share anxieties and concerns in a secure environment with another caring adult.

Hold a departmental Open House (before or after school or during lunch) on a regularly scheduled basis for students to visit counseling offices to obtain information, brochures, and to review their present program of studies (e.g., Wednesday is Junior Day and Thursday is Senior Day).

Be visible and accessible, both are critical components in order to be held in high esteem. Eat with the students in the cafeteria, walk in the halls in the morning before school and say hello to the teacher out in the portable classroom.

Make your phone available to others during appropriate times. Teachers frequently do not have access to a private phone in the building. This demonstrates equality and a cooperative spirit to staff members.

Develop a schedule of evening hours for counselors to meet the changing needs of families and the labor force. Compensate the counselor with a later morning arrival the following day.

Offer staff members as speakers for local service clubs. Most staff members have great credibility and take great pride in professionally representing their discipline.

Enlist the help of parent volunteers to cut down on routine paperwork. The volunteers will feel they are contributing to the school program. The counselor will have at least two or more hours to meet with "people rather than paper."

Have students conduct polls, design school questionnaires on student interests and needs related to counseling. Report findings in the school newspaper for feature articles providing a supportive data based on counseling knowledge.

Develop a "Teacher-Advisor System" where teachers are advisors to students and serve to disseminate and clarify educational and occupational information on a routine basis.

Designate different counselors as liaisons to the various academic and vocational departments within the school. Have them attend departmental meetings and field questions or concerns.

Establish a "Guidance Advisory Committee" to establish goals, identify needs, and develop and plan activities.

Meet with new staff socially before the total staff return to school to welcome and explain programs.

Meet with specific departments within the school to explain programs, services, and resources that the counseling department can offer in their particular discipline.

Establish a building public relations committee composed of members of all staff groups as well as parents. Give the committee specific objectives to generate timely activities.

Recognize

Recognize outstanding efforts on the part of individual teachers in working with students, e.g., charitable or service activities.

Recognize administrators for their interest, support, and contribution to counseling. Invite them to your local professional meetings.

Periodically express appreciation to custodians, secretaries, and parent volunteers. Reinforce that their contributions make the counseling program successful. Send letters of appreciation recognizing contributions to their supervisor.

Put up a bulletin board with outstanding graduates as the focus. It provides both a follow-up of activities of graduates and a positive incentive for younger students to excel.

Start a "Secret Pal"/"Secret Friend" Program. The idea is simple—every staff member draws another's name and does kind deeds and favors for that person all year anonymously. This could also work with students (such as peer helpers) or with all counselors in your district.

Sponsor a teacher recognition campaign at your school. Enlist the fiscal support from local businesses. Develop inexpensive, yet thoughtful ways to show appreciation, such as letters, small gifts in mailboxes, gift certificates at local retail stores, etc.

Have a staff appreciation luncheon. Invite central office leadership and VIPs from the local community.

Highlight special programs and services that specific teachers or departments provide, e.g., highlight a "teacher feature" in the school's weekly bulletin or monthly newsletter.

Develop an "upclose and personal" file on colleagues and other helping professionals. Note details of their accomplishments, particular areas of expertise, hobbies, interests, and children. This adds a personal dimension to communication and builds rapport among peers.

EXTERNAL MARKETING STRATEGIES

Create a file of addresses and phone numbers of city hall, state representatives and senators, the newsrooms of local papers, the names of editors, television and radio station managers, and presidents or chairman of local clubs such as the Rotary or the Chamber of Commerce, for future contacts.

Share educational goals and school-based needs with other helping professionals in both the public and private sector. Many private agencies who employ "referral development representatives" welcome any opportunity to educate the public about their programs. Many sponsor workshops for the community on a variety of topics such as "teenage depression, stress, or chemical dependency" which in turn provides a valuable resource for students and their families.

Develop a reference list of parents, community organizations, and student organizations who support and promote the school guidance and counseling program.

If your division or district has an on-going adopt-a-school program, involve them in your program.

When a local newspaper publishes a feature article about your program or students, reproduce the article and distribute it to your faculty, administration, support personnel, school board members, and P.T.A./P.T.O.

Have business cards printed for distribution to key community persons (include your name, special interests, and phone number).

Network with feeder schools. Send copies of bulletins, newsletters, and other material to feeder schools. This reinforces how important they are to the success of your program. Send copies of honor roles, merit awards, and other accomplishments to feeder schools. They will appreciate your sharing the successes of their former students with them.

Educate

Organize a district-wide speaker's bureau consisting of counselors within your school system to speak to special interest groups to highlight individual expertise and to promote the value of counseling. A district-wide Parent Night also could be conducted to showcase counselor skills and expertise.

Offer one day workshops for special audiences in the community, either on-campus or at a community center (e.g., job seeking and job keeping skills, parenting skills, how to prepare for tests, etc.).

Develop a regular newsletter for distribution to parents, school P.T.A./P.T.O., school board members, feeder schools, senior citizen clubs, church groups, community agencies, etc. In Figure 15.3 is a sample newsletter.

Develop a brief talk/presentation on a timely subject for use with local clubs, organizations, or interest groups. Send information in August and December to program chairpersons of community groups telling about your offerings. Topics may include human relations, stress management, wellness, career forecasts, time-management, etc. In Figure 15.4 is an example of a sample contact letter.

Provide information or brief reports for school board meetings on a periodic basis (e.g., explain changing student demographics, percentage going to college, universities, military service; percentage who dropout; teen pregnancy, drug and alcohol related problems). In Figure 15.5 is an example of a report that could be shared with various groups and individuals.

Write short articles for the local newspaper.

Maintain a current file of "read and rip" clips about current issues related or focused on counseling issues as a timely frame-of-reference for the well-informed counselor (e.g., Does coaching for the S.A.T. really work? Would developing a "homework hotline" be helpful? Will engineering majors be required to bring their own computers to school at State U?).

Send press memos, or news articles to local media about counseling related events, programs, and activities. To further ensure the chance of getting media coverage of an event, schedule it for the "fifth something of the month." Most organizations and news-making organizations meet on the first and third Wednesday or on the second Tuesday. Editors looking for news will generally find less on the days following the "fifth something."

(Continued on Page 337)

COUNSELOR'S KALEIDOSCOPE

October 19--

TO: ALL STUDENTS

FROM: COUNSELING DEPARTMENT

SUBJECT: NEWS ON CAREER INFORMATION, COLLEGE OPPORTUNITIES & STUDENT
ACHIEVEMENT

By now you are all settled in your classes and hard at work.
We hope this year will be the most rewarding school year that you
have experienced and that you are looking forward to it with great
anticipation.

In order to keep informed and up-to-date on items of interest
and importance to you, The Counselor's Kaleidoscope will be issued
periodically. If you have questions or desire more information
concerning any items appearing, please see one of the counselors.
If you have questions concerning matters which are not included
or if I can be of service to you in any way, please feel free to
come by the Counseling Department anytime.

College Boards and American Testing Programs

Most colleges require that students take the S.A.T. (college
boards) or A.C.T. (American College Testing) for admission. Some
of you took S.A.T. last spring. If you did not take it or you did
not do as well as you would like, you should register for the S.A.T.
(or A.C.T., if the college of your choice requires this test) as
early as possible. Registration forms may be obtained in the guidance
office.

Test dates for the S.A.T. and Achievement Tests* are as follows:

TEST DATE	REGISTRATION DEADLINE
November 5	September 30
December 3	October 28
January 28	December 23
April 7	March 2
May 5	March 30
June 2	April 27

*Some colleges require that students take Achievement Tests in
subject areas in addition to the S.A.T. Achievement Tests are given
on the same dates as the S.A.T., but you cannot take both on the
same date.

Figure 15.3. Counselor's Kaleidoscope (shown in typewritten form).

```
Your Name:   _____

  School:    _____

 Address:    _____

   Phone:    _____
```

Dear Program Chairperson:

Your organization may have need for a speaker with my experience and qualifications. I am a licensed professional counselor with 10 years experience in the field. I have had numerous speaking engagements and written several articles on counseling issues. My most frequently requested topics are

        Alternatives to college

        Goal Setting for Career Development

        How to Help Your Child Choose a Career

        The Future Job Market

        Adolescence: Storm or Stress?

        How to Find Your First Professional Job

        Financial Aid and Money for College

        Stress and the Family

        How to Write a Winning Resume

        Homework Strategies for Better Grades

Your interest is appreciated. Feel free to call me at the number above to discuss any of the topics listed.

        Yours truly,

        NAME

Figure 15.4. Sample contact letter (shown in typewritten form).

TO: ALL FACULTY & STAFF

FROM: COUNSELING DEPARTMENT

DATE: February 15, 19--

With the end of first semester, we have decided to outline the counseling programs and activities that the counseling department has generated to date. Routine counseling, consultations, partent/ teacher/student contacts, and attention to administrative details are assumptions of our role as counselors on the secondary level. We thought, however, that we would capsule some of the additional programs and services that we offered the students and staff in our continuing efforts to meet the variety of needs of our particular population.

Activity/Program/Service	No. of Students Served
PSAT/SAT Preparation & Test-taking Skills	138
Targeted Support Groups for students	342
Armed Services Vocational Aptitude Battery administered & interpreted	128
Post-secondary Fair for college bound	272
Inservice by planning bells: Implementation of Student Assistance Core Teams	All Faculty
Selecting a college and how to apply for scholarships	232
Administered JOB-O and follow-up with career planning	205
Small group counseling—Life skills	246
Apprenticeship Representative	30
College Representatives from: Longwood University of Virginia Averett Atlantic Christian Old Dominion University Norfolk State University Bridgewater College Christopher Newport George Mason College of William & Mary	20 per session

Figure 15.5. Counselor's report card (shown in typewritten form).

Work with the local public television or cable station to develop a locally aired forum on counseling concerns for parents such as a local and state college/ university forum. The program can be co-hosted by counselor/ teachers/administrators or deans of admissions at local colleges. Topics could include financing a college education, admissions tests, college life, etc.

If your local newspaper carries a feature article about your program, duplicate the article and distribute it to your school's faculty and administrators. If the article is especially positive, have a number of copies made for distribution to external audiences and any other person or groups with whom your department is involved. Be assertive in marketing and promoting a new image of counseling to internal and external audiences.

Develop a radio or public service message on S.A.T./ P.S.A.T. deadlines, financial aid information, college and career night, youth services support group resources, parenting clases, and wellness issues.

Involve

Provide supervisors and other support personnel with information that will assist them in effective decision making and sound policy formation.

Invite past and present student leadership groups to discuss their impressions of guidance and counseling services.

Obtain periodic rankings of important guidance and counseling services from different groups—students, parents, employers, administrators, and community organizations.

Become an active participant in a community civic organization or public affairs group (e.g., Rotary Club, Lions Club, Kiwanis, Chamber of Commerce, Junior League, etc.).

Establish and utilize a board school and community-based guidance advisory committee for identification of consumer needs and articulation of programs and services.

Conduct a periodic needs assessment of parents, students, faculty, and administration.

Schedule on a semester basis, opportunities for peer program visitation to local feeder schools.

Write letters of congratulations to individuals in the community who have achieved recognition for something related to counseling interests; to individuals who have expressed support for counseling and school counselors.

Spotlight outstanding graduates by placing advertisements in the local newspaper or sponsor a special reunion in their honor. Invite school supporters.

Present "Certificates of Appreciation" or recognition to persons helpful to the goals of the counseling department.

PARENT/TEACHER ORGANIZATIONS: ALIEN OR ALLY

The Parent Teacher Association (PTA) or Parent Teacher Organization (PTO) is perhaps the most overlooked resource for school counseling programs. Their fundamental interests, from a lay person's perspective, is the well-being of the educational climate and the students it serves. Counselors who become involved with these organizations can greatly enhance programs, as well as provide accurate information to anxious parents who yearn to be involved, yet hesitate to participate. Community support for your counseling program is achieved only through hard work and spending time fostering a productive interchange between school program and parent interest. A continuum of parent involvement is illustrated in Figure 15.6. As supportive organizations, they have unlimited

(Continued on Page 340)

No Involvement	Parents as Volunteers	Parents as Partners
No PTA or PTO	PTA, PTO is strong	PTA, PTO advocate of partnership
No volunteer program	Program support is provided	Direct communication between parent and teacher
Interaction with principal only	Parents engaged in volunteer activities	Focus on individual child
Parents come to school only when requested	Balance of teacher and administrative contact	Parent involved with intructional activities
	Indirect awareness of classroom activities and expectations	Parent knowledgeable of course expectation and class activities

Source: Sandfort, J.A. (1987). Putting Parents in their place. *NASSP Bulletin,* Vol. 71, No. 496, P. 36. Reprinted by permission.

Figure 15.6. When parents are partners.

possibilities. For a list of activities by parents and teaching staff see Figure 15.7. The following activities are suggested opportunities which could strengthen the guidance and counseling program:

Select a number of parents to survey opinions and attitudes of other community members—both parents and nonparents.

Make presentations to parent/teacher associations about counseling services and elicit specific interests or needs.

Enlist the support of interested parents as volunteers to assist in hall monitoring during testing, to prepare mass mailings, or to call absentees, etc.

Start a scholarship fund with the parent/teacher organization and provide a comprehensive scholarship directory listing local scholarships and selection criteria.

Annually recognize members and the organization for the services they provide to the school and counseling department.

Annually plan a cooperative "Parent Information Night" with the counseling department and the parent/teacher organization for local as well as feeder school populations about a series of topics in which the community might be interested. In Figure 15.8 is an example of a brochure to inform parents.

Parent Volunteers: Parents
Actively Serving School (PASS)

The P.A.S.S. program can be sponsored by the parent/ teacher association as part of a "Volunteers in Education" project. The program is beneficial in providing the school with valuable and needed human resources while allowing parents to obtain firsthand knowledge and experience of quality information.

(Continued on Page 343)

Parents	Teaching Staff
• Assist with homework	• Invites parent to school (conferences/classes)
• Consult with teachers	
• Review assignments	• Informs parents of expectations
• Assist with schedule planning	• Writes educational prescriptions
• Serve as resource	• Calls home
• Assist in classrooms	• Solicits parent help
• Initiate conferences	• Provides suggestions
• Provide study time and environment	• Assigns "do-able" tasks
• Read with students	• Shares with parents
• Promote writing in the home	• Develops observable learning objectives
• Provide educational resources	
• Model appropriate skills and behaviors	
• Blend education and family activities	
• Talk about goals	
• Post examples of good work	
• Visit classes	
• Reinforce skills	
• Encourage improvement	
• Reinforce good behavior	

Source: Sandfort, J.A. (1987). Putting parents in their place. *NASSP Bulletin,* Vol. 71, No. 4, p. 37. Reprinted by permission.

Figure 15.7. Partnership activities.

**PARENT INFORMATION:
A SERIES OF WORKSHOPS**

7:00 p.m.

Jan 9— Financing a College Education
              Jim Brown, School Counselor

Jan 15— Sensitive Parenting
              Ruth Hamilton, School Counselor

Jan 22— Reducing Family Discord
              Jack Whitehall, School Counselor

Feb 6— Keeping Your Kids Off Drugs
              Jim Brown, School Counselor

March 3— Working at School, Schooling for Work
              Ruth Hamilton, School Counselor

You are invited
No fee is charged

Offered by
School Counselors
Northside High School
Guidance Department & P.T.S.A.

Figure 15.8. Parent information night: A series of workshops.

Volunteer activities fall into three broad categories:

- clerical assistance such as working in the library, in the main offices, or collecting fees;

- classroom assistance such as tutorial aids, distribution of classroom materials, or working with groups; and

- special areas such as chaperoning, assisting in the clinic, or working in the career center.

MULTIMEDIA APPROACHES

A public relations activity can take on many forms from general feature articles and talk show interviews to public service announcements on radio, television, and the newspaper. Use of the media reaches a wider audience. Promotion is an important, yet often neglected component of any worthwhile program. In each school guidance and counseling program, certain individuals enjoy working with the media. Designate one person in the department to be the public relations liaison. A public relations philosophy also would be helpful.

Face-to-face contact, telephone contacts, and mail exchanges are three processes which, when incorporated into any program, tend to assure media exposure. Recordkeeping and systematic organization save time and energy. Since most media sources are overwhelmed with calls and releases, they frequently misplace, discard, or "never receive" your materials (especially if they went to the wrong person). Recognize the need to maintain a ready reference of media contact and pertinent information. It is wise to follow up all calls with written data and all written data with a phone call. A uniform contact sheet may be helpful to expedite an otherwise arduous chore.

**Checklist of Vital Components
of a Public Service Announcement**

Submission should be on 8 1/2 x 11 white typing paper and double spaced to allow space for editing.

Provide name, address, phone number, and department name on the "upper left corner."

Start the release of information one-third of the way down the page, leaving four or five inches of blank space at the top.

Provide spacious margins on sides, bottom, and top.

Keep the release as short as possible. If a second page is necessary, type "more" at the bottom of the first page.

Start the next page with the page number and an identification phrase such as "page 2 . . . Parent Information Night," in the upper left corner.

Indicate the end of the story by typing "-30-" or "###"

Indicate when the announcement should be released.

Follow-up anything that gets "aired" or printed with a "thank you" letter.

Don't burden your media contact by asking for copies of printed material. Collect them from your colleagues.

Hand deliver whenever possible and follow-up with a phone call.

Recognize that most weekly papers are printed on Wednesday nights, so editors must have news copy in hand by Tuesday at the latest. If your release is timed to coincide with an actual event such as a workshop or conference, mark it "for immediate release"

Procedures for Photos and Captions

Send to newspapers 8 x 10 or 5 x 7 black and white photos with only two to three people in the frame at a time.

Make sure people in the photo are doing what you say they are doing.

Do not ask for your photo to be returned.

Type or write captions with felt marker on a separate sheet of paper and attach it to the back of the photo by a strip of cellophane tape.

Note on the caption all individuals in the photo (from left to right) and state their full name, what they are doing, and might include what school.

Recognize that the amount of media space available for stories, photos, etc., is determined by the advertising space sold. Not getting your data in means no space was available at the time you needed it.

Newspaper or Organizational Bulletin
Proposal Outline

Format. "The Counselors' Corner" (if so named) will provide current weekly information and resources to subscribers of the local newspaper. It will center around various themes that may be of interest to readers. Feature stories or articles provide an opportunity for favorable coverage of guidance and counseling programs and services.

Information. Information should be factual; not opinion or advice, and should provide readers with current information about careers, financial aid, or vocational and educational programs.

Rationale. The newspaper column should communicate local and state-wide information about programs, services, and opportunities pertaining to career, vocational, and post-secondary planning of students. It should also serve to

- bridge the gap of communicative accuracy that sometimes exists between prospective programs and parents, counselors and students;

- actively articulate the services and information school counseling programs can provide;

- increase the public visibility of school counseling services;

- increase the accountability of school counseling programs and services; and

- provide a means of accurate communication to parents and the community, and provide a more efficient use of time and energy by reaching the public through a popular medium.

Suggested Topics. The following are suggested topics. Many others could be included.

- Applying for Financial Aid
- Tuition Assistance for Independent Colleges
- College Admission Test Dates and Deadlines
- Test Taking Tips
- Postsecondary College and Training Fair
- How to Apply to the Service Academies
- National Merit Scholarships
- Apprentice Programs
- Tips for the Job Interview
- How to Get Job Experience Through Volunteer Opportunities
- Occupational Outlook to the Year 2000
- What Colleges Consider to Be Important Entrance Requirements

Journalism Principles. The following journalism principles also should be considered:

Fundamentally, include in most stories six basic facts: whom, what, when, where, how, and why.

Strive for easy readability by using short words and simple sentences. Use short paragraphs and try to keep the story to a single page.

Write the "lead" or first paragraph of the story so as to provide the most important facts. The "body" or remainder of the story should contain further details in order of descending importance. Essentially, make the first paragraph complete with essential facts so that the story can be cut from the bottom (if space and time dictates) without losing important information.

Make sure the story is complete so that the reader is not left with an unanswered question about time, place, or participants.

Before sending in the article, check for accuracy, grammar, spelling, punctuation, and typing. Also keep a file copy.

Double space the article. This allows space for copy readers to write in any necessary instructions.

A Systematic Approach for Organizing a Feature Column

Collect the Facts. Many informational resources are available to counselors, e.g., local newsletters from postsecondary training or educational opportunities, and publications from the U.S. Department of Labor such as the *Occupational Outlook Handbook*. In the interest of saving time, it is helpful to implement "rip and read" or "clip and save" procedure of collecting articles or information. Categorize information into categories such as educational, occupational, or counseling.

Determine Your Approach. Once you have enough facts, look over the materials you have assembled and decide how you want to approach it. How, for example, would you handle a story about a learning disabled student who has enrolled in a nearby college which offers special services and has become an honor graduate? Would you tell the story from his/her point of view? Or would you arrange the facts about him/her into a narrative that would simply report the story? The question of the approach must be answered before you start writing.

Write a Suitable Lead. For a feature column, the lead does not have to follow the strict one-paragraph format (i.e., giving a summary of the entire story) of a straight news lead or include all the essential facts. Instead it must emphasize attention-getting statements, make clear what kind of information to expect, and set the tone. It should also establish the angle from which your readers will view the story and should encourage them to want to read further.

The first three or four words in your lead must attract readers to your story. Types of leads which have been most useful in an educational-informational column such as the "Counselor's Corner" have been leads which begin with

- a striking statement,
- with a quotation, or
- with a question.

Focus on Significant Details. The impression your column makes depends not only on the way it is organized, but also on the details it includes. For example, if you write an article on financial aid for college bound students, make sure terms, abbreviations, deadlines, and dates are clear and up-to-date. Highlighting eligibility criteria or alternatives for the borderline candidate also should be considered.

Write With Purpose and Personality. Collect and organize your material and write your column informally but clearly in a lively, appealing style. One practical approach often used is to write an opening lead that is "catchy," or thought provoking, followed by an informative body with examples and illustrations and a closing which is encouraging or upbeat.

Ethical Considerations. A guidance and counseling program provides for direct service to students, staff, and community, and strives to achieve the following goals:

- to assist persons in developing a better understanding and acceptance of themselves; their strengths and limitations; aptitudes, needs values, and interests; and their worth as unique individuals;

- to assist individuals in problem solving and decision making; and

- to accept increased responsibility for their educational, occupational, and vocational development (American School Counselor Association, 1983).

A column of this nature needs to promote a professional tone and serve as a one vehicle of many for delivering accurate, timely information. Caution should be employed not to permit the column to evolve into an "advice" column. All sources of information also should receive the proper citation, as well as credit given to the author(s).

Public Speaking

Practicing counselors who are reluctant to present programs at professional conferences, or in-service training for their faculty are missing a tremendous opportunity to encourage interest and support from colleagues. Many school counselors do not realize that the routine activities they perform on a daily basis would be valued in the public domain. Many also may lack self-confidence in their skills and abilities. Nonetheless, the investment in a timely presentation generates a more positive image of school counselors. The following strategies and suggestions are provided to enhance the school counselor professional presentations:

Deliver your initial presentation to strangers, away from people who are familiar with you. It's easier to present to strangers, because you may never see them again! They also can provide more objective feedback if you elicit an evaluation of your presentation.

Survey the literature and current attitudes about timely topics. Topics held in high esteem by peers are usually those which are practical in developing and presenting ideas.

Provide an illustration of a new concept, or better yet, demonstrate a new skill. Audience participation such as role-playing also is well received.

Timing is critical. Most of us cannot pay attention for a long period of time, so break your presentation into segments:

- introduction or "anticipatory set" raise the consciousness of your audience by asking questions, or giving a unique illustration, etc. (5 minutes);

- presentation of new information, strategies, or skills (20 minutes); and

- closure of information with time for questions (10 to 15 minutes).

Provide handouts. Announce that handouts are available at the beginning of the presentation, however, hold them to the end. This approach serves as a motivator for listening and participating. Getting the audience involved as active participants also is successful. Provide key concepts, brief examples, a bibliography of other sources, and any potential limitations. If more requests are made for your information than you have on hand, mail materials to participants. Such is an important follow-up component in public relations.

Annoying mannerisms or behaviors which call attention to themselves also can slip into your delivery and should be avoided. Here are a few classics:

- talking too fast;
- fiddling with paper, pencils, jewelry, or eye glasses;
- adjusting clothes;
- winding your watch;
- misusing the lectern such as continually adjusting or leaning on it;
- a slumping or dejected posture;

- lack of eye contact with your audience; and
- vocalizing pauses such as "ah" or with phrases like "you know", "where as," "therefore," "on the other hand," etc.

Presentation Planning Guide. The following are guidelines to use in your planning and presentation.

Topic

Date to be presented

Location

Time needed

Time allowed

Objective of presentation

How will the audience benefit?

What reactions or concerns should I anticipate?

What style of presentation will be most effective?

- lecture
- demonstration
- audiovisual
- panel discussion
- combination

Technical resources needed:

- lectern
- microphone
- overhead
- tv/vcr

Handouts provided

Finally, read your entire speech to yourself aloud. Change any language that is awkward to pronounce or to listen to. Audiotape or videotape yourself and review your taping for diction, inflection, delivery, voice quality, sequence, and organization of material.

Enhancing Your Delivery

Begin your presentation with a smile and a warm thank you to the person (by first name) who introduced you. Acknowledging the introducer by his/her first name reinforces their credibility and initiates your own acceptance by the audience.

Have a high-impact opening and memorize your first sentence thoroughly. The opening should get attention, stimulate thought, and reflect the theme of your talk. In the beginning, people sit a little straighter in their chairs and listen more critically.

Obtain the audience's attention by such things as

- asking a question,
- making a thought provoking statement,
- giving a stimulating illustration,
- telling a story that's unique or humorous, and/or
- speaking to the special interest of your listeners.

Maintain their interest by

- stating clearly what you want your audience to know,
- using illustrations to support your central idea,
- repeating ideas to make them stick,
- relating each idea to the others for clarity, and/or
- including an occasional quote or anecdote to illustrate the points you make.

Maintain constant eye contact with your audience, especially if questioning becomes intense. Eye contact establishes credibility in what you are saying.

Keep smiling unless the subject matter is sensitive or somber. In that case, reflect the proper demeanor but return to the optimistic or more positive as soon as possible.

Be clear and concise. When presenting or answering questions make short, simple, concrete statements.

Use familiar illustrations and comparisons to make your points. Simplicity communicates best.

Anticipate any negative questions. Don't let an outrageous accusation or statement go unchallenged. Refute it politely and with a smile, offering a brief positive explanation, then move on to issues you or the rest of the audience want to discuss.

Close your presentation with a reference to the opening remarks. Memorize your last closing sentence thoroughly. Convey your appreciation to the audience and for the opportunity to be with them.

How To Get On Talk Shows

If you have an interesting story to tell and a stimulating way to tell it, talk shows may be looking for you! Radio and television time is unlimited. Producers are anxious for new ideas. The following are some suggestions to help put you in front of the camera.

Know Your Local Stations. Each station has its own personality. Design your proposal for air time so that it fits into the station's image.

Also get to know the station people. A small station may have a program director who takes care of all guest shows. Some stations also will have a public affairs director. A large station will have these people, but also will have a producer, director, and secretary for the show. Call the station to find out the chain of command, including the names of the hosts of talk shows.

Know Your Message. You'll never get on the air to talk about "good counseling." Decide what specific issues you want to discuss and why they are timely. What can you tell people that they do not already know. As an illustration, you might decide to discuss the various forms of treatment programs for substance abusing adolescents and their families. Prepare a background briefing about the aspect of professional counseling you want to portray. Talk show hosts do not need a lot of material, but they need enough to give them a sense of the subject. You should include facts about treatment strategies and other details that make the process valuable.

Prepare a one-page fact sheet telling the "who, what, when, where, why, and how" for the host. You also may want to prepare a list of ten open-ended questions about professional counseling that cannot be answered with a simple "yes" or "no." Your ultimate goal is to get this information into the public domain; for example, to demystify drug treatment alternatives and to increase counselor credibility.

Developing a School Counseling Brochure

Desktop publishing offers an unlimited possibility for creating and disseminating information. Computer technology can be used to produce counselor brochures, newsletters, specialized forms, course descriptions, handbooks quickly, economically, and with quality. New information can be added or deleted. Formats can be changed, type size can be decreased or increased, and illustrations can be added, taken out, or moved with the touch of a key. In developing such public relations items as brochures consider the following:

> Define your service: counseling, group guidance, career information, parent consultation, community human service liaison, etc.

> Define your market: parents, teachers, students, pupil personnel, churches, local business, etc.

> Understand perceptions and preferences of your market and their educational frame of reference. For example, poorly drawn cartoons may not be well received by

an adolescent population. Conversely, parents may not respond well to brochures written in "educanese."

Create an image that promotes credibility.

Use catchy phrases which elicit personal reactions, such as "counselors help America work" for a brochure on job-seeking skills.

Make sure your method of distribution gets to the source intended. For example, a brochure on an upcoming financial aid seminar may not go home with a student (who jams it into their locker between homeroom and lunch), but would by direct mail to the home.

EVALUATING YOUR PUBLIC RELATIONS STRATEGIES IN YOUR SCHOOL

Read each of the following questions and answer yes (Y) or no (N). Keep account of the number of yes and number of no responses.

Y N

__ __ Is the notion of good public relations at your school accepted and recognized as a shared responsibility between administrators, teachers, and counselors?

__ __ Are there annual school plans and prioritized goals focused entirely on public relations established at the beginning of each year?

__ __ Does your public relations program receive financial support?

__ __ Is input for public relationship activities and programs elicited from teaches, parents, students, and all who interface with the school?

___ ___ Are there many means of communicating activities, programs, and services available and utilized (e.g., newsletters, message boards, computers, fax machines, brochures, pamphlets, etc.)?

___ ___ Is there an annual systematic evaluation of public relations efforts?

___ ___ Are all communications to internal and external audiences designed to reach them at their level of understanding?

___ ___ Do you use all available communication mediums to reach internal and external audiences (e.g., the school newspaper, PTA/PTO newsletters, yearbook, athletic programs, local educational cable networks and radio stations, etc.)?

___ ___ Do you routinely recognize designated counseling weeks or months such as American School Counseling Week or Vocational Counseling Month by focusing on the value and role of such programs?

___ ___ Is your guidance and counseling department represented at regular meetings with faculty, administration, district-wide steering committees, and school board?

___ ___ Do you have an orientation package for new students which explains programs, services, policies, and regulations?

___ ___ Do you have an exit package for transfer students or school leavers advising them of contact persons or outreach services which are available to them?

___ ___ Do you maintain a personal contact with local newspaper, television, and radio media personnel who follow and feature school stories or public service announcements?

___ ___ Do you have a minimum of three articles or feature stories about the guidance and counseling program in the school and local newspaper each year?

__ __ Do you seize the opportunity to award or recognize significant people who support your program at annual award ceremonies with certificates of appreciation or placques of recognition?

__ __ Do you maintain a strong network and renewed professional commitment among colleagues?

__ __ Does your department utilize and recognize volunteers in the implementation of the guidance and counseling program?

__ __ Do you maintain an on-going advisory board made up of representatives from the school and community to advise on programs, services, and student assistance?

__ __ Do you have a system for informing internal and external publics about the programs and services of your counseling program?

__ __ Do you have one counselor in your department who assumes the responsibilities for all public relations activities?

Now determine your score. For each item that you answered yes, give yourself 5 points.

A score of 90 and above—"You are public relations"

80-89—Looking good, but see if you can motivate more people to support your program

70-79—Keep the ball rolling

60-69—Invite a marketing director to lunch and "pick their brain"

SUMMARY

Public relations is an expanded perspective for professional counseling. Purkey and Schmidt (1987) aptly stated, "It's

never a matter of whether or not a counseling department
has public relations; it's a matter of what kind. To invite
positive public relations, make sure that the majority of messages
sent to colleagues, students, and their families are positive"
(p. 161).

CHAPTER **16**

ASSIMILATING THE PRINCIPLES OF TIME MANAGEMENT

Finish each day and be done with it. You have done what you could. Some blunders and absurdities no doubt crept in; forget them as soon as you can. Tomorrow is a new day; begin it well and serenely and with too high a spirit to be cumbered with old nonsense. The day is all that is good and fair. It is too dear with its hopes and invitations to waste a moment on yesterday.

Ralph Waldo Emerson

To the noble art of getting things done we must add the noble art of leaving things undone.

Ancient Oriental Saying

Administering a guidance program and counseling children are demanding and often physically and emotionally exhausting. The pressures on time are continuous and relentless. Yet, though the development of carefully negotiated habits, time can be a resource instead of a threatened commodity.

Counselors do not have to succumb to the Pareto Principle or the 80:20 rule, i.e., spending the bulk of their time doing the clerical, trivial, or mundane with only a small portion for their time on significant activities that contribute to their role as a counselor. Counselors try not to project their roles as enmeshed in clerical and administrative tasks, but since the currency of a bureaucracy is paper, school counselors have often become the designated tellers.

Concurrently, school counselors are expected to be involved in a greater variety of guidance and counseling activities than their predecessors ever envisioned. Role and function include work in the curriculum, conducting placement and follow-up activities, remediation, consultation, specialized testing, observation, and interfacing with business and industry. In addition, they are expected to continue routine activities such as crisis counseling, teacher and parent consultation, mental health referrals, and noncounseling administrative services which often are delegated by insensitive administrators or support personnel.

Counselors lament that "they are all things to all people" (clinically termed the type E person, i.e., being everything to everybody), as peers remark "You can't save them all." Fundamental to implementing time-management techniques is to understand the stress that creates impositions to professional functioning. Stressful activities or responsibilities include

- trying to resolve parent/school/teacher/student conflict;

- having to abide by administrative decisions or school policies that disengage or alienate student (e.g., discipline policies, attendance, or eligibility requirement to participate in extracurricular activities);

- complying with state, federal, and division roles, policies, or mandates which may be incompatible;

- imposing excessively high expectations on self or others;

- not setting healthy limits on personal or professional obligations or commitments;

- trying to gain public/peer approval and/or financial support for counseling programs or activities;

- always feeling overextended with a heavy caseload or workload that never seems to achieve fruition;

- feeling that meetings/committees/conferences take up too much time;

- trying to complete reports and other paperwork on time; and

- being interrupted frequently by colleagues, students, visitors, and phone calls.

ANALYZING TIME CONSUMERS

In addition to understanding your stressors ("pinch points and crunches"), another important aspect is understanding what activities consume large blocks of your time. In a poll reported by Powers (1965), the ten worst time wasters as perceived by more than fifty chairpersons of boards, presidents, or vice-presidents of corporations were

- telephones,
- mail,
- meetings,
- public relations,
- paperwork,
- commuting,
- business lunches,
- civic duties,
- incompetents, and
- family demands.

Mackenzie (1975) identified the following 15 leading time wasters based on experiences of managers in 15 countries:

- telephone interruptions;
- drop-in visitors;
- meetings—scheduled as well as unscheduled;
- crisis situations for which planning ahead was not possible;
- lack of objectives, priorities, and deadlines;

- cluttered desk and personal disorganization;
- involvement in routine and detail that should be delegated;
- attempting too much at one time and under-estimating the time it takes to do it;
- failure to set up clear lines of responsibility and authority;
- inadequate, inaccurate, or delayed information from others;
- indecision and procrastination;
- lack of clear communication and instruction;
- inability to say "no";
- lack of standards and progress reports; and
- fatigue.

When to the foregoing, school counselors add the following list, then one can easily understand why counselors feel "burnout":

- being all things to all people;
- commuting time to confer with teachers, principals, families, etc.;
- changing accreditation standards and new programs;
- heterogeneous, multicultural student populations;
- changing demographics; and
- conferring with business and industry, service organizations, central office personnel, and satellite offices (to name a few).

This caseload is also illustrated by federal mandates and local policy. For example: the flow of communication among support personnel, home-school instructional staff, and parents is often encumbered by federal mandates and local policy. This can be aptly understood by viewing the number of people who sign off, review, interview, assess, or peruse a child's individual educational plan to comply with P.L. 94-142, The Education of All Handicapped Children Act of 1975.

Nearly all support personnel will have interfaced with the guidance and counseling program or staff to obtain the necessary information on a child enrolled in the school for a single semester. Support personnel include nurse, special education coordinator, school psychologist, educational diagnostician, school community worker, resource teacher, counselor, regular education teacher, administrator(s), social worker, probation officer, vocational program liaison, community mental health liaison, parent, foster parent, speech therapist, court liaison, and program administrator (Thompson, 1985, p. 53). Unfortunately, while everyone is signing off, documenting, and pontificating placement decisions, the student has dropped out of school because of feelings, among others, of unrelatedness to the school environment; and the counselor resigns himself/ herself to the notion that "you can't save them all."

Time Management Exercise

Keep a log for several days of how you spend your time. The more frequent the entries, the better will be your data base for analysis and understanding.

MANAGING YOUR PAPER CHASE

Kozoll (1982) maintained that educators often suffer from a condition known as the *battered mind syndrome,* which means that they have many thoughts at one time; worry about what remains to be done; lose their focus as new concerns divert them from the task at hand; and expect to be interrupted and, as a result, don't become deeply involved in their work. The devastating outcome of this syndrome is a belief that one has little or no control over one's time; destined to be battered by other people's priorities. The following suggestions may provide some structure and management to your present modus operandi:

> Follow the OHIO principle (only handle it once) when managing paper; i.e., use it, lose it, or file it away.

> Have incoming mail screened or sorted by the secretary if possible. If that's not possible, move the trash can under your mailbox and leave the junk mail there.

> Don't write if a phone call will do just as well.

If a brief reply to a letter is needed, write it on the incoming letter or memo, make a copy for your file and return to sender.

Avoid unnecessary copies. They waste everyone's time to make, distribute, file, trash, or read. Do not become a disciple of what Rowan (1978) referred to as the "fat paper philosophy, induced by 'memoitis' and spread by copy machines."

Set aside a regular time each day to do paperwork— no more than an hour on a daily basis. Examine how much of your clerical work can be given to a clerical worker. Set aside blocks of time for more detailed concentration such as college recommendations or research activities. Make sure that the first hour of your day, or the last hour of your day, is a productive one.

Read flyers, catalogs, and routine memos at a designated time once a week. Follow the technique of "rip-and-read" (rip out the article that could be used later and throw other irrelevant materials away). Better yet, have a designated reader on the staff who will "rip-and-read" or "clip-and-save" for you.

Implement a time truce or quiet hour to frame a large block of uninterrupted time for your most important tasks or deadlines. Have your secretary screen and guard your door.

Although we learn quickly in Guidance 101 not to label individuals or limit our understanding by convenient descriptions, much is to be gained from the value of minimalism. We also know that we continue to seek a life balance between expectation and effort where getting the "max from the minimum" is the typical contemporary consumer perspective. Ahrens (1988) also provided a number of salient strategies to incorporate minimalism into school counseling:

Decide which guidance information to carry around in your head and which to leave on the bookshelf or in the computer.

Decide what paper to keep and what to recycle.

Know when to do paperwork and when to have someone else do it if it needs to be done.

Resist the urge to have more than one four-drawer filing cabinet. Organize it.

If you are responsible for a flexible system, be sure it is maximally organized; if you have a tightly controlled system, ensure that it is creatively flexible.

Return all phone calls as soon as possible (setting aside a block of time each day for phone calls also is helpful), and gently but quickly refer those that can be made by others.

Control your appointment schedule. If you don't, it will control you.

Know when to say "yes" and when to say "no." Be assertive.

Don't do anything for those you counsel that they can do for themselves.

STRESS MANAGEMENT

The estimate is that the average American will spend 3 years sitting in meetings, 5 years waiting in lines, over 17,000 hours playing telephone tag, 4,000 hours stopped at red lights, and a lifetime . . . trying to wind down (Michael Fortino & Associates, Inc. 1990).

Stress for the school counselor evolves from the imbalance between the demands made from administrators, teachers, students and their families, special populations, and supervisors versus our expectations of what should be accomplished (real or imagined) in the course of a year. Most stressors to which counselors strive to adapt are subtle and symbolic. Situations which can trigger a stress reaction include the threat of rejection, a heated argument with a colleague, the passing of an important milepost, or the pressures of an approaching project deadline.

Chronic and accumulated stress can have a devastating physical, as well as, emotional consequence. Researchers suggest that stress lowers our resistance to illness and can play a contributory role in disease of the kidney, heart, and blood vessels; migraine and tension headaches; gastrointestinal problems, asthma, and allergies or respiratory disease.

The way we feel and behave under these multiple stressors is determined in part by what we think (self-statements as in "shoulds" and "oughts") in a given situation. The stress reaction involves two major elements: heightened physical arousal—increased heart rate, rapid breathing or muscular tension; anxious thoughts (e.g., a sense of helplessness); and panic from being overwhelmed, or a desire to escape. Since behavior and emotions are learned and controlled by inner thoughts or expectations, the best way to exert control over them is by assimilating the appropriate skills (such a progressive relaxation or cognitive restructuring) to change both the sensation and the thought(s). In Figure 16.1 is a list of many of our irrational beliefs.

On the other hand, stress in small amounts can be a very positive life force. It is the impetus for growth, change, and adaptation (Ruben, 1978). To better understand your stress level, complete the awareness exercise in Figure 16.2 which is designed to identify your "pinch points" and "crunch points."

To alleviate negative stress on a routine basis capitalize on existing professional and personal networks to form support groups.

Sometimes it is very helpful to find strengths in a peer network or support group to share ideas, diffuse stress, or access opportunities for personal growth.

If you feel socially isolated, try to share your concerns, experiences or situations with a peer network or with other professionals you can trust.

(Continued on Page 370)

1. **Fear of Rejection:** I must be liked (loved) and respected (approved) by everyone I meet all the time (and it is awful if I am not)

2. **Fear of Failure:** I must be thoroughly competent, adequate, and achieving at everything I do. Extreme: Perfectionism.

3. **Fairness:** People and things should always turn out the way I want them to and I should always be treated fairly (and it is awful when either does not happen).

4. **Blame/Punishment:** If I am rejected, if I fail, or if I am treated wrongly or badly then someone deserves to be strongly blamed or punished. (Sometimes I should blame or punish myself because I decide, "It is my fault.")

5. **Rumination:** If something seems threatening or fearsome, I must become terribly occupied with it, upset about it, and make myself miserable (anticipatory anxiety).

6. **Perfect Solutions Exist:** It is awful and horrible (I can't stand it) when I don't find quick and good solutions to my problems. (A perfect solution exists for every problem.)

7. **Avoidance:** It is easier to avoid difficulties, responsibilities, and uncomfortable situations than to face them.

8. **I Am Not Responsible::** People and external things make me feel the way I do (upset me, make me miserable) and I have very little ability to direct and control my feelings.

9. **Past Conditioned:** Your past remains all-important and because something once strongly influenced your life, it has to keep determining your feelings and behavior today.

10. **Detachment:** You can achieve happiness (safety or security) by getting involved in and doing nothing or by passively and uncommittedly "living."

Source: Gonzales, M., Jones, D., Whitely, R.M., & Whitely, J.M. (1988). *The ACCD stress management manual.* Reprinted by permission.

Figure 16.1. Irrational beliefs.

Complete the following sentence stems as indicated in the example:

Potential Stressor	Visible Reaction "What I say/do"	Inward Reaction "How I feel (+ -)
EXAMPLE		
Professionally inviting "open door policy"—previous student drops in during college break ...	"Alumni are always welcome, nothing is ever too important to pass the time of day with a graduate of Central High."	This will put me behind on my recommendation letters for scholarship deadlines ... I'll have to take them home and finish them later."

Open door policy instructional staff support personnel

Telephone calls/follow-up calls

Administrative/clerical work (memos, letters, grants, reports, etc.)

Compliance with regulation or policy: P.L. 94-142—federal/state/school division

Meetings—routine/requested

Consultation with parents/teachers/community agencies

Caseload 500:1; 400:1; 300:1, homogeneous/heterogeneous

Control of time/agenda/appointment calendar

Influence vs. power in the chain of command

Needs of target populations, e.g., underachievers, special education; potential dropouts

Figure 16.2. Stress awareness exercise.

Figure 16.2. Continued.

Potential Stressor	Visible Reaction "What I say/do"	Inward Reaction "How I feel (+ -)"
Adminstrative policy that hinders or helps school climate		
Managing delegated tasks from administrators		
Identification by staff/students/parents for special programs: governor's school, magnet school, summer school, enrichment activities		
Cooperation from staff and support personnel		
Personal feelings of inadequacy		
Too little authority		
Too little influence		
Socially isolated		
Highly visible/invisible		
Conflicting role expectations		
Personal work style		

Some Strategies to Incorporate in Everyday Living to Reduce Stress

- Plan "down time" or "debriefing time" every day
- Grab a folder (preferably empty) and get out of the office periodically.
- Avoid irritating and overly competitive people prior to lunch or near the end of the day.
- At least three days a week have lunch conversations that are not school or work related.
- Design your daily schedule so you have a chance to perform at least one activity each day that makes you feel successful or that completes a goal.

If you feel unrecognized or unappreciated, inventory what you have accomplished since a year ago. Identify your strengths and successes. Share these with a confidant for feedback and validation.

If you feel emotional overextended, isolated, or overloaded, make an effort to do more non-work related activities for yourself.

If you are intellectually stagnant or understimulated, attend workshops, seminars, or cross disciplines, take a course in business management or English literature.

If you have influence but virtually little power to change things, identify the formal and informal networks and influence what you actually have, and note positive change.

If you are alienated administratively, have one or two professional friends in which you can confide to discuss ways to make positive contributions.

A support group should be based on the willingness and ability to listen, share problems, give assistance, admit mistakes and develop trusting relationships.

Other stress reduction strategies could include the following:

Interact, at least once each day with someone in your school who makes you laugh.

Learn to plan a "free weekend" to "kick back" at least once a month.

Do a small, but in-depth one-to-one activity with each family member during the course of each month. This helps to renew close interpersonal relationships.

Develop a "vacation attitude" after work; treat your home as your vacation home. Read *The Stressless Home* by Robert M. Bramson and Susan Bramson, (1985), Ballantine Books.

Get involved with a friend, spouse, or child in an activity which will teach you a new concept, new skill, or new process (an opportunity to learn an unrelated work skill in itself is refreshing).

Make a date for self-preservation. Periodically plan ahead and mark your calendar scheduling time to be alone with yourself. Perceive these planned occasions as genuine "meetings." Make yourself unavailable to the needs and manipulations of other people. Practice saying, "I have a date" or "I'm sorry, I have other plans" as a way of saying no without feeling guilty.

If you are at the constant mercy of other people's needs (teachers, administrators, coordinators, social service, the courts, parents, students, volunteers, ad inf.), you tend to become frustrated, fragmented, and overextended. This healthy schedule alternative will make you feel focused and back into control over time, and others. Ultimately, you are more likely to face a challenge with equanimity when you plan some rewarding time for self.

Have a holistic approach to physical and mental well-being. Physical exercise does make us feel better and gives us energy especially if it occurs at the beginning or ending of a stressful day. Treat your brain as if it is a muscle and exercise it routinely. Read Rogers, Ellis, Elkind, Prather, Dinkmeyer, or Buscaglia. Concentrate on their wisdom to guide you through the day.

Use imagery to track down the reasons behind anxiety and saying "no" to unreasonable or unwanted requests of your time. Lazarus (1987) suggested that you concentrate on any unwanted or unreasonable request from a person to which you generally say "yes" although you want to refuse. Be specific as to the task. Then picture yourself tactfully but firmly declining. As you picture yourself saying "no" you may become aware of some tense feelings. Concentrate on these tensions and see what other images emerge. To counter the experience, imagine your family and the relaxed relations you would have with them if you were not overextended.

Strategies for Leaving Stress at the Office

End the day as calmly and smoothly as possible. Make it a habit to wind down one-half hour before you leave.

Leave unfinished business at your desk. Bringing work home (into your family space) on a daily basis is a bad habit to break. Ask yourself, is this project an emergency? Can it wait until tomorrow? Can this be delegated? If you feel you'll spend the evening worrying about the unfinished business from the end of the day, try the following exercise. Make a list of all outstanding tasks. Imagine your feeling of accomplishment when every item is completed to your satisfaction. Then forget about it until the morning. If you are a more compulsive type, you might try securing three folders (preferably high-tech plastic) in green, red, and yellow. Red is for "hot" projects that need your attention now; green is for "on-going" projects that need your daily attention; and yellow is for "cautionary" items that will need your attention soon. On the outside of each folder stick a "post-it" note of prioritized items which must be accomplished. Smaller lists on three tracks (red, green, and yellow) will give you a better feeling of having things under control. You also will be able to "put your hands on things" when you need them.

Use your commute home as a decompression time. As counselors, we are often overwhelmed by emotional and information overload. Don't listen to the news or rock 'n roll on the radio because they both tend to overstimulate us. Instead, make this a quiet time to let the thoughts of day filter out of your head. And, since you can't utilize guided imagery on the road, pop one of those "new age" music cassettes/CD's in the player.

At home take a few minutes alone, change clothes or rinse your troubles down the drain with a quick shower. Don't make dinner (or children's homework) into an ordeal. Turn off the television and turn on the answering machine. Learn to maintain a healthy perspective. Despite the day's worst disasters—you arrived late because the bridge was up, spilled coffee on the computerized answer sheets, worried about how well you did in an important presentation, and spent an hour trapped in a meeting with someone you despise—it really could have been worse—you could have come to work with two different colored shoes, which your burned-out colleagues didn't notice until mid-day.

Finally, encourage humor within and without. "Humor is serious business." It can serve as a powerful tool for people at all levels to prevent the buildup of stress to improve communication, to enhance motivation and morale, to build relationships, to encourage creative problem solving, to smooth the way for organization change, and to make workshops fun.

The use of humor decreases problems of discipline, increases listening and attention on the part of participants, decreases the pressure on people to be perfect, increases retention, and increases the comfort level of others. The resulting positive attitude can greatly contribute to achievement and productivity. Humor, according to Goodman (1982) makes it easier to hear feedback and new information. Humor gives us perspective on problems; helps us to get away from a problem situation in order to see the situation and possible solutions in perspective. This is a very important skill for counselors to have.

Is There a Neon "Do-Drop-In" Sign above Your Door?

Being a professionally inviting counselor, many former students and their families will want to share their experiences and successes with you. Drop-in visitors also include salespersons, administrators, colleagues, school psychologists, special education coordinators, probation officers, police, and a multitude of other well-meaning, time-consuming people. The following strategies could redirect the flow of traffic and help you manage interruptions less stressfully.

Locate your secretary's desk physically so that he/she can act as a buffer to anyone who may want to interrupt you. He/she can easily screen the visitors, handle many information seeking questions, or direct inquiries to those who could adequately respond.

Your secretary also could schedule an appointment for the drop-in visitor after such key responses: To the armed forces representative . . . "I am so glad to see you, but I'm scheduled to meet within five minutes!" or to the department chair . . . "We really need to spend some time on this issue, let me see if I can clear my calendar for Thursday!"

Finally, avoid the "Rolls Royce Syndrome." Counselors who feel they must do better than required can be characterized as having the "Rolls Royce Syndrome" (Steinmetz, 1976). Although the Rolls Royce is judged to be the best-quality automobile in the world, most people can get by with a Ford.

Use Secretarial Assistance Efficiently

Secretaries are an unlimited human resource. They also can manage the flow of information and activities. A secretary should know your program goals, routine deadlines (data processing, testing, etc.) priorities, and general time management procedures. Often, they can suggest creative ways to streamline or completely eliminate ineffective or redundant procedures. In Figure 16.3 is a checklist of secretary's responsibilities that, if followed, would help reduce stress.

HOW TO SAY "NO" AND
HELP OTHERS ASSUME RESPONSIBILITY

School counselors often assume the legacy of "being all things to all people" and ultimately loose sight of their own priorities. Too often we assume responsibility for the tasks that others should perform. For example, if a coach comes in to check on a player's eligibility, we are inclined to say, "I don't know, and follow it up with, but I'll check it out for you." Or a teacher may come in during his/her planning bell and remark that "Johnny has been absent for four days, and I don't have time to check on this today. Would you please call his family and find out?" Assuming responsibility

(Continued on Page 378)

Does He or She

- Place outgoing calls for you?

- Handle parental inquiries?

- Deal with requests for information from others schools or organizations

- Make decisions as to which calls are important and which can be handled by someone else in the school (such as nurse or attendance clerk)?

- Answer the phone in a pleasant voice?

- Use good human relations skills when dealing with a complaint or an irate parent?

Correspondence

- Screen all notes leaving the counseling office?

- Respond to some requests using your signature?

- Compose most letters from notes?

- Anticipate a response and initiate a letter?

- Make corrections on language usage, spelling, organization, etc.?

- Do proofreading accurately on your correspondence?

- Read all incoming mail so that you are informed?

- Handle confidential information appropriately?

- Route incoming mail to the proper person on the counseling staff?

- Screen all junk mail?

- Place incoming mail in the "in" basket, in accordance with the schedule for handling it?

- Remove correspondence from the "out" basket on a regular schedule?

- Summarize or highlight information in lengthy reports or letters?

Files

- Have a filing system that is designed for easy retrieval and that your staff can use in your absence?

- Keep up-to-date on your filing?

Source: Adapted from Shipman, Martin, McKay, & Anastiasi (1983). *Effective time-management techniques for school administrators.* Englewood Cliffs, NJ: Prentice-Hall. Reprinted with permission.

Figure 16.3. Checlist of secretary's responsiblities.

Figure 16.3. Continued.

Files (continued)

- Maintain a check out system for information, materials, and videos from the counseling department?

- Maintain a tickler file for future action items?

- Maintain a monthly schedule of routines that happen at the same time, annually?

- File in cumulative folders the results of aptitude and achievement tests, and interest inventories?

- File student data forms, health screenings, physical education records, student activity and student profile sheets, etc.?

- Refill records according to promotions, retentions, withdrawals, graduation, and GED results?

Meetings

- Notify those involved in advance?

- Help gather materials and prepare visuals, handouts, or summaries?

- Make sure space is available?

- Make sure all necessary equipment is in place?

- Keep minutes of all meetings and forward information to participants?

- Prepare the meeting agenda and distribute to participants before the meeting?

Scheduling Appointments

- Keep a calendar of your schedule?

- Update the calendar daily (reconcile the desk calendar with the personal pocket calendar)?

- Make appointments with the appropriate time allocations?

- Avoid scheduling an appointment with a person if they should be seeing someone else?

- Interrupt visitors (tactfully) when allotted time has expired?

Visitors

- Make visitors feel welcome and comfortable?

- Give new students and families a warm, receptive feeilng about the school?

- Help visitors and staff when possible without bothering the counselor?

- Act as a "buffer" to intercept drop-in visitors?

Figure 16.3. Continued.

Miscellaneous

- Keep a folder of all pertinent information for a substitute?
- Help in training new staff members about procedures?
- Demonstrate punctuality, loyalty, and conscientiousness?
- Know where the counselor is and when he or she is expected back?
- Meet with the counselor each day to have questions answered and set priorities for the day?
- Keep aware of deadlines and inform the counselor of the status in relation to deadlines?
- Maintain confidentiality?
- Assist in the updating of program documents such as the student handbook?
- Prepare an eligibility list of students for special programs?
- Verify student names for various lists?
- Disseminate and collect data processing information from faculty and staff?
- Assist in the preparation of letters, awards, scholarships, or other information?
- Prepare the monthly newsletter or parent information bulletins.

---

for the coach or the teacher should not supersede your own priorities. After all, who has the largest caseload, the coach, the teacher, or the counselor? Help them assume their responsibility.

Shipman et al. (1983) listed ten suggestions that would help school administrators say no to time-consuming activities that do not move them toward completion of their major priorities. These ten suggestions have meaning for school counselors too:

- Realize what is being asked of you.

- Think about the consequences of saying "yes."

- Determine why others are asking you rather than someone else or themselves.

- Think about whether or not you are a soft touch.

- Ask, "Why me?" when you are asked to do something.

- Project the amount of time you will need to respond to the request if you say "yes."

- Say "no," but give an alternate suggestion.

- Reroute the request to someone else, i.e., delegate.

- Never promise what you cannot deliver.

- Simply say "no."

Do not let others hold you responsible for things over which you have little control or influence:

- Help others do their jobs, but be sure they take responsibility for handling their problems.

- Help students, teachers, parents—all those with whom you work—know that they have responsibilities too.

- Define the boundaries of your influence, and the responsibilities that others have.

- Do not accept blame for problems caused by others.

- Clarify roles among parties involved in conflicts, i.e., what can each do to help solve the problem?

REFERENCES

REFERENCES

Abdel-Halim, A.A. (1982). Social support and managerial affective responses to job stress. *Journal of Occupational Behavior, 3,* 281.

Ahrens, R. (1988). Minimalism in school counseling. *The School Counselor, 36,* 2, 85-87.

Alan Guttmacher Institute. (1984). *U.S. and cross-national trends in teenage sexual and fertility behavior.* New York: The Alan Guttmacher Institute.

Allen, J., & Anderson, E. (1986). Children and crisis: A classroom guidance approach. *Elementary School Counselor, 21,* 2.

Alschuler, A.S., & Ivey, A.E. (1973). Internalization: The outcome of psychological education. *Personnel and Guidance Journal, 51,* 588-610.

Amatac, E.S., & Fabrick, K.F. (1984). Moving a family into therapy: Critical referral issues for the school counselor. *The School Counselor, 31,* 285-294.

American Institute for Research. (1976). *Planning career goals.* Monterey, CA: McGraw-Hill.

American Medical Association. (1987). *Whitepaper on adolescent health.* Chicago, IL: Author.

American Psychiatric Association. (1987). *Diagnostic and statistical manual of mental disorders DSM-III-R.* (3rd rev. ed). Washington, DC: Author.

American School Counselor Association. (1983). *Accreditation procedures manual and application for counseling and related educational programs.* Alexandria, VA: Author.

American School Counselor Association. (1989). ASCA role statement: The practice of guidance and counseling by school counselors. *The School Counselor, 29,* 7-12.

Astin, H.S. (1967). Patterns of career choice over time. *Personnel and Guidance Journal, 45,* 541-546.

Attkinsson, C.C., Hargreaves, W.A., Horowitz, J.J., & Sorenson, J.E. (Eds.). (1978). *Evaluation of human service programs.* New York: Academic Press.

Aubrey, R.F. (1983). A house divided: Guidance and counseling in 20th Century America. *Personnel and Guidance Journal, 61,* 4.

Avis, J.P. (1987). Applying counselor skills to improving the human environment of schools (IHES) groups. *The School Counselor 34,* 4, 297-302.

Avis, J.P., & Bigelow, E.E. (1984). *Improving the human environment of schools.* Sacramento: California State Department of Education.

Babcock, R.J., & Kaufman, M.A. (1976). Effectiveness of a career course. *Vocational Guidance Quarterly, 24,* 241-266.

Baldwin, B.A. (1977). Crisis intervention in professional practice: Implications for clinical training. *American Journal of Orthopsychiatry, 47,* 659-670.

Balk, D.E. (1983). How teenagers cope with sibling death: Some implications for school counselors. *The School Counselor, 31,* 2, 150-158.

Beck, A., Rush, A., Shaw, B., & Emery, G. (1979). *Cognitive therapy of depression.* New York: Guilford Press.

Beehr, T.A., & Newman, J.E. (1978). Job stress, employee health and organizational effectiveness: A facet analysis model and literature review. *Personnel Psychology, 31,* 654-669.

Bennett, E.C. (1975). *Operation C.O.D.: A program designed to improve pupil self-esteem to reduce future school dropouts.* Chicago, IL: Nova University.

Berenson, B.G. & Carkhuff, R.R. (Eds.). (1967). *Sources of gain in counseling and psychotherapy.* New York: Holt, Rinehart & Winston.

Bertoldi, A.R. (1975). *Remediation for auxiliary services students evaluation period school year 1974-75.* Brooklyn: New York City Board of Education Office of Educational Evaluation.

Birk, J.M., & Blimline, C.A. (1984). Parents as career development facilitators: An untapped resource for the counselor. *The School Counselor, 31,* 4, 310-317.

Blocker, D.H., & Rapoza, R. (1972). A systematic eclectic model for counseling and consulting. *Elementary School Guidance & Counseling 7,* 106-112.

Borg, W.W., & Gall, M.D. (1983). *Educational research: An introduction (4th ed.).* New York: Harper & Row.

Boyer, E. (1983). *High school: A report on secondary education in America.* New York: Harper & Row.

Boyer, E.L. (1987). *College: The undergraduate experience in America*. Report prepared for the Carnegie Foundation for the Advancement of Teaching, New York: Harper & Row.

Boyer, M.C., & Horne, A.M. (1988). Working parents: A family matter. *Counseling and Human Development, 21,* 1.

Bramson, R.M., & Bramsom, S. (1985). *The Stressless home.* New York: Ballantine Books.

Breckenridge, M. (1987). Evaluation of school counselor. *NASSP Bulletin, 36,* 12.

Brown, N.W., Thompson, R.A., Geoffroy, K.E., & Adair, F.L. (1987). Discrepancies in the perceptions of counselor roles in secondary schools. *Capstone Journal of Education, 7,* 4.

Bryan, T., & Pearl, R. (1981). Self-concepts and locus of control of learning disabled children. *Educational Horizons, 59,* 91-96.

Burns, P. (1981). *Feeling good: A new mood therapy.* New York: Signet Books.

Campbell, D.P. (1965). *The results of counseling: Twenty five years later.* Philadelphia, PA: W.B. Saunders Company.

Canady, R.L., & Seyfarth, J.T. (1979). *How parent-teacher conferences build partnerships.* Bloomington, IN: Phi Delta Kappa.

Caplan, N. (1970). The new ghetto man: A review of recent empirical studies. *Journal of Social Sciences, 26,* 59-73.

Capuzzi, D., & Golden, L. (1988). *Preventing adolescent suicide.* Muncie, IN: Accelerated Development.

Capuzzi, D., & Lecog, L.L. (1983). Social and personal determinants of abuse of alcohol and marijuana. *The Personnel and Guidance Journal, 62,* 4, 199-205.

Carey, R. (1977). Trends in counseling and student services. *NASSP Bulletin, 26,* 3-9.

Carkhuff, R.R., & Berenson, B.G. (1976). *Teaching as treatment.* Amherst, MA: Human Resource Development Press.

Carkhuff, R.R., Pierce, R.M., & Cannon, J.R. (1977). *The cut of helping III.* Amherst, MA: Human Resources Development Press.

Carroll, M.R. (1973). The gradual making of psychological education. *The School Counselor, 25,* 5, p. 326.

Carrol, M.R. (1979). Group counseling: The reality and the possibility. *The School Counselor, 27*, 2, 91-96.

Casner-Lotto, J. (1988). Expanding the teacher's role: Hammond's school improvement process. *Phi Delta Kappan, 69*, 5.

Chapman, D., O'Brien, C.H., & DeMasi, M.F. (1987). The effectiveness of the public school counselor in college advising. *The Journal of College Admissions*, 1159, 11-18.

Chartier, M.R. (1985). Functional roles for facilitating organizational change. *The 1985 Annual: Developing human resources*. LaJolla, CA.

Children's Defense Fund (1988). *Model programs: Preventing adolescent pregnancy and building youth self-sufficiency*. Washington, DC: CFD, p. 9.

Cochrane, P., & Mareni, B. (1977). Mainstreaming exceptional children: The counselor's role. *The School Counselor, 25*, 17-22.

Cohen-Sandler, R., Berman, A.L., & King, R.A. (1982). Life stress and syptomatology: Determinants of suicidal behavior in children. *Journal of the American Academy of Child Psychiatry, 21*, 178-186.

College Board Publications. (1986). *College Prep: Counseling students for higher education*. New York, NY: College Board Publications.

Conner, J.D. (1983). Admissions policies and practices. Selected findings of the AACRAD/CEEB Survey. *NASSP Bulletin, 67*, 460.

Cooper-Haber, K., & Bowman, R.P. (1985). The Keenan project: Comprehensive group guidance in high school. *The School Counselor, 33*, 1, 50-53.

Corey, G. & Corey, M. (1983). *Groups: Process and practice* (2nd ed.). Montery, CA: Brooks Cole.

Cox, W.D. & Matthews, C.O. (1977). Parent group education: What does it do for the children? *Journal of School Psychology, 15*, 358-361.

Crouse, J., & Trusheim, D. (1988). *The case against the SAT*. Chicago, IL: University of Chicago Press.

Cutlip, S.M., & Center, A.H. (1971). *Effective public relations*. Englewood Cliffs, NJ: Prentice-Hall.

Dagley, J.C. (1987). A new look at developmental guidance: The hearthstone of school counseling. *The School Counselor, 38*, 2.

Dagley, J.C., & Gazda, G.M. (1984). Alterations for educational reform: Responses of selected leader. *Journal of Counseling and Development, 63*, 221-226.

Daniels, M.H., Karmos, J.S., & Presely, C.A. (1983). *Parents and peers: Their importance in the career decision making process.* Carbondale, IL: Southern Illinois University.

Day, R.W., & Sparacio, R.T. (1980). Impediments to the role and function of school counselors. *The School Counselor, 27,* 270-275.

Dinkmeyer, D. (1968). The counselor as consultant: Rationale and procedures. *Elementary School Guidance and Counseling, 1,* 15-18.

Dinkmeyer, D. (1971). Top priority: Understanding self and others. *Elementary School Journal, 72,* 62-71.

Dinkmeyer, D., & Carlson, J. (1973). *Consulting: Facilitating human potential and change processes.* Columbus, OH: Merrill.

Dinkmeyer, D., Jr., & Dinkmeyer, D. (1977). Concise counseling assessment: The children's life-style guide. *Elementary School Guidance & Counseling, 112,* 117-123.

Dinkmeyer, D., & Dreikurs, R. (1963). *Encouraging children to learn: The encouragement process.* Englewood Cliffs, NJ: Prentice-Hall.

Downing, J.C.. (1983). A positive way to help families. *Elementary School Guidance & Counseling, 17,* 208-213.

Duncan, L.W., & Fitzgerald, P.W. (1969). Increasing the parent-child communication through counselor-parent conferences. *Personnel & Guidance Journal, 47,* 514-517.

Dyer, W.W. & Vriend, J. (1977). *Counseling techniques that work.* New York, NY: Funk & Wagnalls.

Education Week. (1986, May 14). Today's numbers, tomorrow's nation. *Education Week, 4, 14,* p. 15.

Education Week. (1986, June 4). Counselors reassess their role in context of reform movement. *Education Week, 5,* 37, p. 15.

Education Week. (1988, October 26). Dimensions: Financial aid misconceptions, Vol. VIII, No. 8.

Egan, G. (1980). *The skilled helper: A model for systematic helping.* Monterey, CA: Brooks Cole.

Egan, G. (1982). *The skilled helper: A model for systematic helping* (2nd ed.). Monterey, CA: Brooks Cole.

Egan, G. (1986). *The skilled helper: A model for systematic helping* (3rd ed.). Monterey, CA: Brooks Cole.

Egan, G., & Cowan, M. (1979). *People in systems.* Monterey, CA: Brooks Cole.

Elias, D. & David, P. (1983). A guide to problem solving. In J.E. Jones and J.W. Pfeiffer (Eds). *The 1983 annual handbook for facilitators, trainers and consultants.* San Diego, CA: University Associates.

Engen, H.B., Lamb, R.R., & Prediger, D.J. (1982). Are secondary schools still using standardized tests? *Personnel and Guidance Journal, 60,* 287-290.

ERIC Counseling and Personnel Services Clearinghouse. (1983). *150 ways to improve school and classroom environment.* Ann Arbor, MI: The University of Michigan, School of Education.

ERIC Counseling and Personnel Services Clearinghouse. (1986). *Checklist on the organization and administration of the testing program.* Ann Arbor, MI: Author. The University of Michigan School of Education.

Fairman, M. (1983). *Pulaski County special school district board report.* Paper presented at the Pulaski County Special School District Board Meeting, Little Rock, AR.

Fairman, M., & Haddock, J. (1981). Eight ways to improve student attitudes. *Principal, 61,* 35-37.

Flake, M.H., Roach, A.J., & Stenning, W.F. (1975). Effects of short-term counseling on career maturity of tenth grade students. *Journal of Vocational Behavior, 6,* 73-80.

Forrest, A. (1987). Managing the flow of students through the higher education system. *National Forum LXVIII,* No. 4.

Fortino, M., & Associates. (1990).*R.T.W.: Ready to wind-down for Spiegel, Inc.* Chicago, IL: Author.

Frontiers of Possibility. (1986). Report of the National College Counseling Project, National Association of College Admissions Counselors, Burlington, VT: The Instructional Development Center, University of Vermont.

Gallup, G. (1971). The third annual survey of the public's attitude toward public schoolsl. *Phi Delta Kappan, 52,* 33, 48.

Gallup, G. (1982). The 14th annual Gallup poll of the public's attitude toward the public schools. *Phi Delta Kappan, 64,* 37, 50.

Garfinkel, D.B., Frose, A., & Hood, J. (1982). Suicide attempts in children and adolescents. *American Journal of Psychiatry, 139,* 1257-1261.

Gazda, G.M., Childers, W.C. & Brooks, D.J., Jr. (1989). *Foundations 'of counseling and human services.* New York: McGraw-Hill.

Gill, S.J., & Barry, R.A. (1982). Group focused counseling: Classifying the essential skills. *The Personnel and Guidance Journal, 60,* 5.

Gispert, M., Wheeler, K., Marsh, L., & Davis, M.S. (1985). Suicidal adolescents: Factors in emmulation. *Adolescent, 20,* 753-762.

Glasser, W. (1978). Parent anxiety adds to fears. *The School Counselor, 26,* 2, 90-91.

Goodman, J. (1982). *Using humor in workshops.* The 1983 Annual for Facilitators, Trainers and Consultants. San Diego, CA: University Associates.

Gonzaies, M., Jones, D., Whitely, R.M., & Whitely, J.M. (1988). *The American Association for Counseling and Development stress management manual.* Alexandria, VA: American Association for Counseling and Development.

Gordon, E.W., Brownell, C., & Brittell, J. (1972). *Desegregation.* New York: Columbia University.

Griggs, S.A. (1983). Counseling high school students for their individual learning styles. *Clearing House, 56,* 293-296.

Griswold, D. (1947). *Public relations comes of age.* Boston, MA: Boston University School of Public Relations.

Guyton, J.M., & Fielstein, L.L. (1989). Student-led parent conferences: A model for teaching responsibility. *Elementary School Guidance and Counseling, 24,* 169-172.

Hadock, J. (1980). *Relationships between organizational health and student attitudes.* Unpublished doctoral dissertation. University of Arkansas, Fayetteville.

Halmi, K.A. (1983). Anorexia nervosa and bulimia. *Psychosomatics, 24,* 111-129.

Halperin, M. (1979). *Helping maltreated children: School and community involvement.* St Louis: The C.V. Mosby Company.

Hannaford, P. (1987). Consultant offers tips for dealing with the media. *NASSP Newsletter, 34,* 8, p. 4.

Hansen, J.C., Warner, R.W., & Smith, E.J. (1980). *Group counseling: Theory and practice* (2nd ed.). Chicago: Rand McNally.

Hanson, W.B. (1988). Effective school-based approaches to drug abuse prevention. *Educational Leadership 45,* 6.

Hargens, F.M., & Gysberg, N.C. (1984). How to remodel a guidance program while living in it: A case study. *The School Counselor, 32,* 2, 119.

Harmon, F.M., & Baron, A. (1982). The student-focused model for the development of counseling services. *The Personnel and Guidance Journal, 60,* 5, p. 49.

Harrison, W.D. (1980). Role strain and burnout in child protective service workers. *Social Science Review, 54,* 31.

Harvard-Radcliffe Colleges. (1986). Office of admissions and financial aid: Annual report: Class of 1986. Cambridge, MA: Author.

Hassan, T.E., & Reynolds, J.E. (1987). Working class students at selective colleges: Where have they gone? *The College Board Review.* New York: The College Board.

Havighurst, R.J. (1953). *Human development and education.* New York: Longmans.

Havighurst, R.J. (1973). History of developmental psychology: Socialization and personality through the life-span. In P.B. Aaltes & K.W. Schaie (Eds.), *Life-span developmental psychology.* New York: Academic Press.

Hawkins, J.D., & Nederhood, B. (1987). *Handbook for evaluating drug and alcohol prevention programs.* Rockville, MD: National Institute for Drug Abuse (NIDA).

Hawton, K. (1986). *Suicide and attempted suicide among children and adolescents.* Beverly Hills, CA: Sage Publications.

Hawton, K., O'Grady, J., Osborn, M., & Cole, D. (1982). Adolescents who take overdoses: The characteristics, problems, and contacts with helping agencies. *British Journal of Psychiatry, 140,* 118-123.

Hayden, C., & Pohlmann, N. (1981). Accountability and evaluation: Necessaray for the survival of guidance program? *NASSP Bulletin, 65,* 447, 60-63.

Hays, D.G. (1980). The buffalo, the dodo bird, and the whooping crane. *School Counselor, 27,* 252-255.

Herr, E.L. (1976, April). Does counseling work? Paper presented at the Seventh International Round Table for the Advancement of Counseling. University of Wurtzburg, Germany.

Herr, E.L. (1978). *Research in career education: The state of the art.* Commissioned paper. Columbus, OH: The Eric Clearinghouse for Career Education.

Herr, E.L. & Cramer, S.H. (1984). *Career guidance and counseling through the life span* (2nd ed.). Boston: Little, Brown.

Herr, E.L. & Pinson, N.M. (Eds.). (1982). *Foundations for policy in guidance and counseling.* Arlington, VA: American Personnel & Guidance Association.

Higgins, P.S. (1976). *The desegregated counselor aid program of the 1974-75 Minneapolis Emergency School Aid Act Project.* Minneapolis, MN: Minneapolis Public Schools.

Hill, C.E., O'Grady, K.E. (1985). List of therapist intentions illustrated in a case study with therapists of varying theoretical orientations. *Journal of Counseling Psychology, 32,* 3-12, 5.

Hohenshil, T., & Humes, C. (1979). Role of counseling in ensuring the rights of the handicapped. *The Personnel and Guidance Journal, 58,* 226.

Holland, J.L. (1973). *Making vocational choice. A theory of careers.* Englewood Cliffs, NJ: Prentice-Hall. Phi Delta Kappa.

Horton, E. (1985). *Adolescent alcohol abuse.* Bloomington, IN: Phi Delta Kappan, 34, 7.

Hutchins, D.E., & Cole, C.G. (1986). *Helping relationships and strategies.* Monterey, CA: Brooks Cole.

Hutchinson, R.L., & Bottorff, R.L. (1986). Selected high school counseling services: Student assessment. *The School Counselor, 33,* 5, 350.

Ibrahim, F.A., Helms, B.J., Wilson, R.C., & Thompson, D.C. (1984). Secondary school counselor preparation: An innovative approach to curriculum development. *Journal of the Connecticut Association for Counseling and Development, 9,* 2-4.

Ivey, A.E. (1973). Demystifying the group process: Adapting microcounseling procedures to counseling groups. *Educational Technology, 13,* 27-31.

Ivey, A.E., & Authier, J. (1978). *Microcounseling* (2nd ed.). Springfield, IL: Thomas.

Jackson, P. (1986). How to build public relationships that motivate real support. *NASSP Bulletin, 70,* 494, 25-34.

Janosik, E. (1983). *Crisis counseling: A contemporary approach.* Belmont, CA: Wadsworth.

Jenkins, D.E. (1986). The counselor of tomorrow: Counseling at the crossroads. *The American School Counselor Association, 23,* 3, 6.

Joan, P. (1986). *Preventing teenage suicide: The living alternative handbook.* New York: Human Science Press.

Johnson, J.J. (1986). *Life events as stressors in childhood and adolescence.* Beverly Hills, CA: Sage Publications.

Johnston, L.D., Bachman, J.G., & O'Malley, C.T. (1982). *Student drug use attitudes and beliefs: National trends 1975-1982.* Washington, DC: U.S. Government Printing Office.

Jones, J.E. (1981). The organizational universe model. In J.E. Jones and J.W. Pfeiffer (Eds.), *The annual handbook for group facilitators.* San Diego, CA: University Associates.

Jones, V.H. (1980). *Adolescents with behavior problems: Strategies for teaching, counseling and parenting.* Boston: Allyn & Bacon.

Joyce, B.R., Hersh, R.H. & McKibbin, M. (1983). *The structure of school improvement.* New York: Longman.

Kahn, R., Wolfe, D., Quinn, D., Snoek, R., & Rosenthal, J. (1964). *Organizational stress: Studies in role conflict and role ambiguity.* New York: John Wiley & Sons.

Karnes, M.B. (1979). The use of volunteers and parents in mainstreaming. *Viewpoints in Teaching and Learning, 55,* 44-56.

Katz, P.A., & Zalk, S.R. (1978). Modification of children's racial attitudes. *Developmental Psychology, 14,* 447-461.

Kaufman, T.D., & English, R.A. (1979). *Experimental and quasi-experimental designs for research.* Chicago, IL: Rand McNally.

Kazdin, A.E., French, N.H., Unis, A.S., Esveldt-Dawson, K., & Sherick, R.B. (1983). Hopelessness, depression and suicidal intent among psychiatrically disturbed inpatient children. *Journal of Consulting and Clinical Psychology, 51,* 504-510.

Keeping the Options Open: Final Report of the Commission on Precollege Guidance and Counseling. (1986). New York: College Entrance Examination Board, October.

King, P.T., & Bennington, K.F. (1972). Psychoanalysis and counseling. In B. Steffle and W.H. Grant (Eds.), *Theories of Counseling.* New York: McGraw-Hill.

Kolb, D.A., Rubin, I.M. & McIntyre, J.M. (1984). *Organizational psychology: an experimental approach to organizational behavior.* Englewood Cliffs, NJ: Prentice-Hall.

Kotler, P. (1975). *Marketing for nonprofit organizations.* Englewood Cliffs, NJ: Prentice-Hall.

Kottler, J. (1983). *Pragmatic group leadership.* Monterey, CA: Brooks Cole.

Krumboltz, J.D. (1974). An accountability model for counselors. *The Personnel & Guidance Journal, 52,* 639.

Krumboltz, J.D., & Thorensen, D.F. (1964). The effects of behavior counseling in groups and individual settings on information seeking behavior. *Journal of Counseling Psychology, 11*, 324-332.

Krumboltz, J.D., & Thorensen, D.F. (1976). *Counseling methods.* New York: Holt, Rinehart, & Winston.

Kuder, F. (1976). *Kuder general interest survey—Form E.* Chicago: Science Research Associates.

L'Abate, L., & Milan, M.A. (Eds.) (1985). *Handbook of social skills training research.* New York: John Wiley.

Laport, R., & Noth, R. (1976). Roles of performance goals in prose learning. *Journal of Educational Psychology, 3*, 260-264.

Larrabee, M.J., & Terres, C.K. (1984). Group: The future of school counseling. *The School Counselor, 32, 3*, 256.

Larsen, D., Attkisson, C., Hargreaves, W., & Nguyen, T. (1979). Assessment of client/patient satisfaction: Development of general scale. *Evaluation and Program Planning, 2*, 197-207.

Larson, D. (1984). *Teaching psychological skills: Models for giving psychology away.* Monterey, CA: Brooks Cole.

Lazarus, A. (1987). *In the mind's eye.* New York: The Guilford Press.

Lee, V.E. & Elkstrom, R.B. (1987). Student access to guidance and counseling in high school. *American Educational Research Journal, 24, 2*, 287-310.

Levitson, H.S. (1977). Consumer feedback on a secondary school guidance program. *The School Counselor, 20, 6*, 242.

Lewis, J., & Schaffner, M. (1970). Draft counseling in the secondary school. *The School Counselor, 18*, 89-90.

Lewis, J.P., & Boyle, R. (1976). Evaluation of the 1975-76 vocational and basic educational programs in the eight Pennsylvania state correctional institutes. Harrisburg, PA: State Deprtment of Education.

Lewis, M., & Lewis, J. (1970). Relevant training for relevant roles: A model for educating inner-city counselors. *Counselor Educator, 36, 4.*

Lieberman, M.A., Yalom, I.D., & Miles, M.D. (1973). *Encounter groups: First facts.* New York: Basic Books.

Lightfoot, J.L. (1983). *The good high school: Portraits of character and culture.* New York: Basic Books.

Little, A.W., & Allen, J. (1989). Student-led-parent-teacher conferences. *Elementary School Guidance and Counseling, 23*, 210-218.

Lombana, J.H. (1985). Guidance accountability: A new look at an old problem. *The School Counselor, 32,* 5, 340-346.

Lombana, J.H., & Lombana, A.E. (1982). The home-school partnership: A model for counselors. *Personnel & Guidance Journal, 61,* 1, 35-39.

MacDevitt, M., & MacDevitt, J. (1987). Low cost needs assessment for a rural mental health center. *Journal of Counseling and Development, 65,* 505-507.

Mackenzie, R.A. (1975). *The time trap.* New York: McGraw-Hill.

Mann, D. (1978). *Making change happen.* New York: Teachers College Press.

Martin, D., & Stone, G.L. (1977). Psychological education: A skill oriented approach. *Journal of Counseling Psychology, 24,* 153-157.

Maslow, A.H. (1954). *Motivation and personality.* New York: Harper & Brothers.

Matthay, E.R. (1989). A critical study of the college selection process. *The School Counselor, 36,* 5, 359-370.

Mayer, G.G. (1972). Behavioral consulting: Using behavior modicications procedures in the consulting relationship. *Elementary School Guidance & Counseling, 7,* 115-119.

McDowell, W., Coren, A., & Eash, V. (1979). The handicapped: Special needs & strategies for counseling. *The Personnel & Guidance Journal, 58,* 228-232.

McGrath, J.E. (1976). Stress and behavior in organizations. In M.D. Dunnette (Ed.), *Handbook of industrial and organizational psychology.* Chicago: Rand McNally.

Medway, R.J. (1979). How effective is school consultation? A review of recent research. *Journal of School Psychology, 17,* 275-282.

Meyer, J.B., Strowig, W., & Hosford, R.E. (1970). Behavioral reinforcement counseling with rural youth. *Journal of Counseling Psychology, 17,* 117.

Meyers, S.J., Parsons, R.D., & Martin, R. (1979). *Mental health consultation in the schools.* San Francisco, CA: Jossey-Bass.

Mickelson, D.J., & Davis, J.L. (1977). A consultation model for school counselors. *The School Counselor, 5,* 32.

Miles, M.B. (1971). Planned change and organizational health: Figure and ground. In F.M. Trusty (Ed.), *Administering human resources.* Berkeley, CA: McCutchan.

Morrison, T.L., & Thomas, M.D. (1975). Self-esteem and classroom participation. *Journal of Educational Research, 68,* 374.

Morse, D. (1977). Counseling the young adolescent with learning disablilities. *The School Counselor, 25,* 8.

Myrick, R.D. (1987). *Developmental guidance and counseling: A practical approach.* Minneapolis, MN: Education Media.

Naisbitt, J. (1984). *Megatrends.* New York: Warner Books.

National Education Association. (1985). *The strategic context of education in America, 1985-95.* Washington, DC: Author.

National P.T.A. (1988). *School is what we make it.* Chicago, IL: National PTA.

Nicoll, W.G. (1984). School counseling as family counselors: A rationale and training model. *The School Counselor, 31,* 279-284.

Noeth, R.J., Engen, H.B., & Noeth, P.E. (1984). Making career decisions: A self-report of factors that help high school students. *The Vocational Guidance Quarterly, 32,* 4, 240-248.

O'Dell, S. (1974). Training parents in behavior modification: A review. *Psychological Bulletin, 81,* 418-433.

Odiorne, G.S. (1981). *The change resisters.* Englewood Cliffs, NJ: Prentice-Hall.

Ohlsen, M.M. (1977). *Group counseling.* New York: Holt, Rinehart & Winston.

Olson, L. (1989). Governors say investment in children can curb long-term costs for states. *Education Week, X,* 130, February 22.

Orthner, D.K., Smith, S., & Wright, D.V. (1986). Measuring program needs: A stategic design. *Evaluation and Program Planning, 9,* 199-207.

Otto, L.B., & Call, V.R.A. (1985). Parental influences on young people's career development. *Journal of Career Development, 12,* 1, 65-69.

Patton, L.D.. (1980). *Quasi-experimental design and analysis for field settings.* Chicago, IL: Rand McNally.

Peer, G.G. (1985). The status of secondary school guidance: A national survey. *The School Counselor, 32,* 3, 181.

Pfeffer, C.R. (1981). Suicidal behavior of children: A review with implications for research and practice. *American Journal of Psychiatry, 138,* 154-160.

Pfeffer, C.R. (1986). *The suicidal child.* New York: Guilford Press.

Pfeiffer, I.L., & Dunlap, J.B. (1988). Advertising practices to improve school-community relations. *NASSP Bulletin, 72,* 506.

Pietrofesa, J.J., Hoffman, A., & Splete, H.H. (1984). *Counseling: An introduction* (2nd ed.). Boston: Houghton Mifflin.

Pine, G.J. (1976). Troubled times for school counseling. *Focus on Guidance, 8,* 5, 1-16.

Pinson, N., Gysbers, N., & Drier, H. (1981). *Strengthening work related education and training in the 1980's through guidance programs in the reauthorization of vacational education legislation.* Position paper. Washington, DC: The American Personnel and Guidance Association and The American Vocational Association.

Podemski, R.S., & Childers, J.H., Jr. (1980). The counselors as change agent: An organizational analysis. *The School Counselor, 27,* 169-174.

Powell, A.G., Farrar, E., & Cohen, D.K. (1985). *The shopping mall high school.* Boston: Houghton Mifflin.

Powers, R.C. (1965). *Identifying the community power structure.* Ames, IA: Iowa State University, School of Science and Technology.

Prediger, D.J., Roth, J.D., Noeth, R.J. (1973). *Nationwide study of student career development: Summary of results.* Iowa City, IA: The American College Testing Program.

Prediger, D.J., & Sawyer, R.L. (1985). *Ten years of student career development: A nationwide study.* Paper presented at the convention of the American Association for Counseling & Development.

Procter, W.W., Benefield, W., & Wrenn, G.G. (1931). *Workbook in vocations.* Boston: Houghton Mifflin.

Psychological Corporation (1981). *Ohio Vocational Interest Survey II.* New York: Psychological Corporation.

Pugh, A.J. (1989). Compassion fatigue taking toll among care-giving professionals. *The Virginian-Pilot/Ledger-Star,* November 27, A8.

Purkey, W.W., & Schmidt, J.J. (1987). *The inviting relationship: An expanded perspective for professional counseling.* Englewood Cliffs, N.J.: Prentice Hall.

Rappeport, J.R. (1978). Death education in the school. *The School Counselor, 26,* 2, 93-94.

Reschly, D.L. (1976). School psychology consultation: Frenzied, faddish, or fundamental? *Journal of School Psychology, 4,* 105-113.

Roberts, H.C. (1984). Uncloseting the cumulative record: A parent-counselor conference project. *The School Counselor, 32,* 54-60.

Rogers, C.R. (1942). *Counseling and psychotherapy.* Boston, MA: Houghton Mifflin.

Rogers, C.R. (1951). *Client-centered therapy: Its current practice implications and theory.* Boston: Houghton-Mifflin.

Rogers, C.R. (1980). *A way of being.* Boston: Houghton Mifflin.

Rossi, P.H., & Freeman, H.E. (1982). *Evaluation: A systematic approach.* Beverly Hills, CA: Sage Publications.

Rotter, J.C., & Robinson, E.H. (1982). *Parent/teacher conferencing.* Washington, DC: The National Education Association.

Rowan, R. (1978). Keeping the clock from running out. *Fortune, 98,* 76-78.

Ruben, B.D. (1978). Communication and conflict: A systematic theoretic perspective. *Quarterly Journal of Speech, 64,* 202-210.

Sandfort, J.A. (1987). Putting parents in their place. *NASSP Bulletin, 71,* 496.

Sandoval, J. (1985). Crisis counseling: Conceptualizations and general practices. *School Psychology Riview, 14,* 3, 257-265.

Schmidt, J.A. (1976). Career guidance in the elementary schools. *Elementary School Guidance and Counseling, 11,* 149.

Schunk, D.H. (1981). Modeling and attributional effects on children's achievement: A self-efficancy analysis. *Journal of Educational Psychology, 4,* 73, 93-105.

Schunk, D.H., & Miles, L.D. (1971). The Organizational Development Model. *Journal of Educational Psychology, 4,* 93-105.

Science Research Associates (1978). *SRA Placement and Counseling Program.* Chicago: Sience Research Associates.

Shafii, M., Carrington, S., Whittinghill, J.R., & Derrick, A. (1985). Psychological autopsy of completed suicide in children and adolescesnts. *American Journal of Psychiatry, 142,* 9, 1061-4.

Shaw, M.C. (1977). The development of counseling programs: Priorities, progress and professionalism. *The Personnel and Guidance Journal, 55,* 339-345.

Sherouse, D. (1985). *Adolescent drug and alcohol abuse handbook.* Springfield, IL: Charles C. Thomas.

Shertzer, B., & Stone, S.C. (1974). *Fundamentals of counseling.* Boston: Houghton Mifflin.

Sherwood, J.J. (1972). An introduction to organizational development. In J.W. Pfeiffer, & J.E. Jones (Eds.). *The 1972 annual handbook for group facilitators.* San Diego, CA: University Associates.

Shipman, N.J., Martin, J.B., McKay, A.B., & Anastiasi, R.E. (1983). *Effective time management techniques for school administrators.* Englewood Cliffs, NJ: Prentice-Hall.

Shneidman, E.S. (1972). *Death and the college student.* New York: Behavioral Publications.

Shufflebeam, L. & Webster, M. (1980). Evaluation and accountability. *Educatinal Leadership, 36,* 11.

Slaikeu, K.A., (1984). *Crisis intervention: A handbook for practice and research.* Boston: Allyn & Bacon.

Sloan, R.B., Staples, F.R., Cristol, A.H., Yorkston, N.H., & Whipple, K. (1975). *Psychotherapy versus behavior therapy.* Cambridge, MA: Harvard University.

Smaby, M.H., & Tamminen, A.W. (1978). Counseling for decisions. *Personnel and Guidance Journal, 57,* 1106-110.

Smith, D. (1982). Trends in counseling and psychotherapy. *American Psychologist, 37,* 7, 802-809.

Splete, H., & Freeman-George, A. (1985). Family influences on career development of young adults. *Journal of Career Development, 12,* 1, 55-64.

Sprinthall, N.A. (1984). Primary prevention: A road paved with a plethora of promises and procrastinations. *Personnel and Guidance Journal, 16,* 13, 491-495.

Sprinthall, N.A., & Ojemann, R. (1978). Psychological education and guidance: Counselors as teachers and curriculum advisors. *Texas Journal of Education, 5,* 2, 79-100.

Srebalus, D.J., Marinelli, R.P., & Messing, J.K. (1982). *Career development: Concepts and procedures.* Montery, CA: Brooks Cole.

Stanford, G. (1978). An opportunity missed. *The School Counselor, 26,* 2, 96-98.

Stanton, M.D. (1984). *The suicide watch: An alternative approach to managing self-destructive behavior.* Paper presented at the Departmental Conference, Department of Psychiatry, University of Rochester Medical Center.

Stein, W., & French, J.L. (1984). Teacher consultation in the affective domain: A survey of expert opinion. *The School Counselor, 31,* 339-345.

Steinmetz, L. (1976). *The art and skill of delegation.* Reading, MA: Addison-Wesley.

Stewart, L.H., & Avis, J.P. (1984). Is there a future for school counseling in the United States? *International Journal for the Advancement of Counseling, 7,* 241-251.

Stewart, N.R., & Thoreson, C.R. (1968). *Behavioral group counseling.* Boston: Houghton Mifflin.

Strother, J., & Jacobs, E. (1986). Parent consultation. *The School Counselor, 33,* 24-26.

Strum, D.L. (1982). Direct: A consultation skills training model. *The Personnel and Guidance Journal, 60,* 5.

Sue, D., Sue, D.W., & Sue, S. (1981). *Understanding abnormal behavior.* Boston, MA: Houghton Mifflin.

Sue, D.W. (1978). Counseling across cultures. *Personnel and Guidance Journal, 56,* 451.

Sue, D.W., & Sue, D. (1977). Barriers to cross-cultural counseling. *Journal of Counseling Psychology, 24,* 420-429.

Super, D.E. (1957). Vocational development theory: Persons, positions and process. *The Counseling Psychologist, 1,* 6.

Super, D.E. (1969). Vocational development theory: Persons, positions, process. *The Counseling Psychologist, 1,* 2-9.

Sweeney, T.J. (1989). *Adlerian counseling: Proven concepts and strategies.* Muncie, IN: Accelerated Development.

Tesiny, E.P. (1980). Childhood depression, loss of control, and school achievement. *Journal of Educational Psychology, 72,* 4, 506-510.

The William T. Grant Foundation Commission on Work, Family and Citizenship. (1988). *The forgotten half: Non-college youth in America.* Washington, DC: Author.

Therrium, M.E. (1979). Evaluating empathy skill training for parents. *Social Work, 24,* 417-419.

Thiers, N. (1988, October 20). Non-college youth lose financially. *Guidepost, 31*, 6.

Thompson, C., & Poppen, W. (1979). *Guidance activities for counselors and teachers.* Monterey, CA: Brooks Cole.

Thompson, R.A. (1985). Public Law 94-142: A critical review of it's impact on the secondary level. *The High School Journal, 69*, 246-254.

Thompson, R.A. (1986). Developing a peer facilitator program: An investment with multiple returns. *Small Group Behavior, 11*, 21-26.

Thompson, R.A. (1987). Creating insturctional partnerships to improve the academic performance of underachievers. *The School Counselor, 34*, 32-37.

Tindall, J.A. (1985). *Peer power: Becoming an effective peer helper, book 1, introductory program (2nd ed.).* Muncie, IN: Accelerated Development.

Tindall, J.A. (1989a). *Peer counseling: An in-depth look at training peer helpers (3rd ed.).* Muncie, IN: Accelerated Development.

Tindall, J.A. (1989b). *Peer power: Book 2, applying peer helper skills (2nd ed.).* Muncie, IN: Accelerated Development.

Tindall, J.A., & Salmon-White, S. (1990a). *Peers helping peers: Program for the preadolescent, leader manual.* Muncie,IN: Accelerated Development.

Tindall, J.A., & Salmon-White, S. (1990b). *Peers helping peers: Program for the preadolescent, student workbook.* Muncie, IN: Accelerated Development.

Tishler, C., McKenry, P., & Morgan, K. (1981). Adolescent suicide attempts: Some significant factors. *Suicide and Life Threatening Behavior, 11*, 86-92.

Tittle, C.K., & Zytowski, D.G. (1978). *Sex-fair interest measurement: Research and implications.* Washington, DC: U. S. Government Printing Office.

Toffler, A. (1974). *Learning for tomorrow: The role of the future in education.* New York: Vintage Books.

Treuille, B.B., & Stautberg, S.S. (1988). *Managing it all: Time saving ideas for career, family, relationship & self.* New York: Mastermedia Ltd.

Tugend, A. (1984). College counseling is inadequate. Education Week, *August 10,* 29, 7.

Tyler, L.E. (1969). *The work of the counselor.* New York: Appleton Century Crosts.

U S A Today: Tracking tomorrow's trends. (1986). Kansas City, MO: Gannett News Media Services.

United Stated Department of Commerce. (1984). *Statistical Abstract of the United States.* Washington, DC: Author

United States Department of Education. (1986). *What works: Schools without drugs.* Washington, DC: Author.

United States Department of Education. (1987). *Life values seniors consider important.* Washington, D.C.: Author.

United States Department of Health and Human Services. (1981). *Alcohol, drug abuse & mental health administration.* Rockville, MD: Author.

U.S. Department of Justice (1981). *Teenage crime.* Washington, D.C.: Bureau of Justice Statistics.

United States Department of Labor, Bureau of Statistics. (1986, April). Washington, D.C.: Author.

United State General Accounting Office. (1986). *School dropouts: The extent and nature of theproblem.* Report E HRD-86-106BR. Washington, D.C.: Author.

Van Riper, B.W. (1971). Student perceptions: The counselor is what he does. *The School Counselor, 19,* 54.

Votdin, G.J., & McAlister, A. (1982). Cigarette smoking among children and adolescents: Causes and pervention. *Annual Review of Disease Prevention.* New York: Springer.

Wagenaar, T.C. (1982). Quality counseling: The role of counseling resources and activities. *The School Counselor, 29,* 3, 204.

Waldo, M. (1985). A curative factor framework for conceptualizing group counseling. *Journal of Counseling and Development, 64,* 1, 58.

Washington, K.R. (1977). Success counseling: A model workshop approach to self-concept building. *Adolescesnce, 12,* 47, 405.

Wehlage, G.G. (1983). *Effective programs for the marginal high school student.* Bloomington, IN: Phi Delta Kappa.

Wells, C.B., & Ritter, K.Y. (1979). Paperwork, pressure and discouragement: Student attitudes toward guidance services-Implication for the profession. *The Personnel & Guidance Journal, 58,* 170.

Wiggins, J.L. (1977). Some counseling does help. *The School Counselor, 25,* 196-202.

Wise, P.S., & Ginther, D. (1981). Parent conferences: A brief commentary and an annotated bibliography. *School Psychology Review, 10,* 100-103.

Worrell, J., & Stilwell, W.E. (1981). *Psychology for teachers and students.* New York: Mcgraw-Hill.

Yalom, I. (1975). *The theory and practice of group psychotherapy.* New York: Basic Books.

Yalom, I. (1985). *The theory and practice of group psychotherapy.* New York: John Wiley.

Zaltman, G., Duncan, R., & Holbeck, J. (1973). *Innovations and organizations.* New York: John Wiley.

Zimmerman, B.J., & Ringle, J. (1981). Effects of model persistance and statements of confidence on children's self-efficacy and problem-solving. *Journal of Educational Psychology, 73,* 485.

INDEX

INDEX

A

Abandonment 33
Abdek-Halim, A.A. 271, 381
Abuse
    emotional 33
    physical 33
    sexual 33
Academic and career planning guide,
    Figure 220
Academic performance
    strategies to improve 157-8
Accountability 270
Act Assessment Program (ACT) 221
ACT Career Planning Program 222
Adair, F.L. 6, 383
Adlerian-based
    consultation 126, 128
Administrators
    to improve services 186
    to involve in decision making
        181-2
Admission
    credentials for college, *Table* 235
Adolescence
    developmental tasks, *Figure* 52
Adolescent
    depression 22-8
    emotional disorders 22-8
    health and well being 13-39
    pregnancy 19-22
    sexual behavior 19-22
Advertising practices
    internal and external,
        Figure 327
Advisors
    See teacher advisor
    selection of 136

Advisory committee members 298
Aging workforce
    future forecasts 214-5
Ahrens, R. 364, 381
Alice in Wonderland 269
Allen Guttmacher Institute 20, 381
Allen, J. 81, 153, 381, 391
Alschuler, A.S. 71, 381
Alternative School Program 267
Amatac, E.S. 146, 381
American Institute for Research
    222, 381
American Association of College
    Registrars Admissions Officers
    (AACRAO) 234
American College Testing Program
    246-7
American Medical Association
    119, 381
American Psychiatric Association
    118-9, 381
American School Counselor
    Association 290, 349, 381
Anastiasi, R.E. 174, 195, 375, 378,
    396
Anderson, E. 81, 381
Anger 83
Approaches
    multimedia 343-55
Armed Forces 267
*Armed Services Vocational Aptitude
    Battery (ASVAB)* 221
Arrangements
    short-term 102-4
Assessment
    combined instruments 222-3
    educational and occupational
        219, 221-3
    need 295

Astin, H.S. 256, 381
At-risk students
  assistance 34-8
Attendance
  to improve 178-80
Attendance program 38
Attitude
  to improve 178-80
Attkisson, C.C. 295, 310, 382, 391
Aubrey, R.F. 42, 270, 382
Audit
  program 296-7
Authier, J. 173, 388
Average Child, The 140-1
Avis, J.P. 173, 382, 397

B

Babcock, R.J. 48, 218, 288, 382
Bachman, J.G. 47, 390
Bacon, F. 287
Baldwin, B.A. 80, 382
Balk, D.E. 83, 382
Baron, A. 278-9, 388
Barry, R.A. 63, 64, 66, 67, 68, 387
Baruth, L.G. 160, 382
Baseline data
  school climate 189-94
  school climate profile, *Figure* 190
Battered mind syndrome 363
Beck, A. 47, 289, 382
Beehr, T.A. 272, 382
Behavior
  consultation 128
Behavior, sexual
  intervention, implications 21-2
Beliefs, irrational, *Figure* 367
Benefield, W. 42. 394
Bennett, E.C. 46-7, 289-90, 382
Bennington, K.F. 42, 390
Berenson, B.G. 45, 289, 382, 383
Berman, A.L. 22-3, 384
Bertoldi, A.R. 47, 289, 382
Bigelow, E.E. 173, 382
Birk, J.M. 158, 382
Blame 84
Blimline, C.A. 158, 382
Blocker, D.H. 173, 382
Borg, W.S. 309, 382

Bottorff, R.L. 273, 388
Bowmann, R.P. 62, 384
Boyer, E.L. 3, 237, 251, 383
Boyer, M.C. 159, 382
Boyle, R. 47, 289, 391
Bramson, R.M. 370, 383
Bramson, S. 370, 383
Brechenridge, M. 312, 383
Bridgment, P.W. 231
Brittell, J. 45, 289, 387
Brooks, D.J. 61, 89, 387
Brown, N.W. 6, 383
Brownell, C. 45, 289, 387
Bryan, T. 46, 383
Bulletin
  proposal outline 345-7
Burggraf, M.Z. 160, 382
Burns, P. 47, 289, 383
Business communication resources
  245
Business, unfinished 84

C

*California Occupational Preference
  Survey (COPS)* 222
*California Occupational Preference
  System (COPS)* 223
Call, V.R.A. 158, 393
Campbell, D.P. 45, 383
Canady, R.L. 151, 383
Cannon, J.R. 173, 383
Caplan, N. 128, 383
Capuzzi, D. 18, 91, 93, 383
Career Assessment Inventory (CAI)
  221
Career awareness 62
Career Briefs Kit 223
Career Cluster Booklist 223
Career development education
  versus career education 218-9
Career education
  versus career development
    education 218-9
Careers
  future forecasts 215-6
Carey, R. 272, 383
Carkhuff, R.R. 45, 173, 289, 382,
  383

Carlson, J. 126, 128, 385
Carnage Foundation 237
Carrington, S. 23, 395
Carrol, M.R. 1, 289, 383
Casale, A.M.D. 210, 214
Case manager
    duties 102
Case Study Approach 310
Casner-Lotto, J. 132, 384
Catalyst 166
Center, A.H. 322, 384
Change
    future forecasts 213
    how to influence 171-2
    organizations 163-4
Change agent
    roles of 164-71, *Figure* 165
Chapman, D. 241, 384
Chartier, M.R. 164-5, 384
Childers, J.H., Jr. 172, 394
Childers, W.C. 61, 89, 387
Children and youth
    characteristics of 51-3
Children's Defense Fund 20, 384
Choices and decision making
    future forecasts 212
Clarification
    issues to the media 106-9
Clough, W.O. 133
Cochrane, P. 290, 384
Cohen, D.K. 5, 7, 28, 85, 274, 394
Cohen-Sandler, R. 22-3, 384
Cole, C.G. 46, 388
Cole, D. 25, 388
Collaboration
    public/private 35
College
    attribution 243
    changing profile 231-2
    counselor as catalyst 231-53
    credentials for admission,
        Table 235
    decision making 231-53
    education in the workplace
        236-7
    financial aid 249-52
    keeping options open 237-44
College Board 245
College Board and Educational
    Testing Service 233, 237

College Board Publications, 243, 384
College education
    financing 249-52
College selection
    children of non-college graduate
        parents 241
    helpful resources 238-9,
        Table 240
Communication skills 62
Community
    focused programs 9-10
Community centered model 275-6
Community forum approach 295
Components
    essential to facilitate 109-10
Computer literacy
    future forecasts 209
Conferences
    student led 153
Conflict resolution 62
Conner, J.D. 234-5, 384
Consultant
    as counselor, *Figure* 124
Consultants
    counselors 123-32
Consultation
    activities, *Figure* 127
    Adlerian-based 126, 128
    behavior 128
    benefits 131-2
    DIRECT-technique 129-31
    mental health 128
    models 126, 128-31
    organizational development
        model 129
    problem solving 133-6
    problem-solving model,
        Figure 135
    with families 145-61
    with support personnel 133-44
Consumer
    focused programs 9-10
Consultation
    with teachers 133-44
Contact letter
    sample, *Figure* 335
Contingency plan
    crisis communication 105-9
Cooper-Haber, K. 62, 384

Cooperating Hampton Roads
  Organizations for Minorities
  Engineering (CROME) 246
Cooperative Work Program 245
Coren, A. 290, 392
Corey, G. 289, 384
Corey, M. 289, 384
Council for Accreditation of
  Counseling and Related
  Educational Programs (CACREP)
  123
Counsel or refer
  guidelines 97-8
Counseling 37
  See school counseling
  See school counselor
  activities 274-5
  brochure developing 354-5
  developmental 51-7
  grief 110-2
  inherent benefits 44-8
  intentions 53-6
  interpersonal domain 45-7
  interventions 53-6
  life skills as developmental
    56-62
  marketing 322-6
  mourning 110-2
  resources 274
  services development, *Figure* 279
Counselor
  action plan, *Figure* 93
  activities, code, *Figure* 292-3
  catalyst for college decision
    making 231-53
  consultant, 123-32, *Figure* 124
  demand for 2-3
  facilitator of organizational health
    172-6
  interventions, *Figure* 59
  kaleidoscope, *Figure* 334
  number of 2
  objective versus program
    276-80, *Figure* 277
  occupational conduit non-college
    bound 255-67
  operationalizing efforts 10-11
  partner with teachers 136-44

Renaissance 10
  report card, *Figure* 336
  role expectations 3-6
Counselor's role
  helping people in crisis 79-122
Counselor's Time Study Analysis
  Form 290, *Figure* 291
Cowan, M. 289, 386
Cox, W.D. 146, 384
Cramer, S.H. 219, 388
Crisis
  essential components to facilitate
    109-10
  helping people in 79-122
  intervention 80-1
Crisis Communication Contingency
  Plan 98, 105-9
Crisis Intervention Team
  See School Crisis Intervention
    Team
  mobilization of 100-2
Crisis situation
  process evaluation 120-1
Cristol, A.H. 288, 396
Crouse, J. 233, 234, 384
Curriculum
  extracurricular 6
  horizontal 6
  services 7
  vertical 6
Cutlip, S.M. 322, 384

D

Dagley, J.C. 2, 58, 384
Daniels, M.H. 158, 385
David, P. 125, 386
Davis, J.L. 135, 392
Davis, M.S. 23, 387
Day, R.W. 272, 385
Debriefing 112-20
  stages 113-20
Decision making 62
  college 231-53
  counselor as catalyst 231-53
Definition
  counseling 42-4
Delinquency 29-30
  intervention 30

DeMasi, M.F. 241, 384
Denial 83
Depression
    adolescent 22-8
    intervention, implications
        24-8
Derrick, A. 23, 395
Design
    evaluation 307, 309-12
Development
    program 269-86
Dewey, J. 207
*Dictionary of Occupational Titles
    (DOT)* 223
Differential Aptitude Test (DAT)
    221, 222
Difficulties
    educational 61
    school-behavior 60
    social 60-1
Dinkmeyer, D. 25, 71, 123, 126,
    128, 141, 385
Dinkmeyer, D., Jr. 128, 385
DIRECT 129
DIRECT-technique
    consultation 129-31
Discrepancy Evaluation Approach
    311
Disorders, emotional 22-8
    intervention, implications
        24-8
Diversity in living
    future forecasts 215
Domain
    educational 47-8
    interpersonal 45-7
    vocational 48
Downing, J.C. 146, 385
Dreikurs, R. 141, 385
Drier, H. 2, 394
Dropouts
    intervention 32
Duncan, L.W. 146, 385
Duncan, R. 164, 400
Dunlap, J.B. 327, 393
Duties 102
Dyer, W.W. 43, 63, 65, 385

E

Eash, V. 290, 392
Economic barriers
    vocations 257-63
Education of All Handicapped
    Children Act of 1975, 362
Education Week 8, 9, 253, 385
Effectiveness of program 306
    related to effort and efficiency,
        Figure 306, 308
Efficiency of program 306-7
    related to effort and
        effectiveness, *Figure* 306, 308
Effort of program 302, 306
    related to effectiveness efficiency,
        Figure 306, 308
Egan, G. 43, 45, 63, 125, 289, 385
Elias, D. 125, 386
Elkstrom, R.B. 241, 391
Emerson, R.W. 359
Emery, G. 47, 289, 382
Emotional behavior
    in groups, *Figure* 199
Emotional behavior 197-205
    friendly helper orientation 197
    logical thinking orientation 198
    tough battler orientation 197
Employers
    future forecasts 212-3
Encouragement 140-4
Engen, H.B. 158, 221, 386, 393
English, R.A. 311, 390
ERIC Counseling and Personnel
    Services Clearinghouse 178, 226
Esveldt-Dawson, K. 23, 390
Evaluating
    public relations strategies
        355-7
Evaluation
    See program evaluation
    counselor performance 312
        Figure 315-8
    design 307, 309-12
    performance criteria 312
        Figure 313-4
    process following crisis 120-1
    professionals 312-20
    program 287-320
    program, benefits 294
    services 297-307

Evaluation surveys
    sample forms, *Figures* 300, 301
Expectations
    college and university 233-5
Experimental Research Approach 307
Expert Opinion Approach 310-1

F

Fabrick, K.F. 146, 381
Faculty
    to improve services 186
Faculty Meeting (As Seen by the Principal) 191
Fairman, M. 172, 386
Families
    consulting with 145-61
    dysfunctional behaviors 160
    early intervention 159-61
    empowering 92-6
    functional behaviors 159-60
    primary prevention 159-61
    to improve 184-5
Family concerns 62
Family Safety Watch 92-6
Farrar, E. 5, 7, 28, 85, 274, 394
Fear 84
Feature column
    systematic approach for organizing 347-9
Fielstein, L.L. 153, 387
Financial aid
    for college 249-52
Financial aid, misconceptions, *Figure* 253
Fitzgerald, P.W. 146, 385
Flake, M.H. 48, 386
Flexibility
    future forecasts 212
Flextime
    future forecasts 213
Follow-up Approach 309-10
Forecasts
    skills 208-9
Forecasts, future 208-16
    aging workforce 214-5
    careers 215-6
    change 213
    choices and decision making 212

computer literacy 209
diversity in living 215
employers 212-3
flexibility 212
flextime 213
information 209
marketing 213
old-fashioned values 216
self-employed 214
self-reliance 212
services 210
sunbelt 212
technical skills 210, 212
women and minorities 209
workstyle/life-style 213, *Table* 214
Forrest, A. 237, 386
Fortino, M., & Associates 365, 386
Freeman, H.E. 295, 395
Freeman-George, A. 159, 396
French, J.L. 142, 397
French, N.H. 23, 390
Frontiers of Possiblility 232, 237, 242-3, 386
Frose, A. 85, 386

G

Gallop, G. 322, 386
Garfinkel, D.B. 85, 386
Gaul, M.D. 309, 382
Gazda, G.M. 2, 61, 89, 384, 387
General Aptitude Test Battery (GATB) 222
Geoffroy, H.E. 6, 383
Gill, S.J. 63, 64, 66, 67, 68, 387
Ginther, D. 150, 400
Gispert, M. 23 , 387
Glasser, W. 85, 387
Golden, L. 91, 93, 383
Gonzales, M. 367, 387
Goodlad, J. 163
Goodman, J. 373, 387
Gordon, E.W. 45, 289, 387
Grief 110-2
Griggs, S.A. 48, 387
Griswold, D. 322, 387
Group counseling
    classification system, *Figure* 68

curative factors 67, 69-70
efficacy of 63-70
skill classification systems,
  Figure 64-5
Group
  parent study 160-1
Groups
  emotional behavior 197-205
Growth
  attitudes essential 144
  essential concepts 143
  skills to foster 142-3
Guidance
  developmental 51-7
  educational or occupational
    comprehensive system
    216, 218
  educational 207-29
  occupational 207-29
Guide
  academic and career planning,
    Figure 220
Guidelines
  counsel or refer 97-8
Guilt 84
Guyton, J.M. 153, 387
Gysberg, N.C. 272, 388
Gysbers, N. 2, 394

H

Haddock, J. 172, 386, 387
Halmi, K.A. 47, 387
Halperin, M. 33, 387
Hannaford, D. 108, 387
Hansen, J.C. 17, 387
Hansen, W.B. 67, 387
Hargens, F.M. 272, 388
Hargreaves, W. 310, 391
Hargreaves, W.A. 295, 382
Harmon, F.M. 278-9, 388
Harrington-O'Shea System for Career
  Decision-Making 221
Harrison, W.D. 271, 388
Harvard-Radcliffe Admissions
  244, 388
Hassan, T.E. 251, 388
Havighurst, R.J. 256, 388
Hawkins, J.D. 306, 308, 388

Hawton, K. 23-5, 388
Hayden, C. 270, 313, 388
Hays, D.G. 3, 388
Helms, B.J. 271, 388
Herr, E.L. 4, 45-6, 219, 289, 388
Hersh, R.H. 38, 86, 177, 390
Higgins, P.S. 45-6, 218, 289, 388
Hill, C.E. 53, 388
Hoffman, A. 43, 394
Hohenshil, T. 290, 388
Holbeck, J. 164, 400
Holland, J.L. 221, 388
Home-School Partnerships 146-8
  Figure 147
Hood, J. 85, 386
Horne, A.M. 159, 382
Horowitz, J.J. 295, 382
Horton, E. 16, 388
Hosford, R.E. 48, 218, 392
Hostility 84
Humes, C. 290, 388
Hutchins, D.E. 46, 388
Hutchinson, R.L. 46, 388

I

Ibrahim, F.A. 4, 271, 388
Identification
  early 35
  key helping professionals and
    staff 98-9
  physical resources 99
If For Counselors 41
  See counseling
  See school counselor
Implications
  victimization 33-4
Individualized Adademic Improve-
  ment Plans (IAIP) 266
Influence
  change 171-2
Information
  future forecasts 209
Information process diffusion 169,
  Figure 170
Intellectualization 84
Intervention 13-39
  for families 159-61
  implications for primary
    prevention 13-39

programs for college selection 244-7
self-destruction behavior 92-6
strategies 178
Intervention, implications
adolescent depression 24-8
adolescent pregnancy 21-2
delinquency 30
dropouts 32
emotional disorders 24-8
sexual behavior 21-2
substance abuse 16-9
Interview
student in crisis 89-91
Inventory of Counselor Potential for Facilitating Staff Morale, *Figure* 200-5
profile illustration 205
scoring the inventory 204-5
Ivey, A.E. 63-4, 71, 173, 381, 388

J

Jackson, P. 169-70, 388
Jacobs, E. 22, 23, 150, 397
Janosik, E. 80, 388
Jenkins, D.E. 10-1, 388
Joan, P. 101, 388
Job Corp 266
Job Training Partnership Act (JTPA) 267
Jobs
changing 236
college education needed 236-7
for the future, *Table* 211
Johnson, J.J. 82, 388
Johnston, L.D. 47, 390
Jones, D. 367, 387
Jones, J.E. 167-8, 390
Jones, V.H. 47, 290, 390
Joyce, B.R. 38, 86, 177, 390

K

Kahn, R. 271, 390
Karmos, J.S. 158, 385
Karnes, M.B. 148, 390
Katz, P.A. 45, 289, 390

Kauffman, M.A. 48, 218, 288, 382
Kaufman, T.D. 311, 390
Kazdin, A.E. 23, 390
Keenan Project 62
Keeping options open, 237, 390
Key informant approach 295
King, P.T. 42, 390
King, R.A. 22-3, 384
Kolb, D.A. 175, 197, 199, 390
Kotler, D. 323, 390
Kottler, J. 72, 75, 390
Kozoll, C.E. 363, 390
Krumboltz, J.D. 48, 288, 311, 390
Kuder General Interest Survey 221
Kuder Occupational Interest Survey (Form DD) 222
Kuder Vocational or General Interest Inventory (Form C or E) 2
Kuder, F. 222, 391
Kuder-Form E 222

L

L'Abate, L. 57, 391
Lamb, R.R. 221, 386
Laport, R. 47, 391
Larrabee, M.J. 289, 391
Larsen, D. 310, 391
Larson, D. 57, 391
Lazarus, A. 47, 289, 371, 391
Lecog, L.L. 18, 383
Lee, V.E. 241, 391
Levitson, H.S. 272, 391
Lewis, J.P. 45, 47, 289, 391
Lewis, M. 45, 391
Lieberman, M.A. 63-4, 391
Life skills
developmental counseling 56-62
Life values
seniors consider important, *Table* 217
Lightfoot, J.L. 86, 177, 391
Lincoln Educational Alternative Program (LEAP) 264-5
Little, A.W. 153, 391
Lombana, A.E. 147, 150, 392
Lombana, J.H. 146-7, 150, 276-7, 392
Loss 122-20
behavior manifestations 83-6

M

MacDevitt, J. 294, 392
MacDevitt, M. 294, 392
Mackenzie, R.A. 361, 392
Maltreatment
    multiple 33
Management
    stress 365-74
    time 359-79
Management by Objectives (MBO) 297
Mann, D. 171, 392
Mapping, perceptual 323-4
Mareni, B. 290, 384
Marinelli, R.P. 219, 396
Marketing
    counseling 322-6
    educate 326,328, 332-7
    external strategies 331-8
    future forecasts 213
    internal strategies 326-31
    involve 328-30 337-8
    know your audience 326
    recognize 330-1
    strategies 324
Marsh, L. 23, 387
Martin, D. 48, 218, 288, 392
Martin, J.B. 174, 195, 375, 378, 396
Martin, R. 123, 128, 392
Maslow, A.H. 256, 392
Matthay, E.R. 237-8, 240, 392
Matthews, C.O. 146, 384
Mayer, G.G. 132, 392
Mazza, G.G. 79
McAlister, A. 18, 399
McDowell, W. 290, 392
McGrath, J.E. 272, 392
McIntyre, J.M. 175, 197, 199, 390
McKay, A.B. 174, 195, 375, 378, 396
McKenry, P. 85, 398
McKibbin, M. 38, 86, 177, 390
Media
    clarification of issues to 106
Medway, R.J. 123, 392
Meetings
    committee 194
    debriefing 197

evaluation of, *Figure* 195-6
guidelines to improve 193
managing 193-4
planning and problem solving 197
policy 197
promote a shared commitment 191-4
structured task force 197
types of 194, 197
Memorandum 145-6
Mental health
    consultation 128
Messing, J.K. 219, 396
Meyer, J.B. 48, 218, 392
Meyer, S.J. 123, 128, 392
Michael Fortino & Associates 365, 392
Mickelson, D.J. 135, 392
Milan, M.A. 57, 391
Miles, L.D. 129, 395
Miles, M.B. 172, 392
Miles, M.D. 63-4, 391
Model
    community centered 275-6
    comprehensive consumer 275-6
    consultation 126, 128-31
    developmental guidance, *Figure* 58
    organizational development 129
    student-focused, *Figure* 279
Morgan, K. 85, 398
Morrison, T.L. 288, 392
Morse, D. 290, 393
Motivation 140-4
Mourning 110-2
Multimedia
    approaches 343-55
Murray, E. 231
Myrick, R.D. 51, 59, 77, 393

N

Naisbitt, J. 208, 393
National College Counseling 241
National College Counseling Project 237

National Educational Association
13, 393
National PTA 149, 393
Nederhood, B. 306, 308, 388
Need Analysis
critical steps, 302, *Figure* 303
Need assessment 295
Neglect
educational 33
emotional 33
medical 33
physcial 33
Newman, J.E. 272, 382
Nguyen, T. 310, 391
Nicoll, W.G. 146, 393
Noeth, P.E. 158, 393
Noeth, R.J. 45, 158, 393, 394
Noth, R. 47, 391

O

O'Brien, C.H. 241, 384
O'Dell, S. 146, 393
O'Grady, J. 25, 388
O'Grady, K.E. 53, 388
O'Malley, C.T. 47, 390
Objectives
counselor versus program
276-80, *Figure* 277
Occupational Outlook Handbook 223
Odiorne, G.S. 164, 393
Ohio Vocational Interest Survey
(OVIS) 221, 222, 223
Ohlsen, M.M. 63, 65, 393
Ohlson, L. 21, 393
Ojemann, R. 70, 396
Old-fashioned values
future forecasts 216
Options
keeping open 237-44
Options for Excellence 245
Organization
characteristics of a healthy,
Figure 174
climate questionnaire, *Figure* 175
factors in the forefront 176
Organizational development
model 129
Organizational Universe Model 167,

Figure 168
Organizations
change 163-4
Orientations
helping 126, 128-31
Orthner, D.K. 294, 393
Osborn, M. 25, 388
Otto, L.B. 158, 393

P

P-ACT+ 246
Parent
activities, *Figure* 341
information night, *Figure* 342
networks 161
support groups 161
volunteers 340, 343
Parent conference
step-by-step procedure
150, 151-3
Parent conferences
value 148, 149-55
Parent involvement, *Figure* 149
as career counselors 158-9
strategies 148
Parent involvement child's academic
performance 156-7
career development 156-7
Parent study groups 160-1
Parent Teacher Association (PTA) 338
Parent Teacher Organization (PTO)
338
alien or ally 338-340
Parent-teacher conferences
effective conference continuum,
Figure 155
elements of, *Figure* 154
planning sheet, *Figure* 151
Parents
continuum of involvement,
Figure 155
significant partners 36
to involve in decision making
181-2
Parents Actively Serving School
(PASS) 340, 343
Parsons, R.D. 123, 128, 392
Patton, L.D. 309, 393

Pearl, R. 46, 383
Peer group
    leadership 18
    support 18
Peer helpers
    empowering youth 70-6
    functions of 71-2
    log 76
    program scope 75-6
    training 72-5
Peer, G.G. 4, 270, 272, 393
Perceptual mapping 323-4
Pfeffer, C.R. 22-3, 393
Pffeiffer, I.L. 327, 393
Photo and captions
    procedures 344-5
Pierce, R.M. 173, 383
Pietrofesa, J.J. 43, 394
Pine, G.J. 2, 394
Pinson, N. 2, 394
Pinson, N.M. 4, 388
Podemski, R.S. 172, 394
Pohlmann, N. 270, 313, 388
Positioning 324
Post Traumatic Stress Disorder,
    Figure 119
Post Traumatic Stress Reactions,
    Figure 118
Postcard follow-up, *Figure* 295
Powell, A.G. 5, 7, 28, 85, 274, 394
Power
    to change 171-2
Powers, R.C. 361, 394
Predictors
    quality service 274-6
Prediger, D.J. 45, 158, 221, 386,
394
Pregnancy
    adolescent 19-22
    intervention, implications
        21-2
    sexual behavior 19-22
Preparation
    staff 99-100
    teachers 99-100
Presley, C.A. 158, 385
Prevention
    implications 13-39
    primary 13-39

Prevention, primary
    for families 159-61
Principal
    role and responsibilities 104-5
Process helper 166
Proctor, W.W. 42, 394
Professionals
    evaluation 312-20
Program
    coordinated delivery 35
Program audit 296-7
    constructs 296-7
Program development 269-86
Program development benefits
    269-70
Program development student
    outcome model, *Figure* 281-6
Program evaluation
    See evaluation
    benefits 294
    definition 287
    steps 297-302, *Figure* 304-5
Program evaluation 290-5
Program Planning and Budgeting
    Systems (PPBS) 297
Project Involve 245
Project Stay 245
Psychological Corporation 222, 394
Public relations
    developing effective 321-58
Public speaking 349-52
Purkey, W.W. 357, 394
Pyramiding 132

Q

Quasi-experimental Approach 309
Quinn, D. 271, 390

R

Ramsay, T.B. 81, 395
Rapoza, R. 173, 382
Rappeport, J.R. 85. 394
Reschly, D.L. 132, 394
Research 287
    support 288-90
Resource linker 166

Resources
  helpful for college selection,
    238-9, *Table* 240
Responsibilities
  yours' and theirs' 378-9
Responsibility
  help others assume 374,
    378-9
Responsibility, shared 86-8
Reuther Education at Large (REAL)
  263-4
Reynolds, J.E. 251, 388
Ringle, J. 289, 400
Ritter, K.Y. 272-3, 399
Roach, A.J. 48, 386
Roberts, H.C. 156, 394
Robinson, E.H. 154, 395
Rogers, C.R. 42, 177, 395
Role ambiguity 271
Role conflict 271
Role expectations 3-6
  administrative 5
  theraupetic 5
Role, change
  counseling 1-2
  guidance 1-2
Roles
  change agent 164-71, *Figure* 165
Rolls Royce Syndrome 374
Rosenthal, J. 271, 390
Rossi, P.H. 295, 395
Roth, J.D. 45, 394
Rotter, J.C. 154, 395
Rowan, R. 364, 395
Ruben, B.D. 366, 395
Rubin, I.M. 175, 197, 199, 390
Rush, A. 47, 289, 382

S

Salmon-White, S. 76, 398
Sandfort, J.A. 339-41, 395
Sandler, I.R. 81, 395
Sandoval, J. 80, 395
SAT scores 233
Sawyer, R.L. 158, 394
Schaffner, M. 289, 391
Schmidt, J.A. 47, 289, 395
Schmidt, J.J. 357, 394

Scholastic Aptitude Test (SAT) 234
School based programs
  to increase college selection
    247-9
School climate
  baseline data 189-94
  counselors promoters of 163-205
  creating 36
  improving 176-89
School counseling 41-9
  benefits 41-9
  definition 41-9
  poem 41
School counselors
  See counselors
School Crisis Intervention Team 99,
  102, 102
  mobilization of 100-2
School-as-community 81,83
School/Business Partnerships 245
Schunk, D.H. 46, 129, 288, 395
Science Research Associates,
  222, 395
Secretary
  responsibilities, *Figure* 375-7
Segmentation 323
Self-Directed Search (SDS) 221, 222
Self-employed
  future forecasts 214
Self-reliance
  future forecasts 212
Selling 323
Services
  evaluation 297-307
  future forecasts 210
  predictors of quality 274-6
Seyfarth, J.T. 151, 383
Shafii, M. 23, 395
Shame 84
Shaw, B. 47, 289, 382
Shaw, M.C. 270, 395
Sherick, R.B. 23, 390
Sherouse, D. 16, 396
Shertzer, B. 42, 396
Sherwood, J.J. 167, 396
Shipman, N.J. 174, 195, 375, 378,
  396
Shneidman, E.S. 85, 396
Shufflebeam, L. 312, 396

Skills
  future forecasts 208-9
Slaikeu, K.A. 80, 396
Sloan, R.B. 288, 396
Smaby, M.H. 43, 396
Smith, D. 43, 396
Smith, E.J. 67, 387
Smith, S. 294, 393
Snoek, R. 271, 390
Social change
  influence on counseling 7-9
Solution giver 166
Sorenson, J.E. 295, 382
Sparacio, R.T. 272, 385
Speaking
  enhancing your delivery 352-3
Splete, H. 159, 396
Splete, H.H. 43, 394
Sprinthall, N.A. 25, 70, 396
SRA Achievement and Ability Series
  222
SRA Placement and Counseling
  Program 222
Srebalus, D.J. 219, 396
Stabilizer 166-7
Staff
  development 37
  preparation for crisis 99-100
  to improve services 186
Staff Absenteeism
  to decrease 186-8
Staff request for transfer
  to decrease 186-8
Staff resignations
  to decrease 186-8
Stages
  closure 117, 120
  debriefing 112-20
  fact 114-5
  feeling 115-6
  introductory 113-4
  learning 117
  reaction 116-7
Stanford, G. 85, 396
Stanton, M.D. 92, 397
Staples, F.R. 288, 396
Stautberg, S.S. 193, 398
Stein, W. 142, 397
Steinmetz, L. 374, 397
Stenning, W.F. 48, 386

Stewart, L.H. 173, 397
Stewart, N.R. 48, 288, 397
Stilwell, W.E. 28, 56, 400
Stone, G.L. 48, 218, 288, 392
Stone, S.C. 42, 396
Strategies
  improve academic performance
    157-8
  intervention 178
  marketing 324
  parent involvement 148
  post-traumatic loss debriefing
    112-20
  worksheet for implementing,
    Figure 325
Stress disorder, *Figure* 119
Stress management 365-74
Stress reactions, *Figure* 118
Stressors, *Figure* 82
Strong Vocational Interest Blank
  (SVIB) 222
Strong-Campbell Interest Inventory
  (SCII) 221
Strong-Campbell Interest Survey
  (SCII) 222
Strother, J. 22, 23, 150, 397
Strowig, W. 48, 218, 392
Strum, D.L. 129, 131, 397
Student
  drop-outs 266-7
  intervention with the marginal
    265-6
Student advisor
  advocate for the student
    137-8
Student Assistance Advisory Board
  87-8, 109
Student Assistance Teams
  intervention procedures 88-91
Student Assistant Program
  behavior report, *Figure* 139-40
Student dropouts
  to have fewer 180-1
Student expulsions
  to have fewer 180-1
Student in crisis
  interview 89-91
Student led
  conferences 153

Student morale
    improving 176-89
Student self-concept
    to promote 182-4
Student services
    to improve services 184-5
Student suspensions
    to have fewer 180-1
Students
    at-risk 34-8
    care for suicidal 92
    indicators of crisis, *Figure* 91
    marginal 263-7
    to involve in decision making
    181-2
    vocational 263-7
Study skills 62
Substance abuse 15-9
    intervention implications 16-9
Sudden loss
    contingency plan 98-105
Sue, D. 46, 90, 397
Sue, D.W. 46, 90, 397
Sue, S. 90, 397
Suicidal
    care for 92
Suicide 112-20
    contingency plan 98-105
    number of, *Table* 24
    post-traumatic loss debriefing
    112-20
    referral procedures, *Figure* 94
Sum, A. 260
Sunbelt
    future forecasts 212
Super, D.E. 256, 288, 397
Support group 370
Support personnel
    to involve in decision making
    181-2
Survey sampling 295
Sweeney, T.J. 42, 397

T

Tabulation Approach 309
Talent Search Programs 245
Talk shows
    how to get on 353-4

Tamminen, A.W. 43, 396
Teacher
    preparation for crisis 99-100
Teacher advisor
    benefits 138-40
    implementing 136-44
Teacher advisor's role 137
Teachers
    to involve in decision making
    181-2
Teaching staff
    activities, *Figure* 341
Team leader
    duties 102
Technical skills
    future forecasts 210, 212
Terres, C. K. 289, 391
Tesiny, E.P. 46, 397
Test data
    interpreting 223-5
Test program checklist,
    Figure 226-9
The William T. Grant Foundation
    Commission on Work, Family, and
    Citizenship, 255, 258, 260, 266
Therrium, M.E. 146, 397
Thiers, N. 258, 398
Thomas, M.D. 288, 392
Thompson, D.C. 271, 388
Thompson, R.A. 6, 47, 256, 289,
    311, 383, 398
Thoresen, D.F. 48, 288, 391
Thoreson, C.R. 288, 397
Time consumers
    analyzing 361-3
Time management
    principles 359-79
    suggestions 378
Time/Cost Approach 311
Tindall, J.A. 76, 398
Tishler, C. 85, 398
Tittle, C.K. 221, 398
Toffler, A. 208, 398
Training model 57,60
Treuille, B.B. 193, 398
Trusheim, D. 233, 234, 384
Tugend, A. 2, 398
Tyler, L.E. 288, 290, 398

U

Unis, A.S. 23, 390
Unisex Edition of the Act Interest Inventory (UNIACT) 221
United States Department of Commerce 13, 399
United States Department of Education 13, 217, 399
United States Department of Health & Human Services 304, 399
United States Department of Justice 29, 399
United States Department of Labor 211, 399
United States General Accounting Office 13, 399
Upward Bound 244
USA Today 210, 214, 399

V

Van Riper, B.W. 272, 399
Vandalism
    to decrease 188-9
Victimization 32-4
    intervention 33-4
Violence
    to decrease 188-9
Vocation
    economic barriers 257-63
    plans shifting 256-7
Vocational Preference Inventory (VPI) 221
Vocations
    marginal students 263-7
    strategies to facilitate transition 262-3
    ways of assisting young people 261-2
Votdin, G.J. 18, 399
Vriend, J. 43, 63, 65, 385

W

Warner, R.W. 67, 387
Washington, K.R. 46, 288, 399
Webster, M. 312, 396
Wehlage, G.G. 263, 265, 399
Welch, R.J. 191
Wells, C.B. 272-3, 399
Wheeler, K. 23, 387
Whipple, K. 288, 396
Whitely, J.M. 367, 387
Whitely, R.M. 367, 387
Whittinghill, J.R. 23, 395
Wiggins, J.L. 46, 48, 290, 399
Wilson, R.C. 271, 388
Wise, P.S. 150, 400
Wolfe, D. 271, 390
Women and Minorities
    future forecasts 209
    occupations in which making progress, *Table* 210
Work Style/Life-style 13, *Table* 214
Worrell, J. 28, 56, 400
Wrenn, G.G. 42, 394
Wright, D.V. 294, 393

Y

Yalom, I. 63, 67, 73, 400
Yalom, I.D. 63-4, 391
Yorkston, N.H. 288, 396
Youth
    problems, *Table* 14

Z

Zalk, S.R. 45, 289, 390
Zaltman, G. 164, 400
Zimmerman, B.J. 289, 400
Zytowski, D.G. 221, 398

ABOUT
THE
AUTHOR

Rosemary A. Thompson, Ed.D., NCC, LPC, is Supervisor of Drug Education and Youth Risk Prevention, Chesapeake Public Schools, Chesapeake, Virginia, and Adjunct Professor, Old Dominion University, Norfolk, Virginia.

During her eighteen years in the public school sector, Dr. Thompson has been a high school psychology teacher, school counselor, guidance director, and assistant principal for instruction. She has published widely in national counseling and educational journals, and offers a formidable basis for her expertise as counselor, educator, and practitioner.

A native of Virginia, Dr. Thompson earned a B.S. degree in English and psychology from Radford University; a M.Ed. from the College of William and Mary in counseling; a C.A.S. from Old Dominion University in counseling; and an Ed.D. in counseling with an endoresement in school administration from the College of William and Mary. Dr. Thompson is a National Board Certified Counselor, a Licensed Professional Counselor, and maintains a private practice in educational consultation. She served on the Editorial Board of *The School Counselor*, the Editorial Board of the *Journal of Counseling and Development*, and was editor of the *Virginia Counselor's Journal*. She was named Hampton Roads Counselor of the Year in 1985.

Dr. Thompson currently resides in Virginia Beach, Virginia, with her husband, Charles R. Thompson, a professional engineer, and their children, Ryan and Jessica.